A VIEW FROM THE EDGE

A View from the Edge
An Autobiography

Leslie Griffiths

continuum

Published by the Continuum International Publishing Group
Continuum UK, The Tower Building, 11 York Road, London SE1 7NX
Continuum US, 80 Maiden Lane, Suite 704, New York, NY 10038

www.continuumbooks.com

Copyright © Leslie Griffiths, 2010

First published 2010

British Library Cataloguing-in-Publication Data
A catalogue record for this book is available from the British Library.

ISBN 978 1 44119 429 9

Typeset by Pindar NZ, Auckland, New Zealand
Printed and bound in Great Britain by the MPG Books Group

Contents

For

Olwen Thomas (d. 1976)
and
Margaret Rhodes (m. 1969),

the two women who,
between them,
have known me all my life
and who together
have shaped so much of it.

Deo gratias.

Foreword

Ours is an age of celebrity biographies and memoirs. This book represents a break with current fashion: it is an autobiography written by an anti-celebrity.

Leslie Griffiths had to be persuaded to write the remarkable story of his life so far. It is all the more remarkable for its unrelenting honesty. Those expecting a sweetly told tale of poverty-to-peerage should be warned to turn the pages with caution.

He is a gifted pastor, a notable academic, a talented broadcaster, a distinguished writer, a church leader and a politican. For all that, he remains a modest man. He is also 'thin-skinned' and 'volcanic', by his own admission, and these factors mean that Leslie's story is never predictable.

The Burry Port boy who suffered great hardship in childhood now sits happily on the plush red benches of the Upper House as lord of his old manor. This book in effect charts the transition from plain Leslie Griffiths to the Reverend Dr Lord Griffiths of Burry Port, a transition which involves the richest mix of experience at home and abroad.

There are sparse but poignant accounts of his childhood. His mother emerges as a woman of real courage and spirit; and his absent father is junked. Winning a place at Llanelli Grammar School was one of the events which changed the course of his life.

Another was the discovery of his Christian faith. This happened as a student in Cardiff, and it eventually led him into the Methodist ministry. That ministry has been impressively varied. Two tours of duty in strife-torn Haiti have left their mark: Leslie is instinctively on the side of the 'marginalised poor', and his time in Haiti 'completed [his] formation as a human being'.

His career as a leader of the Methodist church, his pastorate at Wesley's Chapel in the City of London, and his profile as a preacher, lecturer and broadcaster all led naturally to the House of Lords where he sits on the Labour benches.

It's not all plain sailing. The book also presents us with a powerful blend of contradictions. Here is a 'Welshman to the core' who confesses dislike for the Welsh language. Leslie's complex attitudes to Wales and Welshness are by no means unusual, but he analyses the difficulties of a multi-layered identity with insight and awareness.

Those of us who speak Welsh often forget the alienation felt by those who do not share the language. In Leslie's case, that alienation has clearly undermined his sense of Welshness. It is revealing to learn that his elevation to the peerage was the event which (in effect) reconnected him with Burry Port and our part of south-west Wales.

Leslie's hope is that this volume will 'open on to a future that's still waiting to be grasped'. He leads by example: his life story reveals a habit of seizing opportunities with great energy.

I am honoured to write these few words of introduction, and certain that the wisdom of Leslie's words will enrich his readers.

Huw Edwards

Prologue

Sweet chance that led my steps abroad
Beyond the town, where wild flowers grow –
A rainbow and a cuckoo.
Lord, how rich and great the times are now! . . .
. . . A rainbow and a cuckoo's song may never
Come together again – may never come this side the tomb.

W. H. DAVIES, 'A GREAT TIME'

Identity is one of the big subjects of our day. On all sides, people are in search of it. This has become a feature of post-modern, post-colonial, post-Christian times when demographic change and social mobility have so often raised radical questions about who we are and where we belong. In these global times, when there are significant numbers of people migrating from one culture to another, the need to discover, preserve, affirm or reinforce our identities is the subject of keen discussion among faith leaders, community workers, social planners and government departments alike. Perhaps we should settle for multiple identities. After all, we live in so many different worlds and have to play the game of life from so many different rule books. Everything seems in a whirl these days as people try to work out just who they are, how to describe themselves, where to fit in. The erstwhile familiar landmarks which established our identity – faith, social class, geography and even genes – are being washed away by the tides of our times.

No such angst clouded my sky as I grew up. No one could have been more certain than I of the rock from which he'd been hewn. A Welshman to the core, that's what and who I was. How I'd puff up my little chest as a lad when, just before kick-off in an international rugby match at the old Cardiff Arms Park, the crowd launched itself into the singing of the national anthem! My voice was added to theirs as we made yet another musical promise to inform the whole wide world about the old land of our fathers, a land of poetry and song whose fame and rich culture stretch back into the mists of time. And when the anthem turned its corner and moved up a gear with its joyful shout '*Gwlad, gwlad, pleidiol wyf i'm gwlad*' (My country, my country, how proud I am of you, my country), I knew that the angels *in excelsis* had joined us in our song. How could any team lose once they'd been raised aloft in this way?

This purist understanding of my identity was soon to be challenged. I didn't speak the language of the bards for a start and that differentiated me at once from all those in our town who did. It didn't seem to matter in my earliest years but in my late teens everything got heavily politicized and I came to feel, perhaps I was made to feel, that I was possibly only a second-class Welshman. This creeping feeling that I might be marginal to the truest forms of Welshness adulterated my once unaffected love for my country and its culture. My previously unqualified feelings began to be tempered by less wholesome ones – alienation, sadness, loss.

Many years later, my wife's assiduous genealogical research disclosed a further fallacy in what I had understood to be my pedigree. My maternal grandfather died when I was ten. I knew he'd been a painter and decorator in Burry Port, the town of my birth, but he'd told me such colourful tales about his time as a coalminer in the Rhondda Valley in the early years of the twentieth century and long before the move to west Wales. With a name like Thomas, his Welshness seemed secure but even that assumption turned out to be wide of the mark. His maternal antecedents sprang from Shropshire. His mother worked for the Earl of Plymouth in his country home on the Welsh borders before she moved with her employer to his imposing mansion in St Fagans on the outskirts of Cardiff. That's where my grandfather was born and raised. But it was in Llwynypia, in the lower reaches of the Rhondda Valley, that he met and married my grandmother in 1904. I'd always known her as Lillian but it now seems that she'd been born Leah Trotman and that among her immediate family members there were given names like Sarah and Hannah and Aaron. They'd all been open-cast colliers in and around Bristol until 1885, when the building of the Severn Tunnel sounded the death knell for that form of mining. Now vast amounts of coal from the deep mines of south-east Wales fuelled the British economy and the expansion of the British Empire. The Trotmans must have been typical of many others. They lived a nomadic life as they followed new employment opportunities opening up in the neighbouring Sirhowy Valley and Rhondda Valley.

All of these discoveries have shown me beyond reasonable doubt just how much of a mongrel I am, with lots of English as well as Welsh (and possibly Jewish) blood flowing in my veins. But the known employment records of my antecedents – housemaids, farmers, stonemasons, coalminers, painters and decorators – place my origins consistently among the labouring classes. I've often heard talk of modern life as being far more mobile than that of yesteryear. People used to be born, live and die in the same communities, on the same streets, we're told. That's a neat theory that's been knocked firmly on the head by the glimpses I've gained into my own family history which shows how there were significant and consistent migratory movements among Britain's working-class population throughout the period we call the Industrial Revolution. The arrival of my mother's family in Burry Port just before the First World War was entirely brought about by difficult labour conditions in the mining valleys of Glamorgan and Monmouthshire. New jobs were being created in the development of the docks and mines of Carmarthenshire, to say nothing of the large-scale expansion of metal smelting and tin plating. And, of course, the lengthening reach of the Great Western Railway made the whole area so much more accessible. My grandfather's sister and her husband made the first exploratory visit and, as soon as they'd got themselves established in Burry Port, they called my grandparents and their four children to join them and so began their new life in west Wales.

On my father's side, things seemed far less agitated. They remained more local, never moving further than a radius of 20 miles from any given starting point throughout the years we've been able to track them. While some of their occupations have a slightly more fanciful sound to them – shoemaker, victualler, cordwainer, copperworker – there are plenty of stonemasons and general factory labourers to compensate for such sophistication.

I sometimes reflect on these unknown and unsung figures from my past. How did they live? What made them laugh? Or cry? Why did they move so often? What kind of education did they have? Were there any fierce tempers, radical voices, gifts of poetry or music among them? I sometimes go to St Illtyd's Church in Pembrey, where all four of my grandparents are buried, and my heart and mind are filled with the familiar cadences of Thomas Gray's 'Elegy Written in a Country Churchyard':

> Let not Ambition mock their useful toil,
> Their homely joys, and destiny obscure;
> Nor Grandeur hear with a disdainful smile,
> The short and simple annals of the poor.

Or else that verse from the Old Testament which the commentators say is one of the oldest fragments to be found anywhere in the Bible: 'A wandering Aramean was my father,' it declares. And those few words not only paint a vivid picture of the nomadic beginnings of the Jewish people. They also remind us, ironic in view of later strictures about how race contributes so materially to the Jewish sense of identity, of the non-Jewish element that's integral to the story of their origins. Perhaps we're all mongrels, mixed-up people, issue of our wandering, wondering, meandering ancestors and it may be just too silly a task to try to prove a pure and fixed identity for ourselves.

Burry Port was an offspring of the Industrial Revolution. Here stood a number of satanic mills that imposed dark stains on the beauty of Cymru's green and pleasant land. Here copper and silver, blue and white lead were smelted; here the tin plate industry thrived; coal was brought into the little town from the nearby Gwendraeth Valley and what didn't get used in the smelting industry was shipped from the new docks to the furthest corners of the globe or by rail to London and the Midlands to feed the furnaces there. The population of the town grew from 2,645 in 1831 to 4,773 40 years later. It was to maintain that level for a century, but when my grandparents arrived the place must still have had a 'new town', Wild West feel about it. Isambard Kingdom Brunel's wonderful railway (the signalling system through Burry Port is still original to those times) gave impetus to these developments but also a shape to the burgeoning town. It split the whole place in two. Posh houses were built above the line while the older parts of the town became trapped among the industrial sprawl below it. About 500 of us fell into this latter category and we were thought by the rest of the population (some 4,500) to be the 'rough end' of civilization. That railway certainly ghettoized those of us who lived in what was known as the Bache (pronounced 'Bakaye'). Our five streets stood in a huddle with its back turned to the rest of the town and our close-knit community bred intense loyalties and a mesmerizingly low opinion of the attitudes which prevailed in the rest of the town. I wore my designation as a 'Bache boy' with the pride of a war hero sporting his medals.

I was born into this community that was consciously on the edge of Burry Port. And, as my narrative will show, my family were soon pushed even further to its margins. The divorce of my parents led us to find accommodation outside the Bache, in the very midst of the factories and railway sheds and industrial activity which dominated so much of the town that lay south of that railway line. I was raised in a builders' yard in a lean-to room on a road where we had no neighbours. We were outside the ghetto, which itself lay outside the town's mainstream. I felt this double jeopardy keenly. The edge is where I've come from and it's from the edge that I've always somehow managed to see things.

One other significant epoch in my personal history has intensified this feeling of being on the edge. Soon after our marriage, my wife Margaret and I set up home in the Caribbean nation of Haiti. A full account of our extraordinary ten years there and my subsequent continuing involvement in Haiti's affairs appears in the body of this book. Here, it seems appropriate to mention just how much at the edge of things Haiti was and is. It's part of an island that, in the West Indies, is second in size only to Cuba but seems to belong neither to the Caribbean nor to Latin America. Its history and demography are so radically at odds with anything else that happened in the region that it's hard to fit it into any available mould. French (and a French-based Créole) is its language, another factor which isolates it from its Spanish-, English- and Dutch-speaking neighbours. This is a country that prides itself on being 'the first black republic in the world' but its independence, proclaimed in 1804, gave it pariah status in its early years of existence and guaranteed its impoverishment thereafter. Haiti is the poorest state in the western hemisphere. Black intellectuals, even those who champion the achievements of black people and campaign fiercely for their rights, seem to have such little awareness of the greatness of spirit or the sheer achievement of people like Toussaint Louverture and the slaves who, between them, overthrew the mighty armies of the British General Maitland and later – a truly epochal accomplishment that's conveniently airbrushed out of our history books – the army of Napoleon Bonaparte at the very height of his powers. And Haiti was never in the British sphere of influence, which, for missionaries like me, meant little commonality with colleagues in other parts of the world whose endeavours tended to be acted out wherever the Union flag had been unfurled.

Even when we arrived in Haiti, it was with the marginalized rural poor rather than the city-dwelling political class that we found ourselves working. I think that's why I've always tended to look at development work from the angle of the disenfranchised peoples of the world rather than that of their masters or rulers. Our time in Haiti completed my formation as a human being and I'll never be able adequately to repay my debt to these peasant people who were once called 'the wretched of the earth' but to whose warmth of personality and whose generosity of spirit I owe so much. I've done my best over the decades to remain faithful to them and to bring a richer account of the short and simple annals of this poor people to a wider audience. My commitment to them has given a sharpness to the way I tend to see things, a lack of patience with heavy-handedness or over-contrived ways of approaching conflict or social deprivation. This experience together with those of my childhood has given me an aversion to the bureaucratization of compassion and the posturing of petty officials. Even as I write these words, I can sense just how much 'edginess' seems integral to my thin-skinned nature.

I have no doubt that it's my marriage to Margaret that has taken the edge off some of my awkwardness or the brutality of some of my potential outbursts. Her patience and cool, moderating presence have rounded me as a person and channelled some of my surplus energies into more productive directions. But I do feel sometimes as if I have a volcano inside me. The things that made me angry as a child continue to simmer away; they gnaw away at my deepest being. And now and again, they still erupt; I know only too well the reality of that 'spontaneous overflow of powerful feelings' of which William Wordsworth once wrote.

Margaret is the class act in our relationship. Her antecedents go back uninterruptedly into the mists of time. Members of the Rhodes clan were burgesses of Newcastle-under-Lyme from its beginnings. And they were there when John Wesley made his first visit in 1768, to welcome him and to set up the first Methodist society in the old market town. So my wife outscores me both in terms of the respectability of her antecedents and the impeccable nature of her Methodist credentials. But her researches have allowed me to let my imagination run free. My own forebears were open-cast miners in the vicinity of Bristol. In April 1739, John Wesley was challenged by one of his contemporaries to submit 'to be more vile', to put aside his gentlemanly ways and to go out of doors to preach to the working classes. He accepted the challenge and his first recorded preaching of this kind was, yes, to the open-cast coalminers at their work on the outskirts of Bristol. It's said that these artisans were so moved to hear that they, too, had a place within the economy of God's grace that tears sprang to their eyes and traced white rivulets down their grimy faces. Who knows? Why shouldn't my ancestors have been among their number?

This then is the cultural, geographical and genetic matrix out of which I appeared. This is where the wild flowers grew and where the cuckoo and the rainbow came together in those distant days before the arrival of that sweet chance that led my feet abroad.

1

Childhood

And as I was green and carefree . . .
. . . In the sun that is young once only,
Time let me play and be
Golden in the mercy of his means.

DYLAN THOMAS, 'FERN HILL'

My eyes were on a level with the shiny brass doorknob and, as I gazed upwards, the polished mahogany door seemed to go on forever. There were adults present and my younger brother must have been there too, but I have no recollection of them. Just that massive door. On the other side of it, a court was in session and my future was being decided. The short and acrimonious marriage of my parents was coming to an end.

The judge awarded a divorce to my father on the grounds of my mother's desertion. She, although given custody of her children, was ordered to leave the family home. I still have the solicitor's letter and its terms seem so brutal, so final:

> It is the intention [of your husband] to sell his house which you now occupy. We shall be glad, therefore, if you will kindly make arrangements to leave the house, not later than Thursday next, the 16th October 1947. You will no doubt appreciate that in view of your attitude towards your husband, you have no right to occupy his house.

This letter was dated 9 October 1947. Just a week, seven days, to get out. And then what? There was nowhere to go. We had nothing. The winter was coming. How would we survive?

My parents should probably never have married. My mother was the fourth daughter of a manual worker and her life had been just about as hard as it comes. Her parents had led a peripatetic life, with my grandfather taking work wherever he could find it. He began as a stonemason in St Fagans, near Cardiff, but soon added himself to the army of miners digging coal out of the bowels of one Welsh valley or another, working always at the whim of mine owners who regarded their workforce as robots rather than people. *Wrth ddŵr a thân*, that's the slogan that's still to be seen on the old Docks Office in Cardiff: Through water and fire. The British Empire was fuelled by the bituminous coal mined so prodigally in the south Wales valleys. And my grandfather played a grudging part in that vast enterprise.

I was only ten when he died but I've lost count of the number of times I heard him repeat the tale of how he'd been one of the thousands of miners who were locked out of the Penygraig Pit near Pontypridd in 1910. He told me again and again how Winston Churchill, then Home Secretary in a Liberal government, had ordered British troops in to hold the miners at bay in their dispute with their masters. A man named Samuel Rays lost his life in that skirmish and, whatever the dry facts of the case, his death began a myth much cherished by the Welsh working classes; he became a martyr for his cause and a reason for hating the capitalists, usually English, who exploited their workers. This was among the first stories I ever heard and it was one that shaped my earliest consciousness. Later in my life, it helped me to understand why news of Winston Churchill's death was greeted with joy by so many people in the towns and villages of Wales. It made me aware of how myths are made, how they become visceral, and how they determine the way significant groups of people then go on to view themselves and their place in the world.

My grandparents moved from Llwynypia, near Pontypridd in the Rhondda Valley, to Aberbeeg in the neighbouring Sirhowy Valley. That's where my mother was born in 1913. But soon the family was on the move again, this time away from the mines, but still in search of work. A brother of my grandfather had recently moved to west Wales, to the little town of Burry Port just west of Llanelli, where he'd found employment on the railway. He must have suggested to my grandparents that this was a far more promising place to find work and bring up their family than on the coalfields of south-east Wales. And so they came, all six of them, and found rented accommodation in Silver Terrace, a string of houses built 40 years earlier to house the Cornish workers who came to Burry Port to work in the metal-smelting industry then developing apace in our part of Wales.

My grandfather worked in a soft job – as mate to a painter and decorator. His daughters grew up in relative stability compared with the peregrinations of the previous years. My mother left school at 14 and found seasonal work as a parlour maid in a hotel in Ilfracombe. She'd cross over the water on one of the white steamers which, in those days, linked south Wales with the north Devon coast. She scrubbed floors, polished silver, washed dishes, attended to the needs of holiday-makers. Later she was to work in factories and, during the war, on the railways where her work consisted of coupling and uncoupling the endless strings of coal trucks which were shunted around the miles of tracks that had spread across the centre of Burry Port.

Before her marriage, my mother had had a boyfriend from the nearby Neath Valley and it was clear they'd been deeply in love. His name was Dick and my mother kept his photograph and a couple of his letters for the rest of her life. She told me again and again how, when my father turned up and expressed an interest in her, she'd been overwhelmed by the glamour of his naval uniform rather than the strength of her feelings for him. After a very short courtship, and with my father needed on his ship, they were married in October 1939. They lived with my father's parents at 25 Glanmor Terrace, where I was born in February 1942. My brother followed just over a year later. But the marriage was wrong from the start. War service took my father away from home for considerable periods of time. I have a strong suspicion that my mother might have continued to see her beloved Dick during those absences. Certainly, she and my father rowed furiously whenever he was home on leave. Some of my very earliest memories are of the screaming and shouting which seemed part and parcel of my father's visits home. Indeed, his raised voice constitutes the only sense of his presence that I can recall from my childhood. In the end, he left never to return. He just disappeared from our lives. There was no alimony, we got no Christmas or birthday cards, there were no sightings – nothing. Later, we were to discover that he was living in nearby Swansea. But during the critical years of my growing-up, he was quite simply non-existent. I remember explaining this to friends with a convenient lie. I told them that he was dead.

I saw the light of day on 15 February 1942, the day the Japanese army took Singapore as part of their great sweep down towards the oilfields of Indonesia. The newspaper headlines screamed 'DISASTER!', a sentiment which perfectly reflected my mother's feelings. She'd set her heart on my being born on St Valentine's Day. That, together with the fact that she idolized Rudolph Valentino, then at the height of his Hollywood fame, would have led to my bearing a name very different from the one I now sport. As it was, bereft of imagination, she did what dozens of mothers in Burry Port did and named me after the doctor who delivered me. There are so many of my hometown contemporaries named Leslie – enough to make up a rugby team with one or two on the subs bench for good measure.

I don't really remember what happened in the early days after our ejection. There was great uncertainty and we were shunted from one temporary abode to another. That particular winter was to be one of the worst ever and it was fortuitous that we found a solution to our needs before it really set in. Some years earlier, my grandparents had moved into a small caretaker's set of rooms at the Building Trades Supply, rambling premises that had originally lodged a white lead smelting works. It was situated just round the corner from Silver Terrace where they'd previously lived and in a very industrial complex with almost no neighbours. Engine sheds, railway tracks, wagon repairers, a copper smelting factory, a soap factory and, eventually, a coal-fired power station – these were our neighbours. And we were just a stone's throw from the still-busy docks and the 'fishing-boat bobbing sea'.

My grandparents lived in one large room divided by a low wooden partition. Abutting it, and reached by a short covered way, was a lean-to room of modest proportion. It stuck out into part of the builders' yard and every Tuesday and Thursday, the lorries of a local transport company would dump a load of rough bricks just outside its one and only window. My mother's eldest sister and her husband, my Auntie Anne and Uncle Jim, lived in this lowly abode.

Faced with the need to get my mother and her two small boys into accommodation before the winter set in, my aunt and uncle decided to move out and to take up residence with Uncle Jim's parents. The fact that Auntie Anne, at the advanced age of 40, had recently produced her one and only child, helped them to reach this conclusion. Their room was no place for a baby. So they moved out and we moved in. For the next four or five years, my mother and her two sons lived in this one room. We ate, slept, bathed and read in that tiny space. It had a sink with a cold-water tap, an open-grate coal fire and a plain concrete floor. It still seems utterly impossible that my mother could have coped or that we, as a family, survived those early days of our banishment.

From the time of our move, my mother had to go out to work. For the first four or five years, she was employed at the Ashburnham Tin Works as a manual worker. Our part of Wales supplied the major part of the country's demand for tin plate and it was little factories like this one that met that demand. The work was hard and unremitting. From time to time, in school holidays, I used to take my mother's lunch to the factory and I remember seeing her at work. Dressed in protective leather, she would carry a number of sheets of steel from one part of the process to another. Her job was to push these sheets through a giant roller, a machine that looked like a mangle. It was physical, dirty, grim work. In the end, her body was broken by it. She struggled bravely on until 1951 before she collapsed. Although she lived another 25 years, she was never fit for work again and lived a severely restricted life, rarely free from pain.

My brother Jim and I were like twins. We were signed-up members of the local gang and took our full part in the fights that were a regular feature of street life. After the breakdown of our mother's health, we became scavengers, looking for booty to supplement our scarce domestic resources. During those years, the Burry Port Council was reclaiming a tract of marshland for eventual use as a park. Household garbage was being tipped there and we two brothers knew the times and days when the domestic waste of our town's wealthiest streets was collected. We lay in wait and, the moment the trucks had disgorged their contents and driven off, we pounced. We brought home in triumph a variety of objects but nothing was more pleasing than the occasional find of money. Once, a local chip shop had a fire and, when the firemen had gone home leaving the shop a soggy mess, everything had to be shovelled up and taken to the tip. Imagine our glee when, rooting and foraging among this detritus, we found that the day's takings had been dumped along with everything else. It amounted to a few pounds and we strutted home like millionaires.

Once, once only, we resorted to begging. Things had become really tough. My mother was desperately unwell. We wanted to cheer her up. So we chose our spot and hassled the people passing by. They all knew us and many of them coughed up a penny or two. We'd set a target of three pounds and, when we'd got it, bore it proudly home. Only to meet our mother's ire. 'We may be poor,' she shouted, 'but we haven't lost our pride.' She beat us furiously and ordered us to go out, find those who'd given us money, and return it to them. And we did just that.

The winters were worst. We couldn't afford to buy coal, so Jim and I, armed with a sack, would go out in search of winter fuel. The engine drivers in the sheds opposite our house would let us know when they were cleaning out their boilers. There would always be cinders, good stuff with plenty of burning left in them. Once, however, we were too keen and shovelled them up while they were still hot. They burned a hole in our sack and our sad and grimy faces drew the sympathy of the engine drivers who set about finding us replacements. The wooden blocks used in holding railway lines in place were other favourites – they burned long and were almost as good as coal. Brushwood and driftwood, small coal and coal dust – all were grist for our mill. It was so maddening that, in order to get our combustibles together, we had to weave in and out of lines of railway wagons, hundreds of them, all filled with fine anthracite coal awaiting shipment from the nearby docks. From time to time, when the pickings had been particularly bad and we feared the wrath of a disappointed mother, we'd climb onto a wagon and throw lumps of the black stuff down to one another.

I was 16 before I ate meat at home – we could never afford that. Bread was our staple with margarine and sugar, sometimes dripping (or even lard), and tinned tomatoes, too. There must have been more to it than this but I seem to have consigned other culinary delights to oblivion. Christmas was the exception to this pattern, however. We made our own decorations – crayons, newspaper, a flour-based paste and string gave us the raw materials and we hung them up liberally across our humble living space. An early afternoon bus on Christmas Eve took us to Llanelli. We did a little simple shopping and always ended up, near closing time, at the market. In those days before freezers, my mother knew the traders would be wanting to offload their fare before packing up for home. And she had her eyes open for a chicken. When she saw what she wanted, she'd haggle, roll her eyes, show the trader her skinny boys, play on his pity and, invariably, with a smile and a yuletide wish, he'd settle for my mother's asking price and we'd move merrily away, the chicken well wrapped and settled in a brown carrier bag and us, three musketeers, ready to take on the world. The Regal Cinema stood across the road from our bus stop and we generally managed to see the last showing of the film (it always seemed to be *The Glass Mountain*) before getting a late bus home. Jim and I were in a state of rare excitement by the time we rolled out our sleeping mat and settled down for the night.

Sundays were also feast days – not quite up to Christmas but special all the same. We regularly invited a Mrs Reidy to tea. She was a widow, a Roman Catholic, Irish, gnarled, beaten down by life. I never discovered her claim on my mother's affection or the reason for the Sunday bash so lavishly prepared for her. She seemed to belong to several worlds we knew nothing about. But she always took pride of place; my mother sat her in our one posh chair. We used our entire butter ration on that tea party.

There was jam, too, and the supreme miracle, a jelly. I don't ever remember Jim or I grumbling at this old biddy's eating our precious food. On the contrary, her knock on the door was akin to the ringing of Pavlov's bell. It would make us salivate in anticipation of the good things that we were about to eat.

This isn't my only memory of my mother's ability to offer hospitality to strangers. Another brings to mind a nasty November evening, with the wind high and driving the rain almost horizontally across our little town. The three of us were cosily gathered around our little fire when there was a knock on the door. No one should have been out in such gruesome weather. When my mother opened the door, she found two nuns standing there and looking like drowned penguins. They wore full habit in those days and were drenched to the skin. 'Come in, darlings,' my mother said, and in they duly came. We found chairs for them in front of the fire and my mother busied herself with making a cup of tea. We had some good conversation even though their thick Irish brogue meant that we had to guess at half the words they uttered. It transpired that they were out collecting money for the construction of a new Roman Catholic church in Burry Port. The existing one was a tin hut and the Catholic community had set its heart on something better than that. In the end, as my mother led them towards the door, she found a half-crown and put it into their hands. Just before they parted, she said: 'I never asked you who you were, what organization you belong to.' 'Oh,' said one of the nuns, 'we're Little Sisters of the Assumption.' I shall never forget either the startled look on my mother's face or the extraordinary remark that she then came up with. 'There's nice darlings,' she said, 'but tell me something, what exactly is it that you assume?' I still chortle merrily at the memory of that precious moment.

Those days before my tenth birthday, we all seemed to live with whatever came along. There were no plans, no ambitions, nothing to aim at. As well as attending to the business of survival – of necessity, a day-by-day affair – I seem to have enjoyed playing with my friends, running free as the wind, coming home dirty and hungry with the setting of the sun. We played among the railway wagons – brilliant for hide-and-seek or our first kiss. We made dens in the marshland or the hillside and secreted ourselves there for hours on end. When a new sewage farm was built, we dared each other to run down one side of an open-to-the-air inverted cone in order, if sufficient velocity had been achieved, to run up the other side without stopping. One of my friends failed to get up enough speed and ended literally in the shit. We were all dismayed because every one of us would be whopped by our mothers when we got home. The news of our goings-on always got home before we did.

As well as my friendship with all the other urchins of our disreputable part of Burry Port, I found myself specially drawn towards two boys who didn't live in our neighbourhood. One was the grandson of the proprietor of the funfair which visited us every summer. My friend lived in Bristol and used to travel with the fair during his school holidays. Our friendship gave me access behind the scenes and made me aware of an exotic life, full of dark mystery, that lay beyond the ken of most people. I loved climbing into the rather posh caravans, mobile homes of some sophistication, where I stood amazed at the way these tiny spaces could offer such luxury and variety to their inhabitants. This was all different from the travelling home of my other seasonal friend, a Romany boy, whose family would arrive in horse-drawn caravans and camp on a little patch of land just behind the Building Trades Supply. I'd sit by an open fire after dark, with my friend's aunt or sister or grandmother (there was something indeterminate about all of them – they seemed ageless, somehow) as they carved pegs or put sprigs of heather into little bunches. I loved the horses but never went too close to them.

Each of these lads embodied a culture that lay over the rim of my direct experience. They suggested a world bigger than Burry Port, a world I began to get curious about.

And then I was ten.

The year 1952 almost destroyed us. We'd put together a threadbare existence as we faced the need to survive. We built a close-knit unit, as our togetherness would give us the best chance of getting by. And now events were to expose the fragility of our way of life and put it under enormous pressure. Somehow we got through the crisis and lived to fight another day. Not everything was negative, however. Things happened during this same year which were to change both our circumstances and also the direction that we were travelling in. Now that I can look back on it all, that year marked a real turning-point in our lives.

In February, the King died. My mother always remembered that because, at the very same time, her father died, too. After a short illness, he just gave up the ghost. He embodied so much of Welsh working-class life. He'd been an enthusiastic supporter of the Labour Party since its beginnings and had lived through mining disasters, lockouts, unemployment and the Great Depression. I've often wished that I could have known him better and heard him talk more on the great issues of his day.

My mother wasn't at her father's funeral because she was herself in hospital, fighting for her life. Her body had just given up; she could no longer carry those steel sheets or push them through those greedy rollers any more. She underwent serious surgery in nearby Morriston Hospital and it was several weeks before we saw her again. My grandmother, just widowed, had to look after Jim and me. I have almost no recollection of that dark period in our lives. My mother's life hung by a thread and I'm sure the adults in our family were wondering just who would take responsibility for us two boys if the worst were to happen. Or was my father's family, somewhere beyond our gaze, aiming at taking us back into their fold? Everything was touch and go. We weren't allowed to visit our mother in hospital but I remember waiting for her on the day of her return home. We'd been scrubbed by aunties and our grandmother, our hair was slicked down with water, and we waited nervously for the car bringing her home. How emaciated, how drawn, how wraith-like she looked. We didn't recognize her at first. She was in such pain then and, periodically, for the rest of her life. But she was alive. She'd survived. We were together again. That simple fact was enough. I wept for joy.

My grandmother soon saw that it would be impossible, with my moth-er's condition still fragile and us boys growing apace, for us to go on living together in one room. She began to make arrangements to move into the house of another of her daughters. Soon, we had our grandparents' living quarters as well as our own. It felt palatial. Crucially, it gave my mother a room of her own to sleep in and gave us all space from each other.

One other thing happened at about this time which I've always lumped together with our family crisis. At school one day, our teacher announced that he was going to read out a list of names. Everyone whose name was called would have the rest of the day off. They were to go straight home and tell their parents the wonderful news that they'd passed their 11-plus exam and would be going to the grammar school. He proceeded, with great solemnity, to call out the names. And mine was one of them. I couldn't make rhyme or reason of the significance of this moment. I didn't even remember sitting an exam that merited the sense of occasion being built up by our teacher. Nor did I have a clue what a grammar school was. No one in our family, indeed no one in our neighbourhood, had ever gone to such an institution. But I was glad enough to have a half-day off school and I remember running all the way home and breathlessly telling my mother the news. She wasn't expecting me home at that time of day so I found her resting in bed. I could see that she wanted to be glad because I was glad but, in the end, we both gave up being glad because neither of us knew exactly what it was that we were trying to be glad about.

We were soon to find out, however, and what we discovered took the smile from our faces. My new school was in Llanelli and there were going to be expenses we'd have to meet. That was a chilling prospect. The shoes Jim and I wore invariably had holes in them, so our feet made direct contact with the ground. We had three pairs of socks between us, two on our feet and the other in the wash. Pyjamas were unheard of and underwear non-existent items – and remained so until I went away to university. We washed with unscented carbolic soap, the kind still used wherever floors are scrubbed. My knees chapped in the winter, I was as skinny as a rake. And now I had to contemplate going to a posh school. We learned that travel and school meals would be free. Even so, there would be the school uniform and equipment to buy. And my new school mates would be the sons of bank managers and teachers. I wasn't sure about this at all. I could

never have imagined that this one event was going to be the key to everything else that happened to me subsequently. If at the time someone had
offered me a way out of my predicament, I think I'd have jumped at it.

At about that time, a man from the National Assistance Board called on
us. He wanted to talk to my mother on her own but, since my grandmother
hadn't yet moved out of her quarters, we were still cooped up in our one
little room. So he had to interview my mother in the company of her sons
– aged ten and nine respectively. His questions were fierce. He seemed to
doubt my mother's medical condition. He suggested that she should think
about registering for work again as soon as possible. He wondered if she
were really as penniless as she was making out. There must be alimony
coming in from my father. And so it went on and on. Jim and I exchanged
many a glance. This man was humiliating our mother. Evidence of her
condition could hardly have been more obvious yet, with all the disdain
and tyrannical condescension to which petty officials know how to rise,
he was rubbing her nose in the dirt. It was as if it were his own personal
money he was thinking of dispensing. In the end, it got too much to bear.
I told him to stop speaking to her like that. He told me to shut up. He
shouldn't have done that. I launched myself upon him, Jim joined me, and
we hit out at him with our little fists and kicked him hard on the shins,
and drove him ignominiously into the street, slamming the door shut on
his retreating form. Miraculously, the feared retribution didn't fall on us.
Another man was sent, an altogether different specimen, and we were soon
receiving a weekly sum from the benefits office.

This guaranteed income made it possible to contemplate a more
reassuring future. But it wouldn't stretch to getting me equipped for the
grammar school. That conundrum, felt by others on her behalf as well
as by my mother herself, was to produce a situation which, it's now clear,
was to determine the course of everything that came later. These turning-
points are miniscule when they occur, yet in the end they produce radical
change. Huge weights can be lifted with levers that seem to the untutored
eye to operate against the very laws of gravity. The course of one's life can
also turn on events and decisions that seem so utterly insignificant when

they happen. The event in question occurred in, of all possible places, a non-conformist chapel.

No mention has yet been made in this narrative of anything to do with faith or religion. That's because it played very little part in those early years. Indeed, what we saw of organized religion didn't much attract us to it either. The five mean streets on our side of the railway tracks were considered by the people of Burry Port to be rough and uncouth – a miniature version of Tiger Bay or Canning Town – and they offered almost nothing to those who wanted to attend church services. The town as a whole boasted a dozen or so places of worship, most of them operating in the Welsh language; south of the railway line, however, there was only one. And that was an English-language Wesleyan chapel built in 1866 for the Cornish workers who came to work in our smelting factories. So churchgoers, especially if they were Welsh-speaking, tended to cross the railway lines to get to their desired spiritual watering hole. I used to watch them carefully. They seemed so fierce as they made their way to say their prayers and sing their hymns. Their religion was certainly of a denunciatory kind – preachers fulminated from flaming pulpits, offering judgement on the town's latest ways. I disliked what I saw. Those faces which seemed to me to be etched in vinegar were never going to attract me to whatever it was that drove them to their Peniels and Rehoboths Sunday by Sunday.

My mother had attended the Baptist church as a girl. But the hard life she'd lived had left her little time or interest for the spiritual. She spoke rarely of such things but, when she did, it was generally dismissive. She had a little speech whose drift I still remember. 'Look at all those people going to chapel,' she'd say. 'I wonder what their preachers will be telling them today. They'd always have a word for me, mind; I smoke, I do the football pools, I like an occasional tipple, when I can I like to put sixpence each way on a horse, especially in the Derby or the Grand National, I love my bingo and, to cap it all, I'm a divorced woman. Plenty of sermons there! But they'll not catch me in their chapels. I'm not going to give those preachers the pleasure of pointing their finger at the likes of me. I'd rather stay at home.' And stay at home is what she did.

And yet she sent Jim and me to Sunday School. How on earth did that come about? The answer is simple and non-theological. She sent us as a child-minding exercise. She worked five and a half days a week in the factory. On Sunday afternoons, she prepared to entertain Mrs Reidy for tea. And we lived in one room. She needed time and space. So Sunday School it was.

We were a real group of ragamuffins, vagabonds, ruffians, rogues and urchins who were sent along to that Sunday School by mothers wanting to get rid of us for a short while or even, who knows, in the hope that something of value would rub off onto their unpromising offspring. We were taught by a group of ladies who were quite remarkable. There was nothing in it for them. We teased them, ran rings around them, took them for a ride and, strange as it sounds, we respected them. They cared for us. Deeply. They shouted at us when our behaviour was outrageous. And they hardly kept us stimulated or inspired with their ancient pedagogical methods based either on learning by heart or reading verses of scripture (from the Authorized Version) mechanistically and in turn. With one or two exceptions, they were barely educated women themselves. So there was little or nothing on the surface that would seem to commend them. At least, not to children like us. And yet, there was something in their demeanour and much in their dedication that got through to us. I have nothing but fond memories to this day of Nesta and Lorraine, Louie and Evan and Millicent, Mrs Jenkins and Mrs Katherine, who were never ill, never fed up with us, always ready to work with such ungrateful material.

All that is true but I haven't yet described the factor which proved to be life-changing for me. When the chapel members heard that I'd passed the 11-plus exam, there was much serious shaking of heads. 'Olwen [my mother] will never be able to manage this,' they said. 'We'd better see what we can do to help.' And that's what they did. They began a 'Les Fund' and put a penny or two at a time into it. It was that little fund that got my mother out of a hole more than once and saw to it that I was properly equipped to go to the grammar school. The women who acted in this way were not exactly eye-catching. On Saturday nights, many of them would be standing outside the Glanmor Arms waiting for their menfolk to be turned out at closing time. They always seemed to wear pinafores and headscarves and they had biceps that bulged, just like those of Andy Capp's wife, Florrie. If their husbands, who all resembled Andy Capp, were the worse for wear, they'd find themselves strong-armed and foul-mouthed all the way home to the delight of us boys who, in those days before television, thought this was pure theatre. And the same women were in chapel the next day, saying their amens and singing their hymns as if butter wouldn't melt in their mouths. These were the people, working-class saints, who saw to it that I would get my chance in life.

Most children left the Sunday School when they reached their teenage years. That's what Jim did. But I stayed on. I even became a Sunday School teacher. Not that this had much to do with faith. I wasn't sure that I could embrace the whole package being taught by those chapel people. It was out of a sense of loyalty that I stayed. They were, after all, contributing materially to my education. As I look back on it now, and in the light of subsequent experience, I see how some people are brought into the kingdom by the purity of doctrine, others through the beauty of liturgy and yet others under the influence of a charismatic preacher or leader. In my case, I took my first steps in faith for more down-to-earth and practical reasons. Here were people whose faith, whatever it amounted to, saw that helping someone in need was part and parcel of what they'd signed up for. This readiness to add value to life around them and to see the spiritual and material worlds inseparably linked was impressive. And those displaying it were such simple people too. They showed me just how straightforward the Christian faith can be. It was certainly never intended to be complicated.

And so I arrived at the Llanelly (that's how it was spelt in those days) Boys' Grammar School. There were four forms of entry and I was put in the 'top' class – Form 1A1. I came fifth in my class at the end of my first term and first at the end of my first year. Scrap of a lad as I must have been, unused to serious learning and from a background so different from that of my classmates, I found myself able to hold my own from the very first day. I could feel the excitement of it all; it gave me goose pimples. What I lacked in appearance, I knew I could make up for in performance. And so it proved. I was a steady rather than a brilliant student. I had to haul myself up from a pretty basic level and the nine O-levels and three A-levels that I eventually attained represented a very satisfying outcome for my endeavours.

In my first term at the grammar school, my form teacher made an announcement that I never forgot. He told us how a very famous man, someone we were destined to know a lot more about as we got older, had just died in New York. He was referring to Dylan Thomas. Burry Port was just about equidistant from Swansea, where the poet was born, and Laugharne, where he was buried. I got very excited about this and, when I began buying books, one of the very earliest was the *Collected Poems* of our local poet. My awareness of the existence of poetry was stirred into life by this early announcement. Throughout my life, poetry has remained the most consistent stimulus to my imagination and the most consoling activity in times of personal pressure or difficulty.

I'm pretty sure that a number of my teachers were aware of the kind of home and background I'd come from. Their pastoral care was amazing. More importantly, they supplied an adult male presence in my daily life, an element which I'd never previously experienced. I could reel off some of their names (and nicknames) even now in a litany of fond remembrance, each name conjuring up a sense of undying gratitude for their care and even affection: Evans French and Tommy French, Caesar Thomas, Bingo Rees, Froggy Harries, Frank Phillips and the two headmasters, T. V. Shaw and Stan Rees. A few years ago, a television commercial for the recruitment of young people to the teaching profession showed a succession of well-known people recalling a teacher who'd left his mark on them and given direction to the rest of their lives. I'd find it very difficult to limit myself to one single teacher. I was surrounded by men who willed me on, gave me courage, believed in me. It was, and remains, a phenomenal achievement on their part. The raw material that they were working with was, after all, so very rough and unsophisticated.

Not everything at school was bright and sunny, however. There were all the usual personal barriers, so important for teenagers, that had to be overcome. They were even more complex in my case and, to this day, I cringe with embarrassment when I think of some of them. My blazer, ordered by my mother from her Marshall Ward mail order catalogue (rather than the school shop) was never quite the same colour as everyone else's. I wore short trousers long after my classmates had moved elegantly into long ones. My skin chapped terribly in the winters and no amount of leg crossing or careful arrangement of my hands or books could quite hide those open scars from the view of the people around me. My teeth left much to be desired and my mouth has remained the most potent reminder of the poverty of my childhood. And the rooms where we changed for games posed their own problems. I was very skinny and couldn't wait to get my rugby shirt on before someone could offer a comment on my skeletal appearance. And I tried desperately to fold all my clothes so that no one would notice the absence of underwear or the state of my socks. I can't think how I mastered these daily challenges to my self-confidence.

Somehow I did. Nor did they stop me from finding outlets for energies which I began to be aware of at this time. Our school was organized on two sites. After three years we moved from spanking new premises in Pwll to the more traditional buildings of the upper school in nearby Llanelli. By the time I was in my third year, my last in the lower school, I was organizing rotas for the school monitors and timetables for out-of-class activities. The headmaster expressed himself well pleased with my endeavours and some of my friends thought that I should be the head monitor. But it wasn't to be. The son of a civil servant got the position instead.

Something similar happened years later when I'd got to the Sixth Form. I served the Sixth Form Forum Committee for both my years at the top end of the school and as its secretary in my final year. I took part in school plays, was joint editor of the school magazine and active in all kinds of clubs and organizations. I was tipped as a likely head boy. But that didn't happen either. That went to the son of a bank manager.

To cap it all, I remember a conversation with Stan Rees, who'd become headmaster in my fourth year at the school. 'Leslie,' he said, 'I want you to know that I'm putting together a group of boys who stand a chance of getting into Oxford or Cambridge.' In those days, Oxbridge aspirants stayed on for a third year in the Sixth Form, the phenomenon so brilliantly explored by Alan Bennett in his play *The History Boys.* Stan Rees wore a solicitous look as he added, 'I want you to know that you will not be in the group. You're clever enough but I don't think you could cope with Oxford or Cambridge socially.'

Whenever I've mulled over these memories or shared them with others, I've wondered whether these examples of what might be called 'class discrimination' were as devastating when they occurred as they might seem in retrospect. They'd make a good story that could be presented with great melodrama and for effect, of course, to show just how big the obstacles were that had to be surmounted and what personal courage I was possessed of. But it would be dishonest of me to do so. When I search my deepest consciousness, I find no trace of resentment whatsoever. Even now, armed with a heightened sense of my human rights and the wickedness of class distinction, I can't muster any sense of having been hard-done-by. I was disappointed at these failures to gain awards or honours that I thought I might deserve. Of course I was. But none of these outcomes lessened my happiness or sense of well-being. And I've never carried any chips on my shoulder because of them. Indeed, I've never doubted the correctness of Stan Rees's judgement about Oxbridge. For a start, I was never clever enough to pass the entry examination. Nor would I have had the self-confidence or the lateral knowledge to do well in a high-powered interview that was an essential part of the process. The miracle was that I'd been in the frame at all. And no one knew that better than I.

Until the very end of my time at the grammar school, going home was like landing on a different planet. It was impossible for me to bring any friends home since we lived in such Spartan conditions and, to boot, in the middle of a builders' yard. So I found myself enjoying the hospitality of others, especially my old friend John Wilkins and his family, in an altogether disproportionate way. During our holidays, we'd spend hours and hours down at the Memorial Park playing anything at all – football or rugby, putting or bowls, cricket or tennis. And then, usually at nightfall, we'd wend our way to John's house where his mother, always uncomplainingly, would cook something or other to fill our aching stomachs. At some stage in the evening, John's dad would come in and he, too, brought a friend. Councillors Alf Wilkins and Labor Dennis had, as often as not, spent the previous few hours either at meetings of the Burry Port Rural District Council or the Carmarthenshire County Council. They arrived at the Wilkins household via one or another of the town's drinking holes. This had loosened their tongues and they were overflowing with good humour and the latest gossip from whichever chamber they'd spent time in that day. John and I were agog with curiosity as the two hardened politicians regaled us with their take on the goings-on of local government.

In the end, of course, I had to go home. And there my mother would be waiting for me, reading the *Daily Herald* or the *Daily Mirror*, or else doing a crossword. And we'd chat and joke until bedtime. If only my school friends could have seen just how bare this little dwelling place was. I remember the time my mother and I papered its walls for the very first time. We hadn't realized that there was a pattern that needed to be matched as we pasted a succession of sheets alongside each other. We ended up with a very rambling display of roses but, to us, it felt like Buckingham Palace. Even that was nothing compared with the day we put linoleum on the floor for the first time. I carried a large roll home from the Co-op shop and we emptied the room of its simple furniture in readiness for this new sign of our increasingly bourgeois existence. We got into all kinds of trouble cutting the linoleum at the edges and in the corners but, in its generality, the shining and sparkling just took our breath away. My mother was so excited that she went onto the street to find people to bring in to admire this spectacle. We didn't put the furniture back until darkness imposed an obligation to do so. The furniture dimmed the brilliance but, in the end, we had to settle for that.

Jim had failed the 11-plus and so he went on to the local Secondary Modern School. It was a good school with fine teachers but it could never shake itself free from the fact that every one of its pupils was there because he'd failed to pass the fateful exam. My younger brother was just as clever as I – he was a fast talker imbued with native wit and downright intelligence. It seemed so wrong that we shouldn't be enjoying the same educational opportunities. We slept in the same bed until we were in our late teens and our love for each other was unbreakable and lasted till separated by his death at the early age of 57. At home, we were the two noisy sons of Olwen Thomas and we spent hours kicking a rugby ball or playing homespun cricket together whenever we had the opportunity. We seemed to be tuned in to each other and we somehow managed to deal with the fact that I needed at times to be the family's father figure as well as Jim's big brother.

For all this closeness, however, our lives were lived in entirely different registers. Jim left the Sunday School as soon as it was decent to do so. He left school at 15 and took an apprenticeship as a linotype setter with the local newspaper. 'Hot metal' is yesterday's technology now but Jim completed four of the five years needed to gain his qualifications. He wandered off into the air force and later worked in factories of various kinds. Rugby was his passion and he was soon playing for one of our local teams, the Pembrey Youth XV. And he became a heavy drinker and smoker. He loved to dress in the latest 1950's fashions and was an especially visible 'teddy boy' with his suede jacket, bootlace tie, drainpipe trousers and platform shoes – an outfit well set off by his DA (duck's arse) hairstyle. Once, in our mid-teens, I was walking down the main street in Burry Port in the company of some friends. Jim was coming towards us from the other direction with some of his pals. We met and greeted each other warmly, to the astonishment of many of our respective parties. His friends couldn't believe that I was his brother and mine found it hard to credit that he was mine. Our education had pushed us into different worlds, different lifestyles. But that was only on the streets. At home, we were as one.

The one disappointment at the grammar school was the way I was taught Welsh. Burry Port was largely a Welsh-speaking town but, because of my family's origins in the valleys of south-east Wales, we spoke only English. This was never a problem for us in my earliest years but, when I began my secondary studies, I discovered that the study of Welsh history and the Welsh language was obligatory. I had a natural gift for languages and was soon enjoying French and Spanish, Latin and Greek. Because I spoke no Welsh, however, the assumption was made that I was an ignoramus. Didn't everyone in the Llanelli area know Welsh? Only the thick don't, won't or can't speak the language of the bards. That seemed to be the logic used in assessing us. So I was lumped with all the other non-Welsh speakers and taught as if we were either stupid or wilful (or both). As a result of this, I became very hostile about the Welsh language, especially after it became politicized, and to this day feel a distinct disinclination to feel positive about it. This has undoubtedly coloured the way I feel about Wales – the very word triggers what Wordsworth called 'a spontaneous overflow of powerful feeling. These range from a passionate and visceral pride in my ethnic and cultural identity, on the one hand, to what sometimes verges on distaste for or even hatred of the narrow-mindedness and parochialism of those who use ethnicity and culture to define the criteria of social acceptability, on the other.

French and Latin were an altogether different experience. I lapped them up. It was when I came home that things got interesting. My mother, who'd left school at 14, had no inkling of any of the things that I was studying but, gamely, she agreed to help me with my French and Latin homework. The role she liked best was checking the vocabulary lists that I'd brought home to learn. She would shout any word from the English list, in any order, and I'd have to give the French or Latin equivalent. If what I said sounded even vaguely like what the word printed in front of her looked like, then she'd feel at liberty to shout another. In the end, this became quite a game and she loved her part in it.

I could sometimes feel her incredulity as she watched the way my life was going. I acquired my first books at about the age of 15. I remember my pride when I placed a copy of *Pears' Cyclopaedia* on a shelf alongside a book, long lost, called *A Hundred Famous Murders*. That led my mother to add to my library. She bought me a Bible for Christmas, a little cloth-covered book with pastoral illustrations, a volume I still have. I recognize now how life in a bookless environment impoverished me. It's led to huge gaps in my reading, works which my contemporaries were devouring in their teenage years. I was a late starter.

It's truly extraordinary that my mother never once sought to put obstacles in the way of my progress. I know she'd have loved me to go out to work. With nine O-levels, I could have got a very creditable clerical job in a local enterprise. The wages I could expect to earn would have relieved her penury. But she didn't blink when I told her about A-levels. It was only with talk of university that she began to show some anxiety – and that was more to do with the fact that I'd have to leave home than that I was still further delaying the day when I might bring some money home. She was generosity itself. I remember describing her in these terms in an article I wrote later in life. A friend of mine, a very wealthy man, read what I'd written and broke down in tears. He had a professional actor record the piece and he played it to himself regularly. He repeatedly told me how, in his view, my mother was possessed of 'an aristocracy of the spirit'. That captures it for me. As does a short snatch of a poem by R. S. Thomas, who describes a young woman whom he's seen recently:

> . . . a girl from the tip,
> Sheer coal dust
> The blue in her veins . . .

The poet's use of the word 'blue' combines the idea of a physical appearance typical among those living in a coal-mining environment with the notion of the blue blood said to flow through the veins and capillaries of the nobility.

Despite every difficulty and all that deprivation, mine was a happy childhood. Dylan Thomas, in his lovely short story called 'Holiday Memory', gazes wistfully at some children playing in the sand on Swansea Beach. He longs for them to seize the moment and squeeze all they can from it since their whoops of joy and shouts of glee will soon be lost to them forever. 'But, over all the beautiful beach,' he writes, 'I remember most the children playing, boys and girls tumbling, moving jewels, who might never be happy again.' As I look back over my own early years, I remember being happy just like those children. I know that this might amount to little more than an idealization of a past which seems pleasurable to the memory only because of the way my life subsequently worked out. I might well be in denial, refusing to admit, in the words of Welsh comedian Max Boyce, that 'it was hard, bloody hard'. Self-delusion, perhaps? A thinly disguised desire to portray myself as the hero who overcame all those 'hobgoblins and foul fiends' which were seeking to daunt my spirit? After all, the poverty was real. And there were days when we felt that everything might collapse around us at any moment. We certainly cried ourselves to sleep from time to time. All these things are true. But, hand on heart, I believe that we knew happiness of a rare order. The landscape of our lives was a not unusual mixture of sunshine and shadow. The shadows were sometimes very dark but the patches of sunlight never seemed far away. I'm convinced that the happiness of my youth created a great deal of the capital I've been able to draw on again and again in my subsequent life.

As it happens, I don't feel I have to protest too much to defend myself on this point. Something happened to my brother Jim in his later life that throws light on the true nature of our state of being in those early years. I'm happy to take refuge in his testimony.

Jim was in his early forties when the incident with which I want to end this chapter occurred. He was living in Kent with his wife and child and we saw each other only rarely. He'd become a trade union shop steward and rose through the ranks very quickly, eventually becoming an area organizer for the General and Municipal Workers' Union (as it was still called in those days). He was reading philosophy and politics and was being encouraged to go to Ruskin College, Oxford. I was very proud of him.

Out of the blue, one day, he telephoned me and it was obvious that he was in some distress. He wanted to come over to see me as soon as possible. He came that same afternoon. We sat and talked; he was crying as he told me how he'd had a most amazing experience. He'd had a vision and heard a voice – the voice, he said, of Jesus. I was stunned. Jim never spoke like this. He wasn't made like this. He was a hard-drinking, heavy-smoking, pleasure-loving man, a man of the world, the life and soul of any party. A vision? A voice? What was this all about? He sensed my reaction and went on to describe what he'd seen and heard.

He felt that he was gazing down into a dark pit at the bottom of which dirty and swirling waters were rushing into some subterranean hell-hole. He was at risk of falling in. 'I've done bad things,' he said, 'flirted with danger and taken unacceptable risks. That vision helped me see just how near I was to losing my very soul. But,' he added, 'there were other things in the picture, too; things that came from our childhood in Burry Port.' He went on to tell me how he'd been able to see the two of us kicking a rugby ball back and forth to each other on the tarmacked ribbon of a road outside the Building Trades Supply. Our mother was there too, calling us in for dinner. The sky was blue and the day was perfect. And there, in the corner of this blissful picture, was the little chapel that we'd attended as children and which he'd abandoned in his early teens. 'All of that, Les,' he said, 'reminded me of the happiness I once had and have turned my back on.' Then, as if all this weren't enough, he went on to tell me about the voice he'd heard. It spoke directly to him, he said, and called him back from the edge of the abyss. It told him that he must go at once to share this experience with me and to ask my forgiveness for all the wrong he'd done me. 'But Jim,' I protested, 'you haven't done anything I'd feel I needed to forgive you for; I just love you so much.' At that we fell into each other's arms, both of us weeping copiously. For joy, not sorrow. And we felt the bonds between us to be unbreakable.

I tell this tale not to highlight my brother's 'Damascus road' conversion. It was exactly that, of course, but my focus is elsewhere. Whatever the exact nature of Jim's epiphany, he'd clearly been presented with a profound understanding of the polarities of good and evil, misery and happiness. He'd seen and recognized them for what they were. They'd become tangible. And within what he described as his vision, the details of our Burry

Port childhood stood out as the very epitome of happiness, a benchmark against which all other feelings and states of mind were to be measured.

Happiness cannot be bought. It's a gift. The Roman poet Virgil suggested that 'there are tears at the heart of things'. Maybe. But they can be tears of joy just as well as tears of sadness.

Life moves on. This tale began with a huge courtroom door shut against me and behind which my fate was being decided. It must now end with another door, a door of opportunity, that's being opened for me. This time I find myself able to shape my own future, take my own decisions, choose my own way forward. It was time to head for Cardiff to begin my undergraduate studies. As I stood on the platform of our local station with my simple suitcase, my mother stood bravely alongside me. We'd never been parted. I'd not spent a single night away from home. We'd never had a holiday, nor had I ever slept over with friends. And now I was leaving. *Partir, c'est mourir un peu.* It felt a bit like that. My mother didn't leave the station until the train was out of sight. I leaned out of the window waving my goodbyes until I could see her no more. She was crying. So was I. Like a baby. My childhood was over.

2

Education

Heaven lies about us in our infancy!
Shades of the prison-house begin to close
Upon the growing boy,
But he beholds the light, and whence it flows,
He sees it in his joy.

WILLIAM WORDSWORTH,
'ODE: INTIMATIONS OF IMMORTALITY'

In July 2005, in the magnificence of St David's Hall, I became an Honorary Fellow of Cardiff University. It was very moving to see the serried ranks of undergraduate and postgraduate students sitting in front of me – so many of them wearing the same academic colours as I'd sported in 1963. The award was made by the president of the University, Lord Kinnock of Bedwellty who, after all the proper flourishes had been successfully negotiated, invited me to make a short speech. It was a real pleasure to do so. Neil Kinnock and I were undergraduates together and, although his concentration on politics (even then) and his study of History meant that we moved in different circles, there were places where we met both in opposition to one another and as team-mates. We were fierce opponents on the soccer field. I captained the French Society team in the Inter-departmental League and Neil was the History Society skipper. He was a bruiser and I remember shouting at my fullback to keep a close track on him. 'Watch Kinnock,' I shouted. 'Watch him, you idiot, can't you see how he keeps drifting out to the right?'

Neil and I were on the same side when we formed a debating team representing Cardiff in inter-varsity and Observer Mace competitions.

We visited Trinity College, Dublin, on one occasion to debate the motion 'That God wouldn't save the Queen'. We Celts were lined up behind Brendan Behan in support of the motion and, ranged against us, stood a solidly Anglo-Saxon team led by Randolph Churchill. The trouble was that Behan didn't show up. So Churchill volunteered to go looking for him. The debate proceeded without them and was well nigh finished when our two principal speakers came tottering back into the debating chamber, arm in arm and very happy, before making brilliant speeches to sum up a debate of which they'd not heard a syllable. I've forgotten the result of the vote on the motion. But I shall never forget those two extraordinary speeches.

It's strange to think that I was an undergraduate with a future leader of the Labour Party. After all, I'd been at school with Michael Howard, a future leader of the Conservative Party and an important member of Margaret Thatcher's government. Both Neil and Michael have been very friendly to me, giving me a great deal of encouragement and support when I took my first timid steps into parliamentary life. When one wag heard of my acquaintance with these two party leaders, he suggested that the logical sequence of having been at school with Michael and university with Neil seemed to point to the likelihood that I'd end up in a nursing home with Paddy Ashdown or David Steel.

I'd gone to Cardiff with the intention of reading French. In those days, first-year undergraduates chose three subjects for study and I opted for French, English and Philosophy. My A-level Latin grade hadn't been brilliant, so I went for a Philosophy course that introduced me to traditional formal logic and the wonders of Plato's *The Republic*. Little did I know then how Plato and I would keep bumping into each other as, in a later part of my life, I read the theological writings of people like Plotinus and Augustine and the Cambridge Platonists. At the end of that year I had to choose between a place in the French or English Honours School and, despite my love of *la langue de Voltaire*, I chose to take the medieval option in the English school. That first year had introduced me to the delights of Anglo-Saxon and Middle English language and literature. I fell in love with it all on first hearing and had a couple of years of sheer joy as I wrestled with *Beowulf*, wondered at the sparkling beauty of 'The Dream of the Rood' and tried to make historical sense of the Anglo-Saxon chronicle. I loved the alliterative verse and the punchiness of its thumping rhythms, the downright physicality of its themes, and the picture it all created of life in northern Europe during its 'dark age'.

My particular pleasure was to read aloud poems like *Sir Gawain and the Green Knight*. It's something I still do from time to time. When Seamus Heaney brought out his translation of *Beowulf* in 1999, I loved it immediately on reading it but it only finally passed my test after I'd given it a proper airing *viva voce*. I couldn't believe how well Heaney sustained the discipline of the verse form as well as capturing the dynamic of the poem's narrative thrust. Another moment for indulging my love of reading Anglo-Saxon poetry aloud came in 1991. In October of that year, on what I imagined would be the 1,000th anniversary of the Battle of Maldon, I travelled into deepest Essex to give voice to the poem that was inspired by that event. The battle in question was between the Anglo-Saxons and the marauding Danes and it was fought at low tide on a causeway on the River Blackwater. So there I stood, surrounded by a host of seagulls, reciting those magnificent words that urged the Anglo-Saxons, fighting a losing cause, to dig deeper and try harder and to remember that they were fighting for glory as they made a last ditch effort to overcome their foe.

My studies wandered outside the medieval fold only rarely. But who can take a degree in English without encountering the genius of William Shakespeare? My professor, whose academic interests lay in the field of philology, held a fortnightly Shakespeare reading for his honours students. I didn't miss one. Parts were given out as people arrived and we launched into the first three acts without delay. Then came a wonderful interval with cream buns and sandwiches, cold drinks and even a glass of wine before, with the parts redistributed, we addressed the final two acts. In this way, I became familiar with all 37 of the Bard's plays and can claim to have acted the parts of a witch and a fool, a young woman in love and an older man riven with jealousy, and two kings – one fiercely patriotic and the other going mad. When I was asked to preach the commemorative sermon in Stratford-upon-Avon at the Shakespeare birthday festival in 2009, I was thrilled almost beyond words. There, in the church where the Great Man had been baptized and married and where he lay buried, I quoted Samuel Johnson's words: 'Shakespeare has no heroes; his scenes are occupied only by men [and women], who act and speak as the reader thinks that he should himself have spoken or acted on the same occasion: even where the agency is supernatural, the dialogue is level with life.'

The good old doctor always talked such sense. Whoever tires of Johnson must surely tire of life. It's that observation of his, where he claims that, even in the realm of religious belief, the dialogue should be level with life that must now prod me in the direction of my own discovery of faith. For it happened at this time in my life.

I'd noticed the Roath Park Methodist Church on the very day of my arrival in Cardiff. The trolleybus taking me from the station to my hall of residence broke down on the corner of Albany Road and Wellfield Road, exactly opposite its imposing neo-Gothic set of premises. The bus's antennae had become detached from the overhead wires and it took the conductor, wielding an extremely long pole, about 20 minutes to get his vehicle under way again. That gave me plenty of time to view the exterior of the church and familiarize myself with what went on there. Curiously, it had never occurred to me that the little chapel I'd attended in Burry Port was part of a nationwide network of churches. But I put that to the back of my mind once the journey was resumed. I was nervous about my new life and the people I was about to meet. And, in this state of mind, I entered Ty Gwyn Court, the villa of a former coal baron, and found the room that had been allocated to me. It was on the top floor, a lovely room under the gables, oddly shaped and with sloping ceilings. I looked out of the window and gasped at the amazing panorama of Cardiff that it commanded. To my astonishment, I noticed rising above the skyline the tower of the same Roath Park church which I'd so recently viewed from close quarters. My consciousness of its existence had been so serendipitous; I found myself wending my way towards it on my very first Sunday in Cardiff, as if by remote control. This was certainly not part of the game plan with which I'd

left home. I wanted to be free from the obligations of church attendance
– I thought that I'd left all that behind me. But here I was, rolled umbrella
in hand, entering this massive church and being greeted by its minister
who had himself arrived there just a month earlier than I.

Ron Ashman knew exactly how to get me integrated into the life of
his congregation. Soon I was the deputy youth club leader. I was already
committed at the university debating society but now began to share my
Friday evenings between it and the youth club. We performed plays, took
part in public-speaking competitions and played table tennis till our
arms ached. It was great to have an anchor in the 'ordinary' life of Cardiff
as well as the more frantic goings-on of student life. Ron Ashman was a
gracious man, somewhat aloof, a perfect example of how to be religious
without ever being sanctimonious. He helped form a Sunday evening
Youth Fellowship group and hospitality for this was given by Don and
Gladys Gauntlett. Every week, after the evening service, we headed off
for their comfortable home in Llanishen. Don was the city engineer; his
father had been mayor of Wembley when the stadium was opened there
in 1923. Gladys would make enough sandwiches and other good things to
feed an army and Don would ferry most of us home in his big Rover 90 at
the end of the evening. Lifelong friendships and more than one marriage
were made through this Sunday-evening activity. It was also a safe place
to explore the meaning and the demands of faith.

All of these developments were moving me inexorably in the direction
of faith. But it was in another and altogether more secular part of my life
that I sensed the coherence that finally opened my eyes to a truth I'd only
ever previously glimpsed. At our hall of residence, at the end of the day, a
few of us would sit around and chat over a cup of tea or coffee. Our conversation would be wide-ranging. It was in these conversations that I came
to realize just how ignorant I was. My companions were social scientists,
medical students, engineers, scientists and lawyers. But they seemed, or
at least between them they seemed, to know everything. I remember the
imposing list of writers and philosophers whose ideas we talked about.
Karl Marx and *The Communist Manifesto*, Friedrich Nietzsche's *Thus*

Spake Zarathustra, Jack Kerouac's *On the Road*, George Orwell's *1984*, Aldous Huxley's *Brave New World*, A. J. Ayer's *Language, Truth and Logic*, Sigmund Freud's *Totem and Taboo* and Bertrand Russell's *History of Western Philosophy* were just some of the titles. All our discussions were taking place against a backdrop where a bewildering series of events was raising huge questions about the direction that the world was moving in. Colonialism was coming to an end; President Kennedy had brought his own charisma into the White House and world politics; the decadence of Harold Macmillan's administration eventually gave us the Profumo scandal; the Beatles were crafting their songs, with the Rolling Stones and Bob Dylan giving their own lustre to popular culture; the Cold War was at its most frigid and the Campaign for Nuclear Disarmament was raising the spectre of total annihilation; the contraceptive pill was just becoming available, as was LSD; homosexuality was decriminalized. We definitely felt both the thrill and the uncertainty about moving out of the constraints and strictures of the immediate post-war era and into a more permissive age whose exact ramifications we couldn't at that time begin to guess at.

All these things shaped those late-evening discussions. I found myself dashing into the bookshops to buy the books that would equip me to get really involved in them. I felt so stupid, so ignorant. It was into those exchanges that I found myself daring, from time to time, to introduce some of the ideas that flow from the teaching of Jesus. Radical love – for strangers as well as friends, enemies as well as allies; self-sacrifice marking the true road to self-fulfilment; service bringing greater reward than mastery; Christ's ministry of reconciliation; the meaning of the Cross. I threw these and other ideas into the melting-pot of our passionate debates. And to my surprise, the company took them seriously. They responded to them as if they had the same standing and were worthy of the same consideration as the ideas garnered from all the other luminaries who figured in our conversation. I find it hard to explain just what this did to me. It blew my mind. I had so associated the Christian story with my childhood that I found myself thrown into total amazement at the discovery that it could stand up and hold its own in such adult company. This, together with the friendships that I was forming and the activities I was getting involved in, led me to recognize that the person of Christ was the one whose way I wanted to follow. I wanted the tone and drift of my life to be a response to the amazing qualities that I found in him. Not that I wanted to give up my voracious interest in other people's ideas. Not at all. But my guide through the maelstrom of frequently competing philosophies would be Jesus. I was ready to confess myself one of his followers. All this had taken me by surprise; in the end, it all came in something of a rush. I knew that I couldn't just leave things where they'd been. I knew that I had to do something about this new position I found myself in. So I turned to Ron Ashman, explained everything to him, and asked him for baptism.

I began preaching, too. A group of us callow believers went around some of the churches of Cardiff trying out our rough-hewn notions of Christian teaching on unsuspecting congregations. It was all so very homespun. But it seemed to confirm the decision that I'd taken to follow the Christian path. It gave me an opportunity to witness the place that Jesus Christ now occupied in my heart and mind.

I took my final exams in the summer of 1963. I got my BA with upper second-class honours. I also sat my Local Preachers' exams, all four of them in two days, in the home of Ron and Gwen Ashman. I think I was as delighted with my success in the preaching exercises as I was in my degree exams. And I was even more thrilled when three, yes three, sources of funding materialized for a research degree. I turned down a State Studentship and a College grant in favour of an award made by the Pantyfedwen Trust – a body that favoured students from Burry Port and other nearby towns and villages in Carmarthenshire.

So I began my doctoral studies. Inspired by C. S. Lewis's *The Allegory of Love* and by my tutor Bill Evans's expertise in this field of literature, I began to study fourteenth-century English romances to see how their authors dealt with the subject of love. My Burry Port friend John Wilkins had recently come to Cardiff and we shared digs together. It wasn't all we'd shared. Together we'd started a Burry Port cricket team and brought competitive summer sport back to our town. We called it the Pegasus

Cricket Club. I wrote its constitution and was its first captain. John took over from me when I could no longer get home often enough to continue in this role. And then there was the local newspaper. Just before leaving for Cardiff, I'd been asked to gather news for the *Burry Port Star* – a job I loved doing. I dashed around the town finding out what was happening in the chapels and the Council chamber, who'd had babies or announced their wedding plans. Now and again, there was something grander to get my teeth into. Once, when our water supply had been infected, I was able to develop the story over three consecutive weeks. The culmination of this local drama came when a Water Board official lifted a ladle of water from the previously contaminated reservoir, put it to his lips and swallowed the whole lot with lip-smacking relish. Our water was pure again. Unfortunately, a sub-editor of the *Burry Port Star* gave my story the headline 'BOARD MAN PASSES WATER', which caused much merriment in many places. When I could no longer fulfil my duties as ace journalist, again it was John Wilkins who took over the reins.

From the time I was 15, the summers presented a problem for my mother. While I was being fed and watered at school, her meagre finances could just about cope with the needs of a growing family. But the long holidays were a different matter. So I went out to work. The succession of jobs I took suggests a readiness to do anything for the sake of that weekly wage packet. For two summers, I worked with the Forestry Commission; another year, I was the 'van boy' for a local man who distributed cold meat products to local shops and businesses. I spent one summer as part of a team engaged in the demolition of the Royal Ordnance Factory in Pembrey, thus clearing previously contaminated ground for the Countryside Park which has since become such a success. I looked after a petrol station in Kidwelly one summer while its proprietor attended the National Eisteddfod in Llanelli. Another long vacation was spent as a male nurse in St David's mental hospital in Carmarthen! But top of the pops as far as my casual work was concerned was the job of postman. In Christmas as well as summer holidays, I'd be up at 5 a.m. to sort the mail and then deliver it among the scattering of hillside dwellings we called 'the

Graig'. I loved this role for several reasons. First, it gave me much-needed employment in both summer and winter breaks. Second, I loved having a job which began with a heavy bag that became progressively lighter as the shift developed. Third, there was lots of human contact. I felt like Willy Nilly Postman in *Under Milk Wood*, bringing tidings of undying love or unwanted visitors or unwelcome tax demands to the homesteads that I called on. And finally, this was a job that was over and done with by 10.30 a.m., giving me the rest of the day for sport or reading.

All in all, my four years at Cardiff were joyous. I grew up fast. I met people from all over the world – Jews and Arabs, people from the Caribbean and various parts of Africa, as well as those who hailed from England. It's astonishing to think how narrow a life I'd lived in Burry Port. That had all been blown away. Intellectually and socially, I was living a different life. 'Bliss was it in that dawn to be alive, But to be young was very heaven' – Wordsworth got it absolutely right. I looked forward to three more years of this sublime existence.

Then it all came abruptly to an end.

My professor wrote me a note informing me that the post of assistant lecturer in English at St David's College, Lampeter, was being advertised and that he wanted me to apply for it. No amount of protest on my part could change his mind. He explained that the University Grants Committee was refusing to go on supporting two separate universities in Wales. St David's College was, of course, older than the federal University of Wales but had fallen on hard times. The only way to rescue it was by bringing it into the larger body as its fifth college. In order to harmonize ways of working and academic standards, the entry of St David's College would need to be under the supervision of an existing college. Aberystwyth was the logical contender for this role but had refused. Lampeter enjoyed strong and historic links with Oxford and Cambridge and had a theological hall for the training of Anglican priests. This didn't please the Calvinists in Aberystwyth; in their eyes, church and chapel didn't mix. So cosmopolitan Cardiff, though separated from Lampeter by the Black Mountains and the Brecon Beacons and 100 miles, agreed to oversee the entry of this charming college into the University of Wales. Professor Llewellyn said that he wanted 'one of my boys' down there to be sure that the medieval part of the English syllabus was being taught correctly.

The interviews for the job took place in the Park Hotel in Cardiff and it was no less a person than the Archbishop of Wales who took the chair. He was flanked by various other Welsh bishops and I was dimly aware, on the edges of this imposing body, of one or two desultory figures who turned out to be Lampeter professors. They played little part in the proceedings. Everything was managed by the ecclesiastical dignitary sitting across the table from me. He ended his interrogation with a gnomic utterance that could have been a question, a statement of fact, or an accusation: 'You're a Methodist, Mr Griffiths,' he declared, to which I replied with consciously similar ambiguity: 'And you're an Anglican, Mr Morris.' He was not pleased.

But I was offered the job and, in September 1964, I travelled by the still-existing train service to take up my new post. I was 22 and the youngest lecturer ever appointed in the University of Wales. Many of those whom I was to teach were older than I was. My accommodation consisted of a couple of rooms in a house where I'd be warden for half a dozen students. The starting salary mentioned at my interview would be £850 per annum but this was increased to £1,050 before my fledgling career had even begun. The Robbins Report had recommended an expansion of the higher education sector and the government of the day had accepted its proposals and made financial provision to match. I'd grown up in a household where £1,000 per annum was thought to be the income of the 'crachach' – the privileged. Now here I was in a job and with earnings that would have been unimaginable to us.

The main college buildings were designed by Charles Cockerell, the architect responsible for the Ashmolean in Oxford and the Fitzwilliam in Cambridge. Its charters and degree-granting powers were given in 1827 and 1833 – it came into existence at the same time as King's College, London, and the University of Durham. Its external examiners had always come from Oxbridge. In 1964, there were about 400 students, all men at

that time, and a staff of about 30. It was a liberal arts college with a strong
– very strong – theological tradition relating to the Church in Wales. The
College principal was a down-to-earth priest who disliked fuss of any kind.
The warden of the Theological Hall, also a priest, was a former librarian
from Pusey House in Oxford. He was of High-Church temperament and
persuasion, a little camp and very fussy. The misunderstandings between
these two men were ripe and rife – for a chapel boy like myself, this was a
real education in the bipolar realities of the Anglican Church. There was a
sub-warden, too, another priest but of less defined material who, finding
himself constantly between Scylla and Charybdis, took refuge in sport.
Football, cricket and golf had quasi-religious resonance for him. They
offered a retreat from the strife which always seemed to envelop his superiors. One of the professors of Theology, yet another priest, was scholarly
in his view of the scriptures, carnal in his view of women. His two fields
of vision sometimes overlapped with embarrassing consequences. When,
many years later, I saw the BBC production *The Barchester Chronicles*,
I was sure that I recognized the features of all my erstwhile colleagues at St
David's College liberally scattered among Trollope's wonderful characters.
The resemblances were quite surreal.

I set about my teaching duties with great enthusiasm. As well as the
material I'd studied for my degree, there were two courses of which I knew
little and at which I had to work especially hard. 'The History of the
English Language' was one and 'The Origins of English Drama' was the
other. First-year classes could be up to 100 strong. At the other end of the
scale were my honours classes, with half a dozen (or even fewer) students.
We were a staff of five in the English Department at that time and got on
reasonably well. Some of my students were very clever and went on to do
great things. It was never difficult to recognize those whose intellectual and
academic qualities were brighter than mine. It was always a pleasure when
we were able to reward them with the first-class honours they deserved.

Since I was of similar age to the students, I was invited to play for the
college teams. I became a regular member of the Rugby First XV and the
Cricket First XI as well as the badminton team. I was awarded my colours

for all three sports. The most memorable match of any kind in which I played during these years was one which pitted the college rugby team against an International XV to commemorate the club's centenary as a founder member of the Welsh Rugby Union. The stars we played against that day were lustrous: Terry Davies, Ray Williams, John Faull, Delme Thomas, Marlston Morgan, Carwyn James, Barry John – all of whom had played or would play for Wales. We lost the match but were not disgraced. Not long after that momentous game, my rugby career came to an abrupt end when I collided with a stocky forward from the Builth team and suffered a broken femur. It didn't stop me teaching but it did prevent my joining the dozens of members of the college who travelled to Aberfan to help with the rescue operation which saw over 100 children lose their lives as a result of a sliding coal tip which totally destroyed the village school.

Twice during my three years at Lampeter we entertained the poet R. S. Thomas at high table. He was the vicar of Eglwysfach, near Aberystwyth, at the time. I remember how he was described once in the *Church Times* as 'a miserable old bugger'. Nothing that I recall of his conversation or presence would contradict that judgement. But his poetry was out of this world. He wasn't well known in those days, his total published work was still slight, but his gifts of observation and his ultra-spare style, never a word wasted, made it obvious that he was destined for greatness. I've been an avid reader, and a total devotee, of his poetry since those early days.

One of the students living in the hall of residence where I was warden, a brilliant young man who was expected to get a first-class honours degree, asked to see me one day. He told me a sorry tale. He'd begun his life as a Methodist but had been attracted by High-Church Anglicanism. It led him to seek entry to a monastic community where he hoped to spend his life in scholarship and prayer. He was homosexual and had declared this in his application to enter the order. He was turned down instantly. Studying for a degree in a secular university was, for him, a poor second choice. It didn't help that he viewed his sexual orientation as a sin. He told me that he'd asked his doctor to help him find a cure for his condition and he was to begin a course of therapy soon. He asked me if I would support him through this treatment. I said that I would and soon I was driving David the 22 miles to Carmarthen for a course of 'aversion therapy'. We had long conversations about his homosexuality and I couldn't begin to understand what was sinful about it. David was who he was. He was gentle, considerate, deeply pious and ultra-sensitive. The treatment he'd been prescribed revolted me. He sat in a room and was invited to look at a screen on which a succession of images was projected. When pretty girls or beautiful rustic scenes were shown, there would be sweet music. When pictures of good-looking boys or men were put up, however, he was made to vomit. This went on for an hour at a time and when he rejoined me he was totally shattered. It clearly didn't work. After a few months, and again at David's own urging, he received electrical treatment. Several nodes were attached to different parts of his head and an electric shock passed through his brain. This succeeded in eliminating much of his memory. It did nothing about his orientation. Nor his guilt. He felt that he must have offended God mightily to have been afflicted so profoundly with this 'illness'. I just couldn't get it. David was the loveliest young man. And yet his God, the God who could be supposed to act in such a way, was surely gruesome, a cruel tyrant.

David was left a wreck, both emotionally and intellectually. He failed his degree exams and wandered off into a bleak future. It was many years later that our paths crossed again. He'd entered the world of counselling and was now a tutor at the Westminster Pastoral Foundation. He'd somehow come to terms with his homosexuality. He had no partner when we met again but he'd gone through a period of very active sexual engagement with a number of people. He was suffering from AIDS. Not long afterwards, he died. He had a cat and, in our last conversation, when he knew that he was soon going to die, he told me how worried he was about his pet. I wept copiously when David died. At the stupidity of it all. The waste. I formed my view of the inherent humanity of gay people in my very earliest years. I was not blind, in an all-male college, to the promiscuous and licentious activities of a number of students (or members of staff). Such behaviour might well be reprehensible. But no one could be bad or wrong or sick or sinful just for having been born with a nature that attracted him to members of the same sex.

I began attending the little Methodist church on the market square from the time of my arrival in Lampeter. The minister there was more comfortable in Welsh than English so he welcomed me and Phillip Nash, a Presbyterian lay preacher who was studying Philosophy, to occupy his pulpit as often as we could oblige. That fact, together with my involvement in the care of David, did two things. First, it suggested to the students who came to our services that I might be an appropriate person to approach with their pastoral needs. Soon young people with depression, debt, problems with their relationships, pre-examination anxiety and the like came asking if they could talk these things over with me. And second, this involvement in the pastoral needs of the students made me aware of gifts which I seemed to have and which previously I hadn't thought much of. An idea formed within me that, however happy I might be in my academic life and work, I wanted to be doing something that would use all my gifts and skills. I loved teaching and knew that I'd need to go on doing that. I was beginning to warm to the demands of preaching. I would certainly want to continue with that. But I needed to deploy my newfound pastoral skills, too, and not only on 18–24-year-olds in higher education. The genesis of my sense of vocation to the ministry lay in this combination of factors. I knew that soon I'd have to ask people to help me to evaluate all this.

It was during these Lampeter years that I met Margaret. I'd been invited back to Cardiff to give a talk to a Methodist student group that I had myself belonged to until a few months earlier. Most of the faces were the same but there was one striking exception. A young lady was warming her hands at a stove at the far end of a subterranean room where the students met. Who on earth believes in love at first sight? And who'd have thought such a thing would happen to me? And could anyone credit the possibility that, across that crowded room, a spark might fly and ignite the fires of hope in my heart? It was a hope that was soon to be dashed; Margaret Rhodes was wearing a ring on her left hand that warned me off the effusive greeting I was about to give her. She was engaged and I knew that I must behave myself. It will surely be accounted unto me for righteousness that I restrained myself from showing the wrong kind of interest on that initial meeting. But my heart was pumping mightily. I'd had a couple of girlfriends previously. I drove one of them pretty much out of her mind and certainly out of my life by insisting on reciting Baudelaire's *Les Fleurs du Mal* to her while we were walking out. The other was a great person to go out with; she loved dancing and taught me the *paso doble*. But it never got much beyond that. What I was now experiencing was of a different order. I was head over heels in love with a girl I couldn't lay a hand on. This was too much. It was the stuff that melancholic literature and Gothic novels deal with. I wanted either to challenge her fiancé to a duel or hire contract killers to dispose of him. I did neither of these things. I played my poor hand decently. I kept my distance. I did engage the services of spies, however, and they kept me in the picture about Margaret's goings-on. I don't think that she was aware of my obsession. At least, not at first. Thank God that I lived in remotest Cardiganshire. Cardiff would have driven me senseless.

She hailed from Newcastle-under-Lyme and had just qualified as a therapeutic radiographer in Bristol before taking her first job at the Velindre Hospital in Cardiff. She came from good Methodist stock going back to the days of Wesley himself. When we eventually married, she introduced thoroughbred qualities to my mongrel life, gave it class and polish. She still does.

But first, I had to woo her. This began in earnest the moment my agents told me that she'd ended her engagement. I pounced. Between the summer of 1965 and the spring of the following year I asked her to marry me no fewer than nine times. On eight occasions she told me, politely, to get lost. Which makes the ninth and successful occasion unforgettable. We were at a youth conference, sitting in a horseshoe arrangement, listening intently to a speaker. I tore a piece of paper from my notepad and wrote my despairing plea: 'Please, please, please, please say you'll marry me. Les. x.x.x.x.x.' I folded it carefully, wrote her name on the outside and passed it along the row. To my immense frustration, when it got to her, she merely glanced at it and, without opening it to read the desperate message of a man whose heart was breaking, she just went on listening to the speaker. Eventually, she excused herself and went to the toilet. When she returned, she continued giving her rapt attention to the person (who on earth was it?) giving the talk (what on earth was he going on about?). Then, offhandedly, she sent a folded piece of paper in my direction. It was a portion of toilet paper, the shiny and slippery kind whose logic I've never been able to understand. It had my name on it. I opened it at once and there were the magical, romantic, heart-warming words that I'd been waiting, gasping for: 'Oh, all right then. M.', it read. It was her acceptance note. How I rejoiced. It didn't even matter that, when we got together later, she laid down one strict condition. If she were taking on a passionate Welshman like myself, she said, she insisted that our engagement be announced on St George's Day. *Chwarae teg*: Fair enough. I conceded the point at once. And I skipped and jumped for joy for the rest of the livelong day.

As it happened, the 1966 College Ball took place on 22 April. So I spoke to the leader of the band hired for that evening and asked him whether, on the stroke of midnight, he'd announce our glad tidings to the assembled company. He said he'd be delighted. And sure enough, as the clock struck 12, none other than Humphrey Lyttelton stopped the number being played and, to much applause, gave out our joyous news. The ball became a party and went on well into the early hours of the morning.

One of the things that Margaret focused on right from the start was the need to furnish and equip the brand new accommodation which my mother was now living in. The proprietors of the Building Trades Supply, either because they wanted the rooms we'd previously occupied for their own commercial purposes or else because they were uncomfortable with the fact that we were living on their premises in such down-at-heel conditions, had had a prefabricated bungalow built where an old shed had previously stood. The irony was of course that, since my mother was now living on her own, the two-bedroom dwelling, with internal toilet and nicely equipped bathroom, represented a luxury that came just a little late in the day. How she'd have loved such a desirable residence when she was raising her family through all those dark years. But it was welcome, for all that. Margaret made and lined the curtains for the large picture window that faced the road; she chose the carpets and equipped the kitchen. Together we bought a three-piece suite and twin beds – at last, the double bed with the straw mattress on which Jim and I had slept all those years could be consigned to oblivion. And, glory be, I was earning money and could now afford to see my mother well catered for. She certainly deserved any comfort that might come her way.

The son of the proprietor of the Building Trades Supply was the same age as I was. While at school, I used to get some of his hand-downs – a satchel, various pieces of equipment and one or two items of clothing. He'd been educated privately and there had been one or two hold-ups along the way. Imagine my surprise, therefore, when I found John, a jovial and fascinating young man whom I'd never really known during the years I lived on his father's premises, sitting among my students at St David's College, Lampeter. He went on to be a very dedicated schoolteacher.

The time had come for me to leave Cardiganshire's 'sweet, especial, rural scene'. I offered myself for ministry and, after due testing and some daunting hoops held out for me to jump through, I was accepted for training. At that time, the Methodist Church had theological colleges in Birmingham, Bristol, Cambridge, Leeds and Manchester. It was decided to send me to Cambridge. What a turnaround! I was, after all, to get my chance to enjoy the delights of one of our ancient universities. I may not have been ready to cope with Oxbridge when I left school, but now, seven years later, I was ready to soak up everything it had to offer.

Because I was already a graduate, I could take the Cambridge degree in Theology in two (instead of three) years. It would mean a period of very intensive study. So Margaret and I decided to settle for a long-ish engagement and only marry when there was less pressure from my studies to contend with. She left Cardiff to live with her parents in Newcastle-under-Lyme. This would allow us to save a little money. It would also allow me the possibility of spending my long summer vacations in Staffordshire and give me the pleasure of getting to know Alf and Kath Rhodes, my future parents-in-law, better than I could ever have done otherwise.

Kath was secretary to a general medical practice and loved the face-to-face contact with patients. She had a compendious knowledge of the Potteries and seemed to be familiar with the family histories of anyone and everyone in Newcastle. For many years, she'd played an active part in the Guide movement. She was a very skilled pianist and had accompanied some of the leading artistes of her day. Alf was a complicated man. He'd wanted to be a Methodist minister but chose to offer himself in 1932, the year when the various branches of Methodism came together to form The Methodist Church of Great Britain. Since the trainee ministers from all these bodies were accepted into the united church, it meant that there would be a manpower surplus. So perfectly good candidates were turned down. It was a freak situation never likely to occur again. Alf was one of those turned down as a result of this unusual situation. But he threw himself into other activities to compensate for his disappointment. After war service in India, he worked with the National Assistance Board and, as we found out after his death, did extraordinary work with distressed families – work that went well beyond the call of duty. In a quiet but persevering way, he supported a number of released prisoners with their housing and employment needs. In the church, he worked with young people and was tireless in his endeavours. Alf and Kath Rhodes were good people, dedicated church members, who gave themselves unstintingly and often without public knowledge to the causes they espoused.

It was a very nervous journey from Newcastle-under-Lyme to Cambridge. Was all the excitement that I'd felt going to be justified? Would I, after all, feel out of my depth or maladroit? Would a step change be needed after my previous academic experiences? And, if so, would I be able to make it? My head was abuzz with self-interrogation as my future father-in-law chauffeured me and my luggage to those fresh woods and pastures new. And what a sight we must have been. The car was stuffed to the gunwales with my bric-a-brac and an ancient bicycle, strapped atop, rode in state like an elephant-borne maharajah. This velocipede had belonged to a former China missionary (they'd got kicked out in 1949) and I was assured that no thief would contemplate walking away with it. I never once locked it up. It never once went missing.

Wesley House, where I was to spend the next three years, stands on Jesus Lane in the very heart of Cambridge. Next door is Jesus College and across the street Westcott House, an Anglican theological college. Our Methodist college was set up in 1923 and admitted only graduates (one undergraduate could be taken each year). It was viewed with some suspicion by egalitarian Methodists, who were sure it reeked of elitism. We're a funny bunch, we who call ourselves John Wesley's preachers; we're always searching for a lowest common denominator, we're terrified of power or privilege, and yet our suspicions are so often but a thin veil for envy. Wesley House has given the Methodist Church some of its finest leaders. And it's established strong bonds with one of the country's best universities. We should be delighted and ready to do all we can to develop the place as a true centre of excellence. Alas, in all honesty, that's not the way things have turned out.

I found myself sharing a staircase with two others. Mervyn Appleby was the undergraduate of our year. The other was a Greek Orthodox Archimandrite, Gregorios Theocharous. Mervyn and I became very friendly with Gregorios and we learned so much about Orthodoxy, particularly about iconography and liturgy. I spent one Easter with the archimandrite's family and visited his church in Camden Town. Indeed, I was able to meet Archbishop Makarios who was President of Cyprus at that time. My Greek friend has gone on to become His Eminence the Archbishop of Great Britain and Thyatira. In November 2009, Margaret and I were among the 750 guests who sat down for a fabulous dinner in one of London's finest hotels as we all thanked God for Gregorios's 50 years of service in the United Kingdom. We continue to meet and our friendship has greatly enriched my ministry.

I've crossed paths with many of my contemporaries at Wesley House since our time together in Cambridge. One of them stands out somewhat from the others. That's due partly to the fact that we've continued to see each other down the years and our families have come to know each other too. Indeed, our friendship even survived the test of working together in the same Methodist circuit for a few years. But there's more to it than that. I've always looked to Tony Barnes as the perfect embodiment of everything we promised to do and be when we were ordained. He's a pastor, a preacher and a teacher. He's never wavered from his calling. My life has tossed me hither and yon. As I look to Tony's faithfulness in the tasks to which he was called, I'm filled with admiration. His ministry offers me a sort of benchmark against which to measure mine.

The surprise news which greeted us on arrival was that the college had been given a new principal. Gordon Rupp was the country's foremost Luther scholar. He'd left his post as Professor of Ecclesiastical History in Manchester and was soon to become the first Methodist to hold a Chair of Theology in the University of Cambridge. He was a tonic. He had an impish sense of humour, an insatiable passion for detective novels, a polymath's grasp of the details of church history, and a gift for friendship. Long after I left Cambridge, he used to send me parcels of books with the injunction that I should not give up my reading. I'll never forget his lectures on the Reformation, full of wit and subtle humour, never merely a dull accumulation of 'facts'. Luther or Calvin, Bucer or Erasmus, Zwingli or Karlstadt, would spring out of his narrative as if alive and their ideas and stances would challenge us to evaluate their contribution to the intellectual and historical shaping of the Europe of their day. On one occasion, when John Robinson, author of the best-selling *Honest to God*, was lecturing on 'The New Reformation' to a dozen or two on one floor of the Divinity School, Gordon Rupp, on the floor immediately above him, had a packed house of hundreds soaking up every word he uttered on the subject of the old Reformation.

Cambridge was wonderful. I enjoyed the music, the theatre, the seasons, the company, the teaching, the very air I breathed. It was hard to think of the turmoil going on in the world around us. The Vietnam War was at its height. The civil rights movement in America had won its victories and given up its martyrs. African Americans were moving away from peaceful and non-violent means of protest towards something altogether more radicalized, with people like Stokely Carmichael and Muhammad Ali giving voice to deep-seated anger. Student riots were shaking university campuses everywhere. Harold Wilson's government was tottering, the pound had been massively devalued, and we were moving towards serious industrial unrest. The Second Vatican Council had released energies that the Roman Catholic Church would find itself contending with for the rest of the century. We weren't sure whether the forces at work meant that we were witnessing a brave new world or the shaking of the foundations of an older one. For all the anxiety of the times, however, Cambridge seemed cocooned in its own beauty, far from the madding crowds, safe from harm or unruly forces.

In the world of theology, things were pretty bleak. Loud voices were announcing that God was dead. Secularism and positivism were rising forces and made their attacks not only on organized religion but on the truth claims made in their name. I found some refuge from all this in a publication called *Slant*, which carried the views of Terry Eagleton, a student in nearby Jesus College, who combined a Roman Catholic world-view that had been radicalized by the Vatican Council with a passionate Marxist analysis that took no prisoners. Eagleton has continued to inspire and stimulate my thinking down the years. His writing has never lost its energy and his critique of our contemporary world always challenges any reader to serious thought. In recent days, as I write, he gave the most devastating, dismissive and entertaining review of Richard Dawkins' *The God Delusion*.

The theological syllabus that I followed was unchallenging, traditional and predictable. I can't deny that it equipped me with information and a methodology that has undergirded the whole of my ministry. But it seemed the product of another world – one on the point of disappearing. I was soon to experience at first hand the outworkings of Liberation Theology. That would blow with the force of a hurricane compared with the summer breezes wafting around my Cambridge studies of church history, the philosophy of religion and the biblical texts. We studied these in the original languages and according to the desiccated tenets of the historical critical method. I found it worthy but bland, a B+ affair. For all that, it gave me another upper second-class honours degree which pleased me well enough. The most important contribution that my studies left with me was a passion to know more. So many doors and windows on life and learning had been opened for me that I knew I'd only just begun my journey rather than ended it. That, at least, was an invigorating prospect.

The summer of 1969 was a momentous time in my life. First of all, I went as a door steward to the Methodist Conference which was meeting in Birmingham. I wanted to listen to the debate about the proposed union of the Anglican and Methodist churches. Gordon Rupp had made this one of his major themes during his year (1967–68) as president of the Conference. I'd shared platforms with him as we advocated this project across the land. Considering the passion with which people on both sides of the argument held their views, I was struck by the courtesy which marked the occasion. In the end, the required majority was achieved and the Methodist Church had effectively voted itself out of existence. When, a few minutes later, the Church of England notified us that it had just failed to match the Methodist result, a palpable disappointment filled the hall and, it seemed to me, no one knew quite what to do next. This was to be the first of a number of such moments where the Anglican Church has had a failure of nerve as far as its relationship with us Methodists is concerned. We've been jilted at the altar again and again.

Some dolts suggested that it was God's will that the scheme should fail. What nonsense! Two opponents of the proposal, from diametrically opposite wings of the Church of England, cobbled together enough votes to sink the whole thing. The evangelical leader James Packer had at least been honest enough to write a dissentient view to the report we'd been debating. Graham Leonard, the Anglo-Catholic suffragan bishop of Willesden, on the other hand, just sniped from the wings. He'd only accept us if we came in on his terms, accepting ordination within the threefold ministry of the Church of England. For him, the bishop was 'the focus of unity'. We didn't have bishops and so, in his eyes, we simply weren't a proper church. Evangelicals and Anglo-Catholics hadn't united in a common cause like this since the publication of *Essays and Reviews*, a radical and modernist collection of writings that was published in 1860. The trial of honest scholars for heresy that followed that intervention was a scandal. And so too was the hiatus which followed the subversive work of the Anglican opponents of this scheme over a century later.

Graham Leonard's subsequent career is interesting to trace. He was 'promoted' to full diocesan status as Bishop of Truro. In this most Methodist of places he wreaked havoc by undoing existing ecumenical initiatives between the two churches. Some years later, he came to London, as Mrs Thatcher's choice over David Sheppard whom she considered too left-wing. Leonard ultimately abandoned the Church of England for the Roman Catholic Church because of his opposition to the ordination of women. But, it was widely reported, only when he'd secured his full pension. By then, of course, bishops in the Church of England were anything but a focus for unity. People went to the bishop who best represented their own point of view. You can't get much more post-modern than that. It's a sad tale. But the failure of the 1969 proposal had little to do with God's will. It was far more a failure of imagination and even of faith.

Just three weeks after these ecclesiastical shenanigans, Margaret and I were married. The wedding took place in the Ebenezer Church in Newcastle-under-Lyme where the Rhodes family had been members for generations. There were 160 guests and we tried hard to ensure that sopranos and altos, tenors and basses, were equally represented. The singing was monumental. My brother Jim was one of my best men (David Rhys-Jones, who became a bowls international and later BBC commentator on that arcane sport, was the other). Our mother was present and in good health too. She certainly enjoyed the whole experience. The Gravell car dealership in Kidwelly, for whom I'd worked one summer, loaned us a car for our honeymoon. And Anne and Arthur Valle (Arthur had been Margaret's minister in her teenage years) gave us the use of their house in Foss on the banks of Loch Rannoch for our honeymoon. The summer festival in nearby Pitlochry, together with the beauty of the Perthshire countryside, gave us a stimulating fortnight. Then we headed down to Cambridge together to begin our married life. Margaret took a job at Addenbrooke's Hospital and I made a second effort to start a doctoral degree, this time by examining the poetry and the spiritual writings of Gerard Manley Hopkins. Hopkins was a priest and a poet and, armed as I was with degrees in both English and Theology, I felt that he would be an absorbing person to study. And so he was. He's given me a lifetime of stimulation and also introduced me to the Society of Jesus (the Jesuits), where I've made friendships that have lasted down the years. In all of this, I was egged on by Gordon Rupp.

During my last year at Cambridge, I was to serve as assistant minister to Whitfield Foy at Wesley Church on Christ's Pieces. Whit was a truly amazing man. As chaplain to the Parachute Regiment in the war, he'd bailed out over Arnhem and if you could get him to talk about that, he'd make your spine tingle. His courage knew no bounds. He'd often compare that jump with the leap of faith that undergirds the Christian life. He went on to serve as a missionary in Southern Rhodesia and was a precursor to the great Colin Morris in addressing the difficult question of racially divided churches. He was far too radical for the white population there and, in the end, was obliged to leave. He'd been at Cambridge once before and set the whole place afire with his powerful preaching. I remember sitting at High Table in St John's College with a number of the Fellows asking me whether it was true that Whitfield Foy was back in town. Some of them remembered his preaching from those earlier days. Alas. He suffered a serious heart-attack on the very eve of the new academic year and I was 'acted up' to take his place. This was a frightening prospect. The large congregation included scores of students and a number of academics. There were professors and heads of colleges. I remember the King Edward VII Professor of English Literature, Basil Willey, and the Master of Peterhouse, Herbert Butterfield. For week after week to come, I'd deliver my sermons to such an august congregation and chair all the core committees of the church. It was both invigorating and draining at the same time. Throughout this period, I kept close to Whit and Rae Foy and, as his condition improved, he offered me a great deal of helpful advice and unstinting affirmation. He impressed on me that preaching that had no passion was hardly worth the candle. We only preached, he argued, to convince, to urge, to persuade, to bring people to their senses, to present people with alternatives and to challenge them. And all this should be put across with a note of urgency.

During my last year at Wesley House, an officer of the Methodist Missionary Society came to challenge us to consider working overseas. Her words aroused a real interest in both of us. In no time at all, we were signed up for this new enterprise and we gave the Missionary Society no directions as to where we'd like to go or what kind of work we might want to do. We'd go anywhere, we said. At first, the talk was of Hong Kong and we began to prepare ourselves for this. Meanwhile, of course, my ministry at Wesley Church and my academic work proceeded apace. But our time in Cambridge was drawing to a close. And we faced that prospect with sadness. I was the president of the Theological Colleges Union (the last, I think, before the creation of the Cambridge Theological Federation) and this drew me close to members of Westcott House and Ridley Hall, both Anglican colleges, and also Westminster College and St Edmund's House, Presbyterian and Roman Catholic institutions respectively. I was certain that the whole of my ministry would need to be pursued with an active commitment to ecumenism.

The decision to go overseas meant that, yet again, I had to wind up my doctoral studies. I managed only a long article on Hopkins in the end. 'The Great Sacrifice: The Incarnation in the Thinking of Gerard Manley Hopkins' appeared in the July 1971 issue of the *Church Quarterly*. This was a study of a retreat undertaken by Hopkins in 1881, as he readied himself for his final vows before becoming a fully professed member of the Society of Jesus. It was good to have something tangible to show for my hard work in this extraordinary year.

Suddenly, out of the blue, we learned that we were not to go to Hong Kong after all. A key member of the small ministerial team in Haiti had died unexpectedly. Because I had reasonable French, they decided to send me in his place. This was a shock to the system. But I was now under discipline as a Methodist minister and Margaret and I agreed to this change without hesitation.

And so the 1960s came to an end. After a childhood spent entirely in Burry Port, I'd had this unique opportunity to enter the world of higher education. And I'd lived in that world for ten consecutive years. I'd been an undergraduate, a research Fellow, an assistant lecturer, an affiliated student and a research student. I'd learned so much and, more importantly, discovered how little I knew. Now, I must show the benefits of my education by committing myself to a lifelong process of study and reflection, thinking and teaching. Otherwise, these years would just be a badge I could wear, a set of objectives I'd accomplished, something to add to my *curriculum vitae*.

In a state of shock, Margaret and I came out of the meeting where we were told that we'd be going to Haiti. For the sake of appearance, we'd nodded where necessary and eventually signed on the dotted line. We walked home in silence as we came to terms with the fact that we were no longer going to South East Asia but to the Caribbean. We brought out our atlas and turned its pages. As we prepared for this great adventure, the first thing we needed to do was to find out exactly where Haiti was.

3

Haiti

The caged bird sings with a fearful trill
of things unknown but longed for still
and his tune is heard on the distant hill
for the caged bird sings of freedom.

MAYA ANGELOU,
'I KNOW WHY THE CAGED BIRD SINGS'

There were four or five of us in our group and we approached the presidential palace with trepidation. The Methodist Church of Haiti had been commanded to pay its respects to the president of the republic and, since this was none other than François ('Papa Doc') Duvalier, we did as we were told. Ours was only one of a number of delegations making their way into the state room where the old dictator was waiting for us. I'd seen Alan Whicker's extraordinary BBC television interview of Duvalier and had also read Graham Greene's novel *The Comedians*. As I shook the tyrant's hand, I'm sure I shuddered. This was someone who'd imposed a rule of terror on the people of Haiti since his arrival in office in 1957. His notorious Tontons Macoutes (secret police) were everywhere. At their hands, thousands had been tortured or killed. Others had simply disappeared. Duvalier had maintained an air of mystery throughout this period. He was widely supposed to hold regular Voodoo sessions within the palace and, in the way he dressed, he was said to cultivate an identification with Baron Samedi, a Voodoo figure closely linked to cemeteries and death. By the time I met him in this way, he'd got rid of all opposition in the army, the church, the business community and the university, either by having them killed or driving them into exile. He was a despot who'd fit readily into the company of Pol Pot, Idi Amin and Saddam Hussein.

This meeting was carefully orchestrated. Our names were noted and appeared in the following morning's government newspaper, thus giving the world the impression that we Methodists were signed-up supporters of Duvalier. It taught us a painful lesson. We wouldn't be caught out that way a second time.

François Duvalier died in April 1971, just six months after our arrival in Haiti. Once his funeral was out of the way, moves were afoot to get his son, Jean-Claude ('Baby Doc'), established as head of state. Once again, delegations were summoned to the palace to pay homage; this time we were ready with a plan. All Methodist ministers based in the capital, Port-au-Prince, headed out of town. The chairman of our district, Alain Rocourt, and Patrick McConnell travelled to Jérémie on the northern side of the long, snaking peninsula that heads west in the general direction of Jamaica. I went to Haiti's third largest city, Aux Cayes, on the southern side of the same strip of land, separated from my colleagues by a range of towering mountains. Our families remained in the capital.

We'd reckoned that a week's absence from Port-au-Prince should see us through our difficulty and I made arrangements accordingly to book a return flight on the little plane that offered a daily link to the capital. On the day of travel, I was horrified to learn that all tickets had been cancelled. The plane would fly empty to Jérémie and it would pick up its complement of passengers there. There was a fierce discussion but the authorities, backed now by a menacing group of armed men, were insistent. Only one person, Alain Rocourt, would be allowed to board the plane at Aux Cayes. My ears pricked up. Alain wasn't in Aux Cayes but I, his colleague, was. I argued my case at the desk and a bewildered official reluctantly allowed me to board the aircraft. I was the only passenger as we flew over the mountains to Jérémie. When we landed, I soon understood the reason for all these shenanigans. The plane filled up with Tontons Macoutes, all dressed in their quasi-military uniforms and carrying automatic rifles across their laps. The mayor of Jérémie and some assorted officials were also brought aboard. Then, through a window, I spotted Alain Rocourt and Patrick McConnell arguing with an official. Alain was sure a place had been kept for him. It had. I was sitting in it. He caught sight of me and all I could do was shrug my shoulders. The plane took off, carrying the Jérémie delegation summoned to pay homage to Jean-Claude Duvalier (and me!) towards Port-au-Prince. It was easily the most uncomfortable journey I've ever taken. And the worst of it was that, for all our avoidance tactics, our names appeared in the official newspaper anyway as if we had after all gone to pay our respects and swear our unswerving loyalty to the new regime.

The first six months of our time in Haiti were overshadowed by the political uncertainties that surrounded the death of Papa Doc. But for us personally, the time between leaving Cambridge and our arrival in Haiti had not been easy either. We spent a month in Paris to get our French up to scratch and we lived in a flat over our Rue Roquépine church in the fashionable eighth *arrondissement,* just off the Champs-Élysées and at the very heart of picturesque Paris. My mother came to spend our final week with us. She'd only ever left Wales once before, in the 1930s, to help her sister in London at the birth of her first child. So it's still a source of amazement to us that she successfully undertook a journey that involved three trains, a tube link and a ferry. We were mightily relieved to see her at the Gare du Nord but she greeted us as if she were alighting at Swansea High Street.

Margaret was pregnant when we travelled to Paris and we were excited beyond words at the prospect of becoming parents. But towards the end of our French sojourn, it was obvious that all was not well with her. We had to make the decision whether to consult doctors in Paris or try to get home first so that we could enjoy medical support in our own language. My mother had one of her bad turns at this same time. Our journey home was touch-and-go for her and for Margaret. It was a great relief to get both of them into the hands of our Burry Port doctor, who sent Margaret off to hospital at once. She made a brave but forlorn attempt to save our child, a little boy of sixteen weeks. We were heartbroken. It hadn't helped that

Margaret was sharing a ward with half a dozen other young women, all of whom were seeking to lose the children they were carrying. That was a cruel irony and difficult to bear. It took Margaret a few weeks and some extra in-patient treatment to get over her miscarriage. In the end, we travelled to Haiti just one day after she left hospital. Her parents didn't think much of this arrangement. It didn't do much for our own self-confidence either. But it spoke volumes about the courage of Margaret, who would not be deterred from making our journey as planned.

Just before leaving, we'd received the news that a senior member of the small ministerial team in Haiti had died suddenly while on furlough in England. We travelled out with this sad news and we knew that there would be serious repercussions for us. And so it turned out. Instead of a posting alongside an experienced superintendent minister, probably in an urban setting where there would be a smattering of French-speakers, I was asked to go out to Petit-Goâve to take serious responsibility for a circuit of 48 churches scattered across a major chunk of Haiti's southern peninsula. There would be almost no French-speakers among my church members – just speakers of Créole, of which I had not a word. A very remarkable Haitian minister would be my superintendent but, because he'd been ill, he would only travel out to Petit-Goâve over the first weekend of every month for the celebration of the circuit Eucharist and the conduct of necessary business. Apart from that, I would be on my own.

There was no map showing where my four dozen churches were located and absolutely no public transport system to get me to them. The furthest was in Bainet. This lay over the mountains from where we lived, on Haiti's Caribbean coast, and involved a 24-hour mule ride with the last few miles spent crossing a meandering river a seemingly endless number of times. Seven of my churches were on the island of La Gonâve and getting there took a three-hour drive into Port-au-Prince and a seven-hour boat trip across the bay with a connecting horse on the other side, if I was lucky. It took me a whole year to find and map out the churches in my care.

A typical weekend would see me leave home in the early hours of a Friday morning astride a mule and accompanied by two or three people who'd carry my effects and cook my dinners. We aimed to get well into the mountains before the sun got too hot. Then we'd continue for an indeterminate number of hours. Eventually, we'd arrive at one of our churches and there would be huge excitement at the arrival of the *pasteur blanc* – the white minister. One of the church leaders would put their two-room, mud-and-wattle house at my disposal and I'd freshen up after my journey. This involved bowls of water being brought to a makeshift bathroom area in the yard whose simple aim was to protect my modesty. The whole community came to wonder at the sight of me washing myself. Then we'd get down to the business of my trip. There were some bureaucratic tasks to accomplish, such as checking membership lists, tallying financial records, inspecting various bits and pieces of equipment. Then I'd visit the sick. I saw so much poverty and avoidable disease in those early days. Often I'd anoint the dying, give communion to the housebound and meet various community officials.

The climax of each visit was the celebration of Holy Communion. These little churches had often not received a ministerial visit for many years. They kept in touch with circuit life by sending delegations down to Petit-Goâve for the monthly communion service. Indeed, one of the truly unforgettable experiences of Haiti was that monthly event. Groups from most of our 48 churches would make the long journey to Petit-Goâve and they'd sit in church under banners which declared their provenance. There would never be fewer than a thousand worshippers; at the major festivals, there might be two or even three times that number. It was awe-inspiring to see the crowd in front of me filling the church and standing around every doorway or window that might offer a vantage point for the service.

The Eucharist that I was able to offer in the different communities I visited was so special. The minister had come out to the people rather than, as was normal, the other way round. And the rejoicing was palpable. In these distant communities, the last thing to happen, when darkness had fallen, was to eat a simple meal around a dying fire. Everyone gathered together. There was no electricity, just a few oil lamps to light our proceedings.

When the meal was over, a little ritual took place which began with a village elder snapping his fingers and shouting the word 'Cric!' Immediately, everyone would reply by clicking their fingers too and replying 'Crac!' This simple exchange prefaced a series of interventions which included jokes or news of the day's events, proverbs or folktales or the singing of haunting songs that had their origins in faraway Africa. It was all very moving.

I'd often be absent from home in this way for four or five days at a time, with Margaret left on her own in Petit-Goâve. We'd been given an apartment above a shop on the main street. We had electrical current between 5 p.m. and 6.30 p.m. and water between 5 a.m. and 6.30 a.m. Our cooking stove and refrigerator were fuelled by kerosene. We didn't seem able to get the stove to work. So Margaret cooked our meals on a charcoal fire in the yard down below our apartment. She shared this space with many a Haitian woman whose identity remained forever mysterious. And she had to run up and down the stairs several times every morning to keep an eye on her culinary efforts.

There was no expatriate community in Petit-Goâve. We were the only foreigners in a commune of 250,000 Haitians. And we neither of us spoke a word of Créole when we arrived there. Margaret had no clue about much of the food on sale in the local market and she had to stand at the place of slaughter to claim and buy an acceptable cut of meat. She spent long periods on her own with just a maid to keep her company. Since La Bénie spoke no English and Margaret very little Créole, and since we couldn't cope with having servants but insisted that La Bénie live with us as a member of our family, there were inevitably long and embarrassing pools of silence to endure.

Our stay in Petit-Goâve lasted just a year. But its contribution to my growth and personal development has lasted down to the present day. I was ministering among Haiti's peasant population, those described by sociologist Frantz Fanon as 'the wretched of the earth'. Their life expectancy was low, their risk from a whole clutch of diseases was high, the land from which they eked out their living was unproductive and they were largely illiterate. Yet I was totally dependent on them. I'd come to Haiti armed with a couple of university degrees and a good knowledge of French. None of these qualifications proved helpful. I was totally disempowered. I could do nothing. And these big-hearted people came to my rescue. They taught me their language, their wit and their wisdom; they offered me the use of their simple homes and their hospitality was astonishing. Out of their dire poverty (Haiti is the poorest country in the Western hemisphere, one of the poorest in the world) they gave me riches beyond price – their trust, their affection, their humour and their humanity. I know I shall never be able to repay the debt I owe them. My education had undoubtedly given me a swagger, more than a touch of arrogance, a conviction that I could change the world. It was all a veneer, of course, a mask behind which I could hide my real self. Social gifts can often be used this way. The peasant people of Haiti put me back in touch with the poor boy I'd once been. They did for me what all the king's horses and all the king's men failed to do for Humpty Dumpty – they put me back together again. They made me whole. And that first year – a year when we cried ourselves to sleep so many times, a year of great difficulty when we genuinely didn't know if we had what it took – ensured that ever thereafter I'd see Haiti, and countries like Haiti, through the eyes of its disenfranchised and marginalized poor rather than from the vantage point of its political class.

The time came, however, when logic simply had to prevail. We were a very small team and an English colleague, Derek Poole, who was made for a rural ministry but who'd been ministering in Port-au-Prince, came out to replace me in Petit-Goâve while I moved into the capital. There I became deputy head of Nouveau Collège Bird (NCB), one of Haiti's best schools. And this brought me into partnership with a man who's remained one of my best friends and who's given me constant inspiration down the years. Rosny Desroches was in his twenties when we met in 1971. He'd just returned from university study in Geneva, where he'd earned top honours in both Philosophy and Theology. He became head of Nouveau Collège Bird and some viewed his appointment with suspicion. He was young and black; the school had been patronized by Haiti's leading families, so many of whom were mulatto. When François Duvalier was excommunicated by the Roman Catholic Church in the 1960s, he'd taken his children out of Catholic schools and placed them with us. Jean-Claude Duvalier had only just left the school at the time when his father died and he became president-for-life of Haiti.

My appointment alongside Rosny was, I'm certain, intended to be a sop to parents who might have balked at sending their children to a school run by a young, black Protestant. I was young and Protestant, too, but my white skin served its purpose. In any case, it was nothing other than a privilege to work with Rosny as he gave the school (which had passed through some rough times) an injection of energy and direction that were truly amazing. My responsibilities included the teaching of English in the senior school, the formulation of a Religious Education curriculum and the training of teachers in the junior school to teach it, the making of the timetable and, finally, school discipline. We educated children from kindergarten to the end of the secondary cycle. We drew pupils from the wealthiest families and the poorest. We charged the rich handsomely in order to make scholarships for the poor. A number of our charges were the children of Tontons Macoutes – so we were sure that our every word was monitored and reported on. That, of course, made the teaching of religion, especially in the senior school, a potentially subversive activity and replete with danger. We explored the meaning of morality, how to build communities, the nature of justice and how to develop a sense of responsibility for each other. It was all based firmly in the Bible but no one had to think too hard to work out how it would all play if applied to Haitian society.

One of the aspects of Haitian life which I met very early in our stay there was Voodoo. There is so much rubbish written on this subject and I was determined to find out for myself. From my earliest days, I sought out the local *bokor* (priest) in his *houmfort* (place of meeting) and sat down with him and got him to describe the Voodoo belief system for me. He explained the various items that stood on or around the altar – a snake in a bottle, a skull, other artefacts. But more importantly, he helped me see how Voodoo had come into being. I should just say that this process of understanding on my part took a number of years to develop but it may be best to bring it all together here.

In the eighteenth century, Haiti was France's richest colony. It brought more revenue to the French exchequer than all of Britain's overseas territories put together. It was truly *la perle des Antilles*, and its wealth led to many a French planter's being described as 'rich as a Créole'. And all this, of course, was built on an economy driven by slave labour. At the time of Haiti's independence in 1804, there were some half a million slaves working the productive land across the 10,000 square miles of its territory and about 36,000 members of the 'plantocracy'. This is easily the most intensive ratio of slave labour anywhere in the New World.

The slaves were shipped in from a swathe of Africa ranging from Senegal in the north to the Congo Basin in the south. They were deliberately separated from each other when they were sold in order to avoid tribal affiliations feeding any form of sectarianism on the plantations. So the African slaves found themselves separated from each other by language, religion and culture. They had to learn to communicate with each other despite these differences and, at the same time, they needed to heed the orders given them by their French overlords. It was out of this pressure pot that the two strongest marks of Haitian identity emerged during the struggle for independence that took place with increasing intensity across the last decade of the eighteenth century. The first was the Créole language, the other the Voodoo religion. Both were constituted by an amalgam of inter-tribal linguistic or spiritual elements that had lost almost all tribally specific features and they gave the first black republic in the world a truly unique identity.

The slaves' god was a distant figure, too far removed from the daily lives of ordinary people to be invoked directly for help or guidance. He was the *Gran Mèt*, the Great Master, who reigned implacably over human life. He was to be approached via the mediation of a whole range of spirits who were much more closely related to the various aspects of everyday living. The Voodoo ceremonies, full of movement and drum-driven dance, would often end with the 'possession' of one of the worshippers by the spirit being invoked. Out of this epiphany might come guidance or counsel, matters which lay within the province of the *bokor* whose ability to interpret what was happening, together with his (or her) knowledge of the mystical qualities of various plants, gave him a strong role in shaping the daily lives of the people of his community.

These were the people I made it my business to talk to as soon as my language skills allowed. It's certainly true that a malign form of Voodoo exists within which spells and curses and the like constitute a definite feature. And there were unexplained phenomena too – the making of zombies, for example, with their reduced human capacities turning them into shambling creatures good only for obeying orders and living shadowy lives. But on the whole, Voodoo amounted to little more than a composite religion formed through the alchemy of the slaves' daily lives and having recognizable similarities with various kinds of animism whose origins lay in distant Africa.

The darker side of Voodoo impacted directly on my work from time to time. On one occasion, a young girl disappeared from her home and we all set out to look for her. It appeared that she had been snatched away by members of a Voodoo sect for ritual purposes. She was eventually returned to us unharmed and we were given to understand that she had been of little use to her captors once they found out that she was *moun levangil*, a Protestant. On another occasion, the day after I'd conducted the funeral of an 18-year-old boy, his mother's only child, who'd died tragically in a drowning accident, I was called out by his family who were frantic with fear because his body had been dug up from its grave and taken off into some mysterious hinterland. The suggestion was that he was exactly the kind of person who might be useful as a zombie, young and fit as he'd undoubtedly been before his death. On that occasion I felt obliged to ask for airtime on the local Roman Catholic radio station to put out an appeal for the return of the boy's body. Since I knew that I was speaking into the fears of so many people, I felt that I must make my position as clear as could be. 'If anyone can show me this boy alive in any conceivable way,' I declared, 'then I will publicly renounce my Christian faith in favour of the Voodoo spirits.' I suppose that this was quite dramatic but it wasn't nearly as outrageous as it might seem. I'd seen the efforts to resuscitate the boy after his accident; I'd carried his body in the back of my Land Rover all the way to his home; I'd seen him lying in his coffin and had myself shovelled the first layers of earth over it. I felt very confident in my challenge. Nothing was ever discovered of the boy's remains – another of Haiti's unrecorded tragedies.

On another occasion, when I was driving through a school-building programme against the delaying tactics of local bureaucrats, I made myself deeply unpopular with several people. I recall more than one pavement argument with tax officials or truck drivers or local workers who wanted to cream off some of the financial benefits of our building project for themselves. I remained unbending on such matters. There were to be no kickbacks, no losses of material, no untoward payouts to anyone. It didn't surprise me, one fine morning, to discover a little package containing some unidentifiable powder with pins and thorns sticking out all over it that had been laid carefully on the driving seat of my vehicle. I went to the building site, held this irksome item aloft, and proceeded to dismantle it in front of a large and largely incredulous audience.

Despite these incidents, my real quarrel with Voodoo was its fatalism. It seemed that no one could be held accountable for things that went wrong, even when there might be an obvious explanation. When, for example, one of our church employees drove a car directly into a solid wall and destroyed the vehicle at one bound, he climbed out of the wreck and would only attribute responsibility to the *Gran Mèt*, to that distant divinity which shaped their ends and rough-hewed them every day. 'Bondieu bon,' he said endearingly in the most common and infuriating of all Haitian mantras – 'God is good' – which, interpreted, means 'It's God's fault, blame him'.

In our medical work as well as our agricultural and educational work, we were constantly battling against this deep-seated determinism. Our clinics received patients whose gangrene or secondary syphilis or malaria could have been addressed very effectively if they'd come to us sooner.

But they'd inevitably spent time with the *bokor* before they thought of us. My contact with the world of the Voodoo religion began at the very outset of our stay in Haiti and remained a common feature till the end of our time there.

In July 1972, I travelled to Aux Cayes to lead a teaching weekend for about 20 lay preachers. We gathered on the ground floor of the spacious manse and began our work well enough. Then the rains began to fall. For 36 hours they beat upon the whole region until, so it was reported later, 972 millimetres (over 30 inches) had fallen. We were all forced upstairs into the pastor's living quarters and soon we were running short of food and fresh water. When we eventually got out into the streets, we couldn't believe our eyes. The whole town was under water. I found my way to the dwelling of the Roman Catholic priests and we formed a rescue team. The town was cut off from the outside world but, *mirabile dictu*, there was a telephone link to Port-au-Prince. I was able to put in a call to London and several thousand pounds were wired at once to our church headquarters via the Methodist Church Relief Fund's New York account. We began to assess the damage. There was widespread loss of life. Over 100 bodies were counted but, since we were unable to get far beyond the footpaths or highway, it's highly likely that there were many more. And the Duvalier government showed what it was made of by refusing our request to use its helicopters to bring in emergency supplies. It took several days for the first convoy of relief vehicles to reach us. We were terrified that there might be an outbreak of contagious disease.

All this time, I'd left Margaret with Allen and Betty-Ann Darby in Petit-Goâve. They'd arrived in Haiti about a year after us and their friendship became very precious. Margaret was almost at the end of her second pregnancy and worried sick by my forced absence. But she couldn't have been with better people, a fine Canadian couple whose work in rural development and functional literacy was to become so impressive. For all that, we were glad to be reunited and returned to Port-au-Prince as soon as possible to prepare ourselves for the arrival of our first child.

He chose a Sunday. Margaret had played the organ in church and we were busying ourselves with preparations for lunch. Her labour began. We raced to the Canapé Vert hospital via the home of Margaret's gynaecologist, Dr Ulrick Francillon. He was sitting in his yard with some of his friends. Under the shade of a spreading flamboyant tree they were playing a serious game of poker. The good doctor, faithful to his Hippocratic oath, threw his hand in, leapt up and followed us to the hospital. Timothy Richard, weighing nine and a half pounds, was born at 5.30 p.m. with Haitian medical care earning five stars for its efforts. I might add here that Jonathan Andrew, weighing eight and three-quarter pounds, was born 16 months later under almost identical circumstances. Again it was a Sunday, with the merry playing of the organ, the almost-ready lunch, the interrupted poker game and the smiling Haitian medical team all following the same pattern. Somehow, I've tried hard not to let my negative feelings about those two missed Sunday lunches affect the upbringing of the boys.

Margaret's mum and dad spent a few weeks with us at the beginning of 1973. They came for Tim's baptism and my ordination. The first took place in our newly opened church at Carrefour, on the outskirts of Port-au-Prince, and was a very happy affair. The second took place on 21 January in our large church in the capital. I was the only ordinand and this was an amazing moment in my life and one which, I believe, set the agenda for the rest of my ministry.

There were two thousand people in church that morning. I remember feeling their gaze as I went forward and knelt at the rail. A number of ministers gathered round me to place a hand on my head and to offer prayer. The president of the Methodist Church in the Caribbean and the Americas, Claude Cadogan, a black Jamaican, was the first. I was ordained by the leader of a Church which had only recently received its autonomy from the Methodist Church in Great Britain. His hand was joined or covered by those of Marco Dépestre and Alain Rocourt, both Haitians, one a black man and the other a mulatto. Mulattos and blacks had fought tooth and nail in Haiti since its independence in 1804. And here were both groups joined together over me at this critical juncture in my life. The remaining ministers who took part in this ceremony were Henry Keys and

Allen Darby, an Irishman and a Canadian. This spread of people from the developed and the developing world, from such a variety of ethnic and cultural backgrounds, gave me a real sense of direction for my ministry. I committed myself to building inclusivity and to healing social, cultural or even political divisions wherever opportunity presented itself. But that wasn't the only understanding that impressed itself on me that day.

My ordination took place during the Week of Prayer for Christian Unity. I was an active member of the Groupe Oecuménique de Recherches (Ecumenical Research Group) and all its members are present. One Roman Catholic priest had brought his boss, the recently appointed Papal Nuncio in Port-au-Prince, Monsignor Luigi Barbarito. Little did I know then that our paths would cross again when he became the Vatican's man in London. I've often hinted to my Anglican friends that the presence of a Papal Nuncio, an archbishop to boot, just a few feet away from me at the moment of my ordination might just mean that my orders are more valid than theirs! There were Anglican as well as Roman Catholic priests present, Salvation Army officers, ministers and pastors of straight (as well as corybantic) Baptists, some very excitable Pentecostalists and various independent churches, too. As I got to my feet and turned back to my place at the front of the church, I saw this ecclesiastical spectrum, a rainbow of colours, and felt that I must commit myself unremittingly to the cause of church unity.

All these developments were taking place at a time when something we were about to call 'Liberation Theology' was taking a hold on the Roman Catholic Church in Haiti. The status of the Church had been re-designated and it was now effectively autonomous rather than being a mission directed from Rome. The Mass was being offered not only in French but also in Créole, and local instruments (drums and pipes) were being brought into church. I kept on discovering priests who were developing the ecclesial base groups and engaged in the 'conscientization' (awareness-raising) of peasant groups in various rural locations – things we were to read of in textbooks a decade later. Teaching methods and materials were reflecting a bottom-up approach to evangelization. Much of the methodology owed a great deal to a neo-Marxist analysis of society and these activities would later be frowned upon and suspected of being subversive – a suspicion that was not far from the truth.

All of this, of course, was the fruit of the Second Vatican Council. The 1968 Medellín Conference of Bishops had been fuelled by the thinking of Paulo Freire, Ivan Illich and, supremely, Dom Helder Camara and it set the future of the Latin American Church in the direction of Liberation Theology. Gustavo Gutiérrez's book on that subject appeared in Spanish only in 1971 and not until 1974 in English. I experienced the actual praxis of this ferment long before anyone was talking or writing about it in Europe.

But for all this heady excitement, or perhaps because of it, I was beginning to get itchy feet. Our four years in Haiti had been an exceedingly demanding time for Margaret, a time which she'd borne with great strength but with real self-questioning. Meanwhile, with my increasing proficiency in the local languages and my deepening knowledge of Haitian history and culture, I found so many Haitian people turning to me for the kind of leadership that I felt they should be looking for from among their own ranks. I was distinctly uneasy and this was forcing me to do some profound thinking about my future.

I wrote a long letter to a colleague in which I set out my worries. This is part of that missive:

For a long time, I tried to work out my unhappiness in terms of the difficulties of the job. Not a mechanic, I have had to grapple with the intricacies of a jeep on terrain that is frightening by any standards; I have had to travel hours and hours on horse and mule up rocky steeps that twist every muscle in my soft and unsupple body; have slept with the fleas and the mosquitoes in the middle of nowhere and had to leave my wife alone for days on end. And so I could go on. And I could just rationalize my dissatisfaction in terms of the physical conditions we have to endure. But that is not the centre of the problem. Or again, there are the personal and psychological problems of a church that has too few ministers and can offer no stable position in which to work. Since we came, we have always been on the edge of being sacrificed to expediency or necessity by being moved from one job to another just to keep the machine

going. And, in these deliberations, one's own aptitudes are usually less important than the need to fill a gap. But even here we do not get to the heart of the
matter, though this uncertainty has sometimes racked us terribly.

What crystallized my thinking and helped me really to see what was
grumblingly at the bottom of my malaise was a chapter I read recently in
T. E. Lawrence's *Seven Pillars of Wisdom*. You will remember that Lawrence
succeeded in identifying with the Arab movement in a unique and deep way.
He mastered the various Arab dialects, understood the Arab way of doing
things, and was able to command his most irregular troops with an authority
based on respect. His spiritual move from Oxford to Mecca amazed me by
its completeness. He loved the desert, though eventually it reduced him body
and mind till he could take no more. He found himself haunted by a deep,
determined and despairing dissatisfaction. He tried to resolve this in terms of
the physical torture that his body had had to suffer month after month, but
he found that it was not in that that his unease lay.

Then comes a paragraph that I want to quote almost in its entirety:

> However, these worries would have taken their due petty place, in despite of
> the body, and of my soiled body in particular, but for the raking fraudulence
> which had to be my mind's habit: that pretence to lead the national uprising
> of another race, the daily posturing in alien dress, preaching in alien speech
> with behind it a sense that the "promises" on which the Arabs worked were
> worth what their armed strength would be when the moment of fulfilment
> came. We had deluded ourselves that perhaps peace might find the Arabs able,
> unhelped and untaught, to defend themselves with paper tools.
>
> Meanwhile we glozed our fraud by conducting their necessary war purely
> and cheaply. But now this gloss had gone from me ... My will had gone and
> I feared to be alone, lest the winds of circumstance, or power, or lust, blow
> my empty soul away.

As I said to my correspondent, too close an identification between me and
Lawrence would be laughable. But the inner dynamics of his anxiety, the
state of his soul and the conclusions that he came to were mine exactly.
It would be wrong for me to play an active part in engineering a social

upheaval among Haiti's poor. That was their job, not mine. It was time to return home.

And home we came. My head was full of unfinished business. I was afraid that I'd cut and run, a shepherd turning his back on his flock. But I had to put that to the back of my mind as we settled in to our new home in Reading. Whenever we've moved from one appointment to another, Margaret and I have always accepted the first invitation that's come our way. We believe that's part of the discipline of itinerancy and what we signed up to. We've never inspected the house we were going to live in ahead of accepting the post. We never felt that we could possibly judge between the merits of, say, Guildford or Gainsborough. So we've always approached a new position ready to be surprised by its secrets and its challenges.

As it happened, Ron Ashman was the superintendent of the Reading circuit and he got in first. So it was a joy to be reunited with him and Gwen in our first real British posting. But our beginnings in the Caversham section of the circuit were less than propitious.

The Methodist Conference had just decided that ministers would henceforth own their own furniture. Furnishing the manse had previously been the responsibility of the circuit. At the time this decision was implemented, incumbents were given the option of buying up the furniture in their houses and taking it with them to their next appointment. That's exactly what my predecessor did and it meant that we arrived in an empty, five-bedroom house with not a stick of furniture to call our own.

The Missionary Society had taken our meagre savings and invested them for us during our time in Haiti. Our return home coincided with one of the worst stockmarket crashes of recent times and we found ourselves having to do what all financial experts advise against: we were obliged to sell our investments at the lowest point in the market. That desultory exercise, together with a small resettlement grant, yielded the princely sum of £600. One of our children slept for a few weeks in an open suitcase and, with great ingenuity and a few embroidered cloths, we turned packing cases into small tables. We begged and borrowed wherever we could and soon had enough to get by on. When Chris Nicholls, one of the church stewards, arrived with a dining table and four chairs, it felt like five Christmases rolled into one. I suspect that he'd persuaded his wife Jo to buy a new dining set for their own home and gave us the old one. It's the furniture that we still use to this day.

I had charge of three churches. At Caversham Heights, we had a lovely suburban congregation and a church impressively committed to serving its community. Martyn Allies, a recently retired RAF officer, and his wife Lilly were overflowing with energy and they'd soon founded a cultural society which attracted top-class speakers and also a lunch club for elderly and lonely people. Meanwhile, down in the 'village' of Caversham stood another church whose members were, on the whole, longer-term Reading residents. There was a massive Boys' Brigade Company and band and a wonderful spirit of fellowship. They provided babysitters galore and lasting friendships to boot. At Caversham Park, a new housing development, an ecumenical community worshipped in a school and I did my best to give some energy to the development of that cause.

One of the traumas of those years was the death of little David Bensley in a road accident. He was only ten. The tragedy yielded unexpected reward – a long and lasting friendship with his parents, Beldon and Margaret. Margaret would eventually type and bind my doctoral thesis – surely the best presented exercise of its kind that year!

Otherwise, the pastoral round and the preaching, the courses I taught and my editorial responsibilities with the Reading Race Relations Council, established the pattern of my working week. I did much of my pastoral visiting by bicycle and generally had one little boy perched behind me on a specially fitted child seat. We had so much fun together as we swooped down slopes and around corners in order to maximize the speed and reduce the need for pedalling. We whooped our way around the streets of Caversham. In one way, I knew I couldn't have been in a better place. But there was a downside, too. Reading lay under the flight path of planes leaving Heathrow Airport for America. The constant burr of this traffic somehow kept my sense of the unfinished business of Haiti naggingly alive. I knew that this would have to be dealt with one day.

Our daughter Ruth was born in Reading. Unlike her brothers, she entered the world on a predetermined day and at an hour that suited the working patterns of the ward where she was born. She weighed ten and a half pounds. Margaret is not a large person, yet she produced three children who all seemed ready to take their O-levels the minute they drew breath. When I was told: 'It's a girl,' I broke down in tears. Then, wiping them away, I jumped into my car and drove from the Royal Berkshire Hospital to the home of our wonderful friends, Gladys and Gerry Alderman, who were looking after the boys – and every single traffic light encountered along the way stood at green. Curmudgeonly friends have told me many times since that it's logistically impossible that all those lights should have favoured my speedy return home in that way. Miserable old so-and-sos. They weren't there. I was. And I'm sticking to my story.

In the summer of 1976, we enjoyed a wonderful holiday in Burry Port. My mother had remarried during our time in Haiti and she was blissfully happy. Harold Rees had been a council workman but, before that, a coal-miner who'd left the pits when his lungs filled up with the dust. He and my mother loved their cigarettes and their crosswords, their car rides and the bungalow they lived in. My mother had suffered deafness since her teens but, miracle of miracles, this had simply disappeared when she married Harold. 'Les,' she'd say in a hushed voice filled with childlike wonder, 'I can hear the clock ticking and the birds singing. Isn't God good?' This mention of God is interesting, for Olwen Rees was now a regular church attender. She'd come to the conclusion that all the sermon fodder her manner of living might once have provided for a finger-wagging preacher was now outweighed by having a son in the ministry. Her logic was both simple and compelling.

Our holiday was brilliant but marred by the news that our five-year-old nephew Michael, the eldest son of John and Kath, Margaret's brother and sister-in-law, had been killed in a road accident. We were all mortified. Margaret and I had to drive from Burry Port to Newcastle-under-Lyme for the funeral, with Ruth in her carrycot behind us and the boys in the care of *mamgu*, their grandmother. When the holiday came to an end, it was with a curious cocktail of sadness and joy that we left Carmarthenshire for Reading, my mother waving us away until we were quite out of sight. It was the last time that we saw her.

Just two or three weeks later, while Margaret was in Newcastle with the children spending time with her grieving family, I got an early morning phone call. It was a Sunday and I was already in my study preparing for the day's services. It was my Auntie Nell, the youngest of my mother's sisters, who told me that my mother had just moments earlier died in the Llanelli General Hospital. She'd been swimming the previous day – an activity she loved, though the way she did it was a precarious variant of that honoured form of exercise. She'd returned home and then, suddenly, the underlying factors which had for so long affected her health cut her down and brought her life speedily to an end. Her *joie de vivre*, her generosity of spirit, her unsophisticated optimism, her ability to make little ado about having next-to-nothing, had made her the person she was and all this overflow of positive and life-affirming energy had drip-fed my deepest self from the moment of my birth. She left no money, not a penny. But her legacy has never been diminished by time and has left me endowed with blessings that money can never buy.

Jim and I travelled to Burry Port where I conducted the funeral in our little chapel before laying her to rest in the cemetery perched on a hillside overlooking the town where she'd spent virtually the whole of her life. It had meant so much to her that Harold, a widower when she married him, had told her there would be room for her in his grave. 'Tidy grave, Olwen,' he'd say reassuringly, 'plenty of room for three.' As we completed the prayers, a large crowd of men standing around the grave gave voice to 'Cwm Rhondda' and its words of hope rang out across the open space: 'When I tread the verge of Jordan, bid my anxious fears subside; death of death and hell's destruction, land me safe on Canaan's side. Songs of praises, songs of praises, I will ever give to thee, I will ever give to thee.' My mother died on 15 August 1976, the Feast of the Assumption of the Virgin Mary, and has surely by now found out just what is being assumed by those who take their name from this doctrine.

It was during our years in Reading that I discovered Hans Küng. I'd seen a two-page spread featuring Küng's latest book in, of all places, the *Observer* newspaper, a journal not usually given over to serious reflection on matters theological. The article gave unstinting praise to Küng in general and to his latest book, *On Being a Christian*, in particular. I was so impressed that the following day I drove in to Oxford to buy myself a copy. Everywhere I went, including Blackwell's (surely the most brilliant of bookshops ever created), I found the same thing: the book had sold out and I'd have to order a copy. Just think of it for a moment. A 700-page, hard-backed book of theology, with 200 pages of footnotes, had sold out in every Oxford bookshop. Disgruntled, I placed my order and waited. When the fat volume eventually arrived, I devoured it in record time. It was exactly what I was thirsting for. Here was some serious, systematic theology done 'from below'. Küng had been a theological expert at the Second Vatican Council, where he and his colleague Joseph Ratzinger had made outstanding contributions. Soon after the Council, however, Küng had angered Roman Catholic traditionalists with the publication of a book which he believed carried forward the thinking of the Council – a book called (provocatively) *Infallible?*

The later careers of Küng and Ratzinger are the stuff of high drama. One has proved too much of a thorn in the side of his superiors and been banished from his teaching role. The other, meanwhile, after many years as the guardian of Catholic orthodoxy in his role as Secretary of State at the Congregation for Doctrine and Faith, became Pope Benedict XVI at the death of John Paul II in 2006. The treatment of Küng has certainly confirmed my feeling that I could never contemplate becoming a Roman Catholic. I had once sent to the Catholic Truth Society for a teaching course. I thought I'd like the authoritative style of self-confident Roman Catholicism. I didn't. Not one bit. And the treatment of Küng made me doubly sure that I'd reached the right conclusion. Küng stands in a long line of those who were ahead of their time and, therefore, viewed with a suspicion bordering on contempt. Alfred Loisy, George Tyrrell, Pierre Teilhard de Chardin (to name but a few) were all banished to outer darkness for the cardinal error of being ahead of their times.

By the mid-1970s, I'd discovered in Hans Küng a theological soulmate, someone who could write about God and faith in a way that avoided the extremes both of scholastic loftiness and sentimental pietism. His style was fresh and accessible. He engaged with the worlds of science, literature and even atheism. My first encounter with his writing drew me in to a narrative that was both biblical and Christocentric. It fed faith without once making me cringe. Küng is a theologian for all people and for all seasons and even the gates of Vatican conservatism will not ultimately prevail against his common sense and brilliance of mind.

One day, we received the visit of the Reverend Alan Kirton. He was a Caribbean minister who'd just been appointed head of the Methodist Church in Haiti. He'd spent a couple of months in France getting his French up to scratch and was calling on us on his way to Port-au-Prince. He made an urgent plea that I should consider returning to Haiti. The group of churches centred on Cap Haitien, Haiti's ancient capital, was in disarray and only someone who already had some experience of Haiti as well as its two languages could hope to rescue it. Would I be that person?

This challenge disturbed me greatly. It raked up the ashes of a fire that had never been extinguished, the deep feeling that I'd somehow left Haiti without finishing my business there. To return for another stint might allow me to address that matter. But at the same time, I was only too aware that Margaret was loath to contemplate such a move. Her reluctance was only reasonable. We had three children who'd all be under five if we were to return. The four years we'd already done had taken a severe toll on her and it would surely be cruel to subject her to all that again. And yet I had all this unresolved stuff grumbling away within me and I didn't know how it would erupt if I tried to suppress it now. Margaret suspected that this question was putting our relationship on a knife-edge. If she insisted on staying, she had no way of knowing how I'd handle what would for-ever be an unanswered question nagging away at my innards. She feared that our marriage might not withstand such a threat. And yet she didn't know if she could survive a second tour of duty and felt keenly that the children didn't need to be so radically disrupted at this stage in their development. She balanced things out and, in the end, encouraged me to respond positively. I still find myself amazed at the downright generosity and guts needed on her part to reach this point. I resolved to do my best to honour her decision by setting our second sojourn in Haiti on an entirely different basis from the outset. I'd try hard to be more detached; I'd identify some fixed objectives and, once these were met, we'd return home again.

Part of my preparation for this second stay in Haiti was to attend a ten-day course offered by an agency called AVEC (after the French word for 'with'). This was run by George Lovell, a Methodist minister who'd served in Burry Port during my teenage years. He worked closely with Catherine Widdicombe, a member of the Grail Community in Pinner. They were work consultants and had developed a non-directive methodology which involved close listening, awareness-raising, and the identification of aims and objectives which then needed to be worked towards by the worker in conjunction with his or her colleagues. One's work was always done 'with' rather than 'for' people. George was to become my mentor over the decades to come, always helping me to see how even a character as forthright as mine and a nature as ebullient as mine could play its part, non-directively, in collaboration with others, in the leadership of a church or community. My attending this course was an important part of fulfilling my commitment made to Margaret that I'd work in a more structured way to set and accomplish appropriate targets which, once achieved, would allow us to leave.

And so, in the late summer of 1977, five of us set out for Haiti. We were met at the airport and taken to our lodging place. The family were shown their quarters and I was whisked away to a meeting of the ministers. There was great rejoicing as we embraced one another after our three-year absence. Then Alan Kirton, now installed as the leader of the Methodist Church in Haiti, invited me to open the meeting with prayer. I invited people to close their eyes and my Créole rolled unhesitatingly into action as I invoked the Almighty. It (the language not the Almighty) had been mothballed in readiness for this day.

Soon we were making our way to the breathtakingly beautiful northern coast of Haiti and our new duties in Cap Haitien. We had a lovely house that stood right by the sea with fabulous views across a wide bay towards the Citadelle Laferrière, a spectacular fortress erected by King Henri Christophe in the early part of the nineteenth century to defend his newly independent nation against any attempt that might be made by France to regain it. It's said that ten thousand men died in the building of this edifice and it, together with the Sans-Souci Palace in the valley down below, is now recognized by the United Nations Educational, Scientific and Cultural Organization (UNESCO) as a world heritage site. The city of Cap Haitien was largely rebuilt after a disastrous earthquake that laid the old French city to waste in 1842. Methodists have been active there throughout this period and have helped to shape the cultural and political life of the city and the region. I had charge of seven (it became nine) churches across the northern department and it became evident to me from the very outset that there would be plenty of work to do.

The first objective I set myself was to create and develop a team. Too much had depended on the minister. So, every Monday morning, three school head teachers, two evangelists, a secretary and I would meet at the manse. I was the only outsider and soon, with local knowledge and an increasing sense of self-confidence, the team came to understand that they were together responsible for strategic thinking across the region of our combined operation. We set budgets together, made difficult decisions together about laying off surplus employees, dealt together with disciplinary problems, had fun together and ate together. It was pure AVEC and made such obvious sense.

The second target was to sort out a large deficit and bring the budget back into balance. To help us achieve this, I made arrangements for an accountant to visit us every three months to bring our books up to date and to give us accurate and useful financial information. Soon, we had a complete set of audited accounts for the first time in years. We could see what was happening and we could work at dealing with our debts. The sense of ownership on the part of my Haitian colleagues was palpable. I'd soon found sources of income to deal with the past overspend and, freed from the encumbrances which went with that, we could set ourselves sensible goals for the future.

The third and most demanding problem area was the state of our plant and premises. We had four schools, one camping site, several acres of good land, and new communities wanting to affiliate with us. The furthest of these needed all the strength of the lowest gears of my Land Rover as I drove up precipitous slopes to reach it. Everything lay within a radius of about 25 miles of Cap Haitien but over roads that could be impassable after the rains and deeply rutted and dangerous in the dry season.

I contacted the United Methodist Committee on Relief in New York. They were happy to set our needs before those of American Methodists. The response was magnificent. Soon, we had a succession of 'work groups' visiting Cap Haitien and helping us with our programmes. I was very strict with these visitors. I insisted that they work with Haitians on a level of absolute equality. So I found tasks which they could undertake together, alongside one another. They planted trees, built schools, mixed and poured concrete together. This gave experiences to our American visitors that were often life-changing. They, of course, would stay in one of our hotels. Margaret would cut peanut butter and jelly sandwiches for their lunch and see to it that the five-gallon water jars were constantly replaced. And every evening, I'd spend half an hour at the hotel to take any questions or deal with any problems that had arisen during the day. No one was to explode with anger or huff and puff with righteous indignation during the day. We held our 'cry sessions' in the evening and generally dealt with any difficulties then. Now and again, I had to suggest that someone wasn't co-operating or was being racist. Then I had to speak severely and even send such visitors packing. All in all, the constant stream of Americans who came to help us were a huge blessing. Their visits almost always brought funding streams that we'd never have enjoyed otherwise. And they led to invitations to Margaret and me (and the children) to visit the United States and friendships that have lasted for decades.

In this way, we rebuilt our entire set of premises. And, in addition to all that, we funded a mobile clinic, a number of wells, irrigation projects and so much else. I became known as *pasteur béton* (Reverend Concrete!) as I left home every morning with a builder's level in one hand and a Bible in the other. There were times when we had two or three building schemes going on at once, but none was as ambitious as the new school that we planned for the town of Cap Haitien itself. That was to be a 16-room brand-new building on two floors. It involved the demolition of an ancient manse (in which several classes met) and it all had to be accomplished within 50 weeks and without the closure of a school of 300 pupils meeting on the site. And so the new buildings of Collège Modèle came to pass. A dozen or so teams of volunteers came from across the United States. The scheme's architect was a young Haitian whom I'd taught during my Port-au-Prince days and this was his first big job. I was the clerk of works and ordered the prodigious amounts of steel, cement, building blocks, timber and related items from a number of sources. I, too, had to keep track of the money. I lost count of the number of times we began a week without the cash we'd need by the end of the week to pay our workers. Several times, I could have suspended the work on these grounds but I was determined, using Haitian and American energies, to prove that great things could happen in this desperate land once there was a will to do so.

We kept all our targets. The old manse was knocked down and the concrete frame of the new building was put up in the three months following the end of the school term and in time for the re-opening in October. The Christmas and Easter holiday periods were intensively used. A well was sunk in one corner of the school yard, window frames were fitted and doors crafted and then, the supreme and finishing touch, the whole edifice was painted in the dark green and yellow colours of the school. It was opened with *éclat* during the annual Conference of the Methodist Church in the Caribbean and Americas in May 1980, with the brass band of the Haitian army and a clutch of town officials in attendance.

All the objectives that I'd set on arrival were met within three years and I kept the promise that I'd made to myself. It was time to go home. I'd engaged with Haiti this time at an entirely different level. I had more detachment, was more focused on tasks. The children had grown up so fast; Tim, Jon and Ruth were going on eight, seven and five respectively and would now need to get into the British educational system. When we first arrived in Cap Haitien, I'd registered the boys at Collège Modèle but that hadn't worked. It really was too much to expect small boys, snatched from a kindergarten in comfortable Caversham, to line up under a hot sun for a school assembly that took place in French and to sit in classrooms within the old and crumbling manse. That experience taught me an important lesson. I may have all the high-sounding principles in the world but I must not use my children to illustrate them. They are individuals in their own right and I must always envisage the best possible options for them. So I got them into a mission school run by an American evangelical group near Cap Haitien. I persuaded those in charge that it would be all right to take the children of a 'liberal' Methodist by offering to teach their children French. It was a deal and led to our eventually becoming great friends with people whose theological style would not immediately have attracted us.

Emotions recollected in tranquillity can so easily distort what's being looked at. As I reflect on a decade dominated by our stay in Haiti, I could so easily paint a picture in the colours of melodrama. Without trying too hard, I could exaggerate the Voodoo elements knowing how well that would play with a Western audience or portray myself as the possessor of heroic qualities. But all that would be false. We did what we had to do and it was as simple as that. We had moments of real depression when everything seemed too much for us. Dengue fever, a hurricane, the lack of contact with home, a never-ending succession of seemingly intractable obstacles to overcome, accidents to the children – all these seemed to take on an extra dimension in a land and a culture so different from our own. Against all this, of course, stood the courage of the Haitian people who, against all the odds, continue to survive. And we had the privilege of working with some extraordinary people. Some of them were truly heroic; they set our endeavours in a proper perspective.

Alain Rocourt was one of these. We'd spent several weeks with Alain and his wife Marlène and their children Françoise, Monique, Ghislaine, Roland and Karine, on our first arrival in Haiti in 1970. We became friends. Alain was the first Haitian to become head of the Methodist Church in Haiti and was universally respected. He took two degrees from the University of London and his sharp intellect was one of his finest features. He gave several years of his ministry to the distant town of Jérémie and its surrounding villages, where he developed an innovative programme of rural development that became a model for such work and attracted visitors and experts from all over the world.

It was while at Jérémie that Alain showed his true colours. It was at the height of 'Papa Doc' Duvalier's reign of terror. Jérémie had a large number of mulatto families among its population and Duvalier, suspecting them of subversion, had ordered his Tontons Macoutes to eliminate as many of them as possible. Hearing of this plan, there was a mass exodus to the hills surrounding Jérémie. But one old man was too frail to leave his home and his family felt obliged to leave him to his fate. When Alain heard of this, he sent his family to seek refuge but insisted on remaining with the old man in town. The Tontons Macoutes arrived under cover of darkness and began pouring petrol over the wooden structures of the empty houses. Alain heard them and went out to remonstrate. He, along with the old man at whose side he'd remained, was arrested and the following day told to prepare himself for summary execution. He was ordered to dig two graves, one for himself and the other for the old man. He did so. The Tontons Macoutes stood ready to shoot when one of them was hailed to take a phone call. It was François Duvalier himself, a chance call, and he asked whether the purge was going as planned. When he heard that Alain Rocourt was standing in front of the caller awaiting his execution, Duvalier gave a direct order not to proceed. Alain was released and later heard that a number of weighty international voices had been putting pressure on Duvalier on Alain's behalf. His name was fresh in the dictator's

Mam, Jim, Les – 1943

Les and Jim – 1946

Lean-to room partly hidden behind bungalow – c.1975

The Bache – Building Trades Supply bottom left

Sixth former – 1959

Going to grammar school – 1953

Cardiff graduation 1963 with
Mam, Jim and a friend

Lampeter v. International XV – spot the stars! 1966
(I am second from left on the front row)

Wedding day – 1969, with Jim

Lampeter College ball – 1967

Family – 1979

Preaching in simple chapel

Ministry – 1984

With President Jean-Bertrand Aristide, 1992

With Rowan Williams

Wesley's Chapel

mind and this had led to the surprising order's being given. You can't come any closer to death than that.

I could have closed this chapter with similar tales of Marco Dépestre, pioneer agriculturalist and Methodist minister; of Paulette Holly, deaconess and intrepid worker in the slums of Port-au-Prince bringing healthcare and education to the poorest of the poor; or Marie-Lyse Desroches, a Swiss woman who has given her life to training teachers for Haiti's rural schools; or Madame Hudicourt who, for 17 years, didn't know whether her husband, picked up by the Tontons Macoutes in one of their regular purges, was dead or alive. It's a long and impressive list.

In the late 1980s, I made a determined effort to get London University to award an honorary degree to Alain Rocourt, one of its alumni. At that time, he'd survived yet another skirmish with death as he held the Electoral Commission planning the very first post-Duvalier presidential election to its task. Again, he'd shown downright heroism in the face of intimidation and the terrorization of his family. But our pleas fell on deaf ears. It seems to me that our universities prefer to give these honours to famous or wealthy people. It's as if such awards are intended to serve the publicity or financial needs of the university rather than to raise awareness of real, if unsung, achievements of the human spirit.

So our Haitian decade came to an end. We travelled by plane to Miami, and then by train to Jacksonville in the north-eastern corner of Florida. There we hired a car and drove through Georgia and the Carolinas up into West Virginia, where we stayed with old friends Lillian and Arlie Queen. Then a long train journey from Huntington to Washington before finally getting our plane home. We had the holiday of a lifetime, staying with and enjoying the hospitality of so many of those who'd worked with us in Cap Haitien.

We left Haiti in the summer of 1980. But Haiti has never left me. For now, however, we brought our direct experience of the Caribbean to an end. It was time to turn to fresh woods and pastures new.

4

One of Mr Wesley's Preachers

My talents, gifts, and graces, Lord,
Into thy blessed hands receive,
And let me live to preach thy word,
And let me to thy glory live;
My every sacred moment spend
In publishing the sinner's friend.

CHARLES WESLEY,
'GIVE ME THE FAITH WHICH CAN REMOVE'

It was a dramatic encounter.

I was standing at the door of a church where I'd been preaching, shaking hands and exchanging pleasantries which had covered a narrow and predictable spectrum with comments ranging between 'nice sermon' and 'lovely weather'. Until, that is, the very last person in the line. He was a thick-set man in his sixties who approached me with tears streaming down his face.

'I don't suppose you know who I am,' he declared. I shook my head. 'I'm your father,' he said and the news almost blew me away. If his claim was true, here was a man who'd disappeared from our lives so completely that I'd consistently and over many years dealt with his absence by announcing his death whenever the subject arose. I'd barely had time to register the impact of what he'd said before he went on: 'It was your mother's fault.'

That statement brought me to my senses and focused my mind. I may have been too young to understand what was happening between my parents when they were together but I definitely knew who'd fought tooth and nail to raise Jim and me. No one had seen more clearly than I how close we'd come to total collapse or what a constant battle we'd fought to ensure that we had even the basics in food, fuel, clothing and shelter. And it wasn't this sobbing wretch standing before me. For 20 years, the whole time Jim and I had been growing up, he'd never once appeared on our radar screens. That's what I knew. So I bade him a peremptory good day and sent him packing.

My mother was still alive and I wasn't yet married. Margaret and I agreed that we should keep this news from my mother. It would be far too painful for her to cope with. Interestingly, my father sent us quite a lavish wedding present and, with it, his address. But we were soon to be heading for Haiti and had plenty to preoccupy us without worrying about him. It wasn't difficult to put him out of our minds.

But the question didn't go away. It arose again when we returned to England in 1980. My father made an early contact and indicated that he'd like very much to see us from time to time. My mother was now dead and we had three lively children. Margaret helped me to overcome my negative feelings by suggesting that it might be a decent – even a Christian – thing for us to allow an old man (he was then 75) to get to know his grand-children. And so it came to pass.

He came to London several times in the next six or seven years. It was always awkward. I couldn't bring myself to like him. The children were our salvation; their antics got us through many an embarrassing moment. He always seemed to want to raise the question of his time with my mother and to put his side of the case as to why everything had broken down between them. I just didn't want to hear any of that. Jim was even more resistant. He was shocked that we'd made contact at all. He showed downright hatred for the man whose name he carried and who'd neglected us so totally. But soon after he'd embraced the Christian faith, and as a direct consequence of his newfound identity, he yielded. He came over to our home in Loughton with his wife Glenys and their son Dylan to meet our father. It was truly the prickliest afternoon I've ever spent. And it was never to be repeated. Jim didn't see his father ever again. I can only take my hat off to him for making such a huge effort that day.

One thing was emerging from all this. While my father showed some curiosity about what was happening to me, his interest in Jim was far more passionate. I remember going down to Swansea to attend the funeral of my father's second wife and meeting relatives whom I didn't even know existed. I overheard remarks spoken in hushed whispers and which purported to be private but which, I'm certain, were intended for my ears. Welsh gossip has its own energies. The barbed comments that came my way were intended to convey the opinion that it was my brother who was the apple of his father's eye. 'We don't rightly know where this one came from,' they said with a mixture of malice and delight, pointing in my direction. 'Just look at him. He doesn't look a bit like Sid. Jim, on the other hand . . .' and so it went on and on. And, of course, it's made me wonder whether I am my father's son. Or whether, during his long wartime absences, my mother might have picked up with her old flame Dick. That would certainly explain why she and my father fell out so catastrophically. Perhaps Jim was the 'consolation child' intended to bring things back together again. Such speculation would go some way to explain the abrupt way in which my father's solicitor had instructed my mother to leave 25 Glanmor Terrace and his command that she should take her children with her. Who knows?

These events unfolded for the most part in Loughton, a lovely township that snuggles within the embrace of Epping Forest to the north-east of London. We'd come there from Haiti in September 1980 and it was to be the perfect location for me to develop some experience in a British circuit and for the family to enjoy a blissful and stable environment as they settled into new rhythms of life. For six years, that's exactly what it proved to be.

When we arrived, I was one of six ministers living and working within the Woodford and Wanstead circuit. Just a year later, I felt like the prophet Elijah who, in a time of persecution, bemoaned his lot with a cry to heaven: 'I, and I alone, am left; and woe is me.' For one reason or another, all my colleagues left. I became the *de facto* superintendent of the circuit and set about building a team. I sent a note to my old college friend Tony Barnes, whose time in Dover was coming to an end, urging him 'to come over to Macedonia to help me'. He and Joyce were soon at my side. So too was Gordon Jones, a man who'd resigned from the ministry some years previously and was now looking for work as an 'active supernumerary'. I welcomed him and Peggy with open arms. He was such a learned man and so gentle. To complete the team, we welcomed Edna Buggey, a local deputy head teacher who would eventually herself become an ordained minister. We became a wonderful team, meeting every Monday morning, enjoying each other's company and stimulating each other at every turn. The Bible tells us that we should love one other. It's a bonus when we discover that we actually like each other as well.

Soon, it became obvious to me that we were going to have to take radical action with our church building in Loughton. We kept getting hefty repair bills for this Edwardian building and yet we didn't seem able to get to the bottom of the problem affecting it. It would need replacing. And we should envisage something altogether more fit for purpose, something that would exploit the church's key position on the High Road. These proposals were soon worked up into a set of drawings and people began to get excited about it. Initial hesitation on the part of those who were understandably fond of the old church was soon overcome. Some key families stood out against spending £500,000 (still a massive sum in those days) on buildings rather than 'mission'. But even these opponents of the scheme eventually became keen enthusiasts. An extremely well-qualified development group, which was not without its eclectic or eccentric elements, was soon hard at work. The money was raised without difficulty and soon a fine building, open every day of the week, began to serve the whole community through its social and cultural (as well as spiritual) programmes.

It took a year to complete the new buildings and, during that time, our Roman Catholic friends at St Edmund's offered us accommodation in their church hall. This was such a gracious offer and forged bonds between the two churches that continue to this day. We shared a vestry and it was great fun, Sunday by Sunday, getting ourselves ready for our main morning act of worship. While Father Adrian Howell SJ and I were getting robed, attention was being given to stoking up the thurible and gales of incense filled the room and our lungs. At the same time, through a door that led to the church hall, we could hear our organist, John Wiffen, creating an atmosphere for Methodist worship by playing some well-known hymn tunes. Both Adrian and I found this combination of incense and Charles Wesley positively inebriating.

The seats in the hall were arranged so that the congregation faced away from the bar. That meant, of course, that the preacher looked directly towards those crystal fountains whence the healing streams would soon be flowing. It was slightly unnerving to see the barman making preparations for opening time with the sermon barely under way. This amounted to a serious external pressure on the preacher and I suspect that it had the effect of turning many a full-blooded sermon into a well-clipped homily. The silent weekly contest between preacher and barman, all done in good humour, was a fascinating extra-liturgical ritual, a fresh expression of church perhaps.

On Easter Sunday 1986, we arrived for our service to find that the hall had been lavishly decorated with banks of trumpeting white lilies and a large notice pinned up in a prominent position. 'A happy Easter to our Methodist brothers and sisters,' it read. However glad we were eventually to cross back to our own brand new church, we went with pangs of sadness at having to leave such generous and friendly hosts.

Ecumenical relationships were brilliant during our time in Loughton. We forged ourselves into an effective team that included a Baptist, three Anglicans, a few Roman Catholics and me. We met and ate regularly and offered ministry to the whole town. My responsibilities lay with the teaching of theology. Every September, I'd sit with a room full of hopefuls in the local high school gymnasium seeking to enrol anyone wanting to do 'Theology on Thursdays' on that year's further education programme. Every year, those signing up for our class outscored their nearest rivals by at least two to one. 'Holiday French', 'Photography for Beginners', 'Cooking for One' were some of the also-rans that I remember. It was fascinating to sense the real thirst for theological knowledge that was abroad in all our churches. We packed in a crowd which generally ran to three figures. I remember sharing courses on early church fathers and modern theologians with Tony Bryer, an Anglican curate. But for the most part, I was on my own. How I had reason to be grateful to Hans Küng! In successive years, we studied *On Being a Christian, Does God Exist?* and *Eternal Life*, all of which had appeared in English between 1976 and 1984. *Does God Exist?* still amazes me as much by the beauty of its construction as by its content. Two wonderful opening chapters centre on the thinking and methodologies of two French scientists of the seventeenth century who also happened to be men of faith. There's a masterly description of the desire of René Descartes to produce 'clear and distinct' explanations of everything. Küng describes his chosen route of methodological doubt and the *eureka* moment: *'Cogito ergo sum'* (I think, therefore I am). This, perhaps as an unintended consequence, led to the privatization of religious belief since faith, after all, remained incapable of the kind of clarity he wanted. Blaise Pascal, on the other hand, believed in revealed religion: *'Le coeur a ses raisons que la Raison ne connaît point,'* he declared (The heart has its reasons, about which Reason itself doesn't have a clue). And he wore a patch on the lining of his coat that attested to the 'Fire!' which burned in his soul. These two brilliant men of science established the parameters within which faith would be discussed in the centuries that followed them.

Then, after a stunning exposition of the thinking of Hegel, we are introduced to an impressive range of secular thinkers and, as we do so, we find ourselves plunging downwards on a course which eventually displaces God. The atheistic determinism of Karl Marx, the forensic skills of psychoanalysis as revealed by Sigmund Freud, the blistering atheism of Ludwig Feuerbach – whose criticism of people of faith was that they tended to create God in their own image – and then the chilling nihilism of Friedrich Nietzsche are all explored on a route that sees God retreat before the forces of rampant secularism. But the road merely bottoms out. Everything now turns on a little phrase which is clearly the key to Küng's whole argument. We've reached the moment where, having seen the uncertainties around us, we must ask ourselves whether there is anything at all in which we can put our trust. Küng reassures us. 'Trust in uncertain reality' becomes his rallying cry – not far off New Testament scholar Tom Wright's description of himself as a 'critical realist'. And then, in a succession of ascending steps, Küng shows how it is possible to say 'Yes' to reality, to God, and to the Christian God. A watchword for this extraordinary exploration of faith, a word which I have kept at the forefront of my mind ever since reading Küng's work all those years ago, is the declaration of Dag Hammarskjöld, the Secretary-General of the United Nations who died in a plane accident in 1961 while on a visit to the Congo:

> You dare your Yes – and experience a meaning,
> You repeat your Yes – and all things acquire a meaning,
> When everything has a meaning, how you can you live anything but a
>   Yes?

As well as the teaching of systematic theology, I launched a study group during these years that invited people to read the New Testament in Greek. So many people complained that I was referring to Greek words in my sermons and they wanted their own chance to get to know the New Testament in its original language. Just over a dozen people gathered once a fortnight, none of them having previously studied Greek and only two of them with Latin. Before I left Loughton, they had all read significant parts of the New Testament in Greek and the class continued for some time after my departure.

The congregation at Loughton had some fascinating characters in it. I can see them now: a banker at the cutting edge of getting his employers and the public ready for the introduction of the first credit cards (and who saw the 1984 Data Protection Act through parliament and onto the statute book); a feisty headmistress who, for the second time, was turning a grammar school into a comprehensive; a former chief executive officer of the Co-operative Movement, the managing director of the UK operation of a leading typewriter company; the stentorian former deputy matron of the London Hospital; the creator of a Christian drama and resource centre; an Assistant Commissioner of the Metropolitan Police who'd played a key role in the arrest of the Kray brothers; teachers, bankers, lawyers, executives of various kinds and, to cap it all, our local undertaker. It was the latter who provided the foundation stone of the new church that we were building – a piece of Westmoreland granite which might otherwise have ended up as someone's tombstone. On it we engraved the words 'TO THE GREATER GLORY OF GOD'. The word 'greater' was included because it figures in the motto of the Society of Jesus – *Ad maiorem dei gloriam* – and we wanted to honour our Jesuit friends for all their wonderful hospitality during the time we lodged under their roof.

When I arrived in Loughton, a previous glut of young people had dried up. We had that rarest of all situations, some splendid leaders with no young people to lead. But there were a number of young wives anchored at home with babies and very young children. We began a mid-week study circle for them and provided a crèche. This proved very successful and soon brought the husbands and fathers into church, too. My baptism arm did double time during these years. Later on, this baby boom produced as good a crop of teenagers as any church could possibly want.

Lionel ('Len') and Heather Murray were regularly present in church. Curiously, so too was Sir Frank Bower. So we had a situation where the general secretary of the Trades Union Congress and a former president of the Confederation of British Industry sat in the same congregation – though noticeably, they sat on different sides of the centre aisle. The Murrays were very friendly to us and we'd often be invited around to their house for beer, sandwiches and snooker. They had a colour television set; this made the sport a natural winner on television and I became hooked. This was a critical period in modern British history for industrial relations and Lionel was rarely out of the news. Again and again he seemed to be locked into (or out of) discussions with Margaret Thatcher about the role of trade unions in the shaping of a modern economic order. He was as demanding of his own supporters as he was of the government, and his doctrine of *Realpolitik* seemed the only sensible one if all sides were to become stakeholders in the future of Britain. This turned out to be at odds both with the reactionary elements within his own movement and with the radical ideas of Mrs Thatcher. I used to get hot news of the latest happenings in the political arena during our snooker sessions and can't say that I was honestly surprised at the sudden announcement of Lionel's retirement in 1984.

Another church member who became a friend of the family was Emily Chisholm. She'd been head of the languages department at our local high school for girls and, on retirement, had found her way to Taizé, the remarkable ecumenical community in Burgundy which was attracting tens of thousands of young people from every corner of the globe for study and reflection, prayer and worship. She soon became a universal grandmother to the young monks who formed the community there and an older sister to Brother Roger Schutz who'd founded it. Taizé was (and remains) a community of reconciliation founded in the immediate aftermath of the Second World War to bring together young people from countries that had only recently been in conflict with each other. Brother Roger was the son of a Swiss pastor but nobody really knew in his later life whether he was a Protestant or a Catholic. He struck up a close personal friendship with Pope John XXIII, who described Taizé as 'that little springtime' for the Church. Communion is offered in semi-darkness and it can be quite difficult to know, when moving forward to receive bread and wine, whether one is standing in the 'Catholic' or the 'Protestant' line. When Brother Roger appeared on the platform for the funeral of Pope John Paul II in 2006, and when it appeared that he'd been given communion by the then Cardinal Ratzinger (later Pope Benedict XVI), the brilliant ambiguity was intensified. I find this blurring of the edges wonderful and Brother Roger pulled it off in spades. It was a shocking moment when we learned how he'd been stabbed to death by a disturbed woman while at worship just a year later.

By the time I met her, Emily Chisholm had become one of the Taizé community's translators. She soon enlisted me as a collaborator. We'd spread out the handwritten journals of Brother Roger, whose writing was almost as inscrutable as his churchmanship, and we'd decipher it as best we could. I remember working on such volumes as *Violent for Peace, The Wonder of a Love, And Your Deserts Shall Flower, The Dynamic of the Provisional* and *A Heart that Trusts*. Soon I was visiting Taizé myself. I struck up an immediate friendship with a number of the brothers and, when they discovered that I'd made a study of Gerard Manley Hopkins, they pressed me into helping them to understand his poetry better. It wasn't easy to explain some of the wordplays of Hopkins, or the nuances of his English style, to people who spoke French or Spanish or Italian. But these were brilliant young men and we had some very stimulating times together. They'd invite me to supper in their refectory and this gave me a number of opportunities to have conversation with Brother Roger himself. I suspect that I was too much in awe of him ever to make the most of those extraordinary moments.

Emily Chisholm was a hymn writer too and her efforts figure in a number of hymn books around the English-speaking world. She made me the executor of her literary remains and I still dip into her jottings and collections from time to time. She became an extra member of our family, hiding Easter eggs for the children, coming on holiday with us, keeping us on our toes with our study of the French language.

Margaret had not resumed her career on our return from Haiti. She'd stayed at home to look after the children. But the time soon came when she itched to get back to work. After a number of locums and a huge effort at retraining with machinery and procedures that had advanced exponentially in the twelve years that she'd been away from the workplace, she was eventually offered a full-time, permanent position at the London Hospital. When she began her time out, she was still making the complicated calculations necessary in her work by slide rule. Who remembers that curious instrument now? Everything had been computerized by the time she resumed her career.

Towards the end of our time in Loughton, we had to make some big decisions about the education of our children. I knew that I'd be moving at least once during the time of their secondary schooling. We agonized over what to do for the best and, in the end, opted for a boarding education – something that would at least give them continuity throughout their secondary years. The boys went to The Leys School in Cambridge. By the time it was Ruth's turn, we'd moved and felt able to say to her that there was a very good chance that she could complete her secondary schooling without having to go away. There were some good local schools that would welcome her with open arms. She was ten when we put this to her. I shall never forget her reply. 'You're telling me this because I'm a girl,' she said. 'You've given the boys their chance to go away but want to keep me at home to cuddle.' Then she added the tart enjoinder: 'I want to go away to school, too. I don't want to be cuddled.' She went to Kingswood School in Bath.

And so our Loughton years came to an end. It was a blissful period in our lives. The children were happy. We had a lovely suburban house with a large garden. There were friends and good neighbours. All that was rudely interrupted when I was invited to consider moving to the West End of London. One of our most renowned ministers, Dr John Newton, had been nominated to become chairman of the Liverpool District where he'd join David Sheppard and Derek Worlock, the Anglican and Roman Catholic leaders who were setting new standards for ecumenical collaboration. The West London Mission would be needing a new superintendent. Would I consider taking this on?

Of course I said that I would and soon we found ourselves in the centre of London, settled into a town house in Marylebone. There were four toilets, each on a different floor and, at my countdown, Margaret and the children brought about a synchronized flush – our very own initiation ceremony – and it gave us a sense of ownership. We discovered that we were next-door-but-one neighbours of Christopher and Mary Hamel Cooke. Christopher was the rector of the parish church of St Marylebone, which had just been completely transformed into a centre for healing and medicine. Its relationship with the Royal Academy of Music made it a centre of excellence in that field also. Just down the road at Spanish Place was the Roman Catholic Church of St James, a somewhat pre-Second Vatican Council sort of place but with a friendly enough priest in charge. Before and behind us lay All Saints, Margaret Street, the cathedral of high Anglicanism and, for balance and good measure, All Souls, Langham Place, the watering hole of low and evangelical Anglicanism. Heythrop College was still at that time in nearby Cavendish Square and that allowed me to continue my friendship with the Jesuits. What with the Oxford Street shops, the mighty BBC, the delights of Regent's Park and proximity of the Wallace Collection in Manchester Square – we found ourselves in some very auspicious company.

The West London Mission has always been a jewel in Methodism's crown. It began its life in 1887, at a time of supreme denominational self-confidence, as one of a number of initiatives directed at the centres of cities across the land. Central Halls mushroomed into existence in London, Manchester, Nottingham, Edinburgh and many other places. They aped the then-popular music halls and sought to avoid feeling or appearing too 'churchy'. There was a platform rather than a pulpit, tip-up seats instead of pews, and service sheets were handed out in the place of hymn books. The West London Mission was by far the most prestigious of all these ventures. It was backed by a number of wealthy Methodist businessmen and set in the fashionable West End of London. Its first superintendent was Hugh Price Hughes.

When my intention to candidate for the ministry was announced to the Local Preachers' Meeting in Kidwelly in the early months of 1967, those who heard the news gave me a round of applause. But one preacher had failed to grasp what had been said. Frank Evans was as deaf as a post. Someone shouted the news into his ear trumpet (the only time that I've ever seen one of these things in use) and it brought deep pleasure to his ancient face and an unforgettable utterance to his lips: 'The first,' he declared with some emotion, 'the first candidate for our ministry since Hugh Price Hughes.' And so I was. It was perfectly true that Hughes and

I have been the only two candidates for ministry produced by the Llanelli and Carmarthen circuit. Hughes was the most dynamic Methodist leader in the second half of the nineteenth century. He'd died in 1902 but Frank Evans had heard him preach several times. He was commonly spoken of as 'a judgement day in trousers'. Christian audacity was his watchword and it suited the mood of the times. Hughes had the ear of statesmen and church leaders alike. He was the very epitome of the self-confident free churchman whose opinions were widely sought and whose influence spread across the land.

I hadn't heard of Hugh Price Hughes when Frank Evans made his outburst. Yet now I was now to take charge of work begun by him and sit at a desk overshadowed by his portrait. Wheels come full circle.

The genius of the West London Mission had always been the way it combined the evangelical claims of Christianity with a commitment to improving the lot of the poor and the marginalized. The hospice movement can trace its origins there. And many a suffragette had become socially and politically aware through serving as one of the Sisters of the Poor. This social outreach was integral to the Mission's life and was still very much alive in my time. We had a day centre for homeless people which specialized in caring for those over 25. It was open every day of the year.

At the St Luke's Centre in Lambeth, we had a fully integrated service for those who misused alcohol or other substances. This ranged from a walk-in, self-referral centre to a detoxification unit, counselling and medical services, and halfway houses for those on the road to recovery. We did work with young people in trouble with the law. And we had a bail hostel with a remarkable therapy routine run by a professor of Criminology from Cambridge University. For those awaiting trial, this was a well-regarded alternative to being remanded in prison.

I was the West London Mission's eighth superintendent. Hugh Price Hughes had been the first. I inherited the sixth as a colleague – none other than the redoubtable Donald Soper, who'd held the reins from 1936 to 1978. When he stepped down, the Kingsway Hall (where the Mission had had its headquarters) was sold and the money realized became the endowment which underpinned the financial needs of the Mission's social work projects. Its new headquarters were located in a newly refurbished suite at the Hinde Street Methodist Church near Manchester Square. On the whole, I didn't find this to be a happy merger. The resource brought into it by the socially committed members of the Kingsway Hall, now just a rump of a once wonderful congregation, was looked after by the managerial class which abounded in the Hinde Street congregation. Though situated so centrally, this church felt just like the suburban one that I'd so recently left behind me in Loughton. It seemed to lack the flair and imagination needed to keep a city centre church alive. It tidied away all invested moneys, as if they were savings accounts or pension funds. Yet they were there to meet social needs, immediate and painful social ones at that. If they'd all been spent on their proper objective and had run dry as a consequence, they'd have done what they were supposed to do. Preserving their 'real value' against inflation with the intention of keeping them in perpetuity seemed to me to deny the very spirit of their existence. We were living in the City of Westminster at a time when the local authority, under the leadership of Margaret Thatcher's close friend Lady Porter, was gerrymandering its housing stock for electoral advantage and starving social projects of matching funding. Our own budgets were always going to be under severe pressure at such a time. I was adamant that existing financial policy should be made more flexible to meet the needs of the time. A keen difference of opinion on this issue was to become one of the reasons for my downfall at the West London Mission.

Donald Soper and I became good friends. He was already in the House of Lords where he took the Labour whip. He came into the office just once during the working week but was always present on Sunday mornings. In addition, of course, were his famous open-air meetings – at Tower Hill on Wednesdays and Speakers' Corner in Hyde Park on Sunday afternoons. He had a patrician air but always sought to encourage me and I appreciated his kindness greatly.

I used to take his place at Hyde Park when he was ill or on holiday. 'Who are you?' members of the crowd bayed on my first appearance, adding: 'We didn't come here to see a young whippersnapper like you. Where's the old man?' It was unnerving, but I was somewhat consoled by others in the crowd who yelled: 'Thank God. They must have shot the old bugger at last!' Donald had given me just one word of advice just before my first outing of this kind. 'I'm not going to patronize you by telling you how to go about things,' he said in that wonderful growl of a voice that could enchant as easily as it could crush his listeners. Then he continued, 'I'll just say this. When you're out there, for God's sake look as if you're enjoying yourself. If you don't, then the British public will have the decency to let you suffer on your own.' What could be more straightforward than that?

I must resist the temptation to bring out all my Donald Soper stories. One more will have to suffice. I called on him once on the day after he'd been on the Wogan show on television. He'd appeared with the Lord Chancellor, Lord Hailsham, and the Lord Chief Justice, Lord Denning. He'd made a good fist of it but I wanted to know from him just how he felt he'd performed. 'No problem,' he said. 'Denning's deaf and Hailsham's daft, so I had a clear run.' I got to know his wife, Marie, as well and became a regular visitor at their home in Hampstead. I admired the range of his competences though I begged leave to disagree fundamentally with him about his pacifism, his teetotalism and his views on Old Labour. On this last subject, I found him a typical bourgeois idealist. His understanding of the working class was a figment of his imagination coloured by his experience of those treated by the Mission's social work projects. He didn't really understand working-class people at all, had no idea what their social aspirations might be or how they lived their lives. The Labour Party produces plenty of people like that. But, for all that, Donald was a wonderful man and it was a great privilege to know him and work with him.

Throughout my years at the West London Mission, I was building a very special relationship with friends in Northern Ireland. David Kerr was superintendent of the Belfast Central Mission and he asked me to be his consultant as he sought to build a fit-for-purpose set of premises on the site then occupied by the historic Grosvenor Hall. This gave me the opportunity to make several visits to Ulster during the time of the troubles, and I built some lasting friendships there which have gone on adding spice to our lives ever since.

The new facilities were to be built on the existing site in Glengal Street. This was next door to the Ulster Unionist Party headquarters and less than 100 yards from the Europa Hotel, the most bombed hotel in the world. It was a key emplacement and would offer space for community activity as well as offices for the administration of an impressive array of social work projects across the city. The new buildings were opened in September 1997 when hopes were beginning to rise for an end to the sectarian troubles that had left so many victims in their wake. I preached at the opening service and the congregation included a former Moderator of the Presbyterian Church, a Roman Catholic and an Anglican bishop and, to crown it all, the first Roman Catholic Lord Mayor of Belfast.

In the ten-year period it took to get these developments off the ground, Margaret and I were drawn into some close and sustaining friendships. Harold Good was the Protestant witness who later testified to the fact that the IRA had indeed destroyed their weapons hordes. David Cooper had the rare knack of cultivating a working relationship with both nationalists and republicans – he once took me to visit an IRA cell; I travelled in the back of a car with my head in a sack! And David Kerr turned a wild dream into a widely appreciated reality – the new Belfast Central Mission was an investment in the new order which we could only see dimly in those distant days. Their wives, Clodagh, Helen and Eileen, shared them with a community that was thirsting for mature leadership. And they suffered calumny and vilification, too, as they put their shoulders to the wheel. I salute them all.

I completed a doctorate while at Hinde Street. It was at the third time of asking. This time, it was in Caribbean History and was submitted at the School of Oriental and African Studies (SOAS). In truth, I hadn't thought to make my history of Methodism in Haiti into a doctoral thesis. The Church there had asked me to write a history for them, knowing that all the best archival sources were likely to be in London. While at Loughton,

I travelled into the University every Monday morning with my next-door neighbour, Albert Perry, who used to drop me off near Euston Station. Then I'd sit in the library and make notes from the vast holdings of missionary archives held there. I would later use the Public Record Office at Kew, the Bibliothèque Nationale in Paris, the New York Public Library and various personal and institutional archives in Haiti itself.

One day, I found a note on my desk in the SOAS library. It was from Richard Gray, Professor of African History. He invited me to call on him and, a week or so later, I did just that. With some curiosity. He asked me about my work and then suggested that I put it forward for a PhD. I was flattered. He explained that the title of the School hides from view the fact that it holds considerable archival collections from parts of the world other than Africa or Asia. It would be doing a favour to the School if I'd register my work, he said. I was happy to do so and found that the University of London and the School itself supported my work more than generously from its research funds. Among other things, this enabled me to do some fieldwork in Haiti.

I compiled my notes systematically every Monday morning. Then, during our annual summer holiday and in the 'dead' week following Christmas and Easter, I'd write it all up. I did a deal with the family: I'd be writing every morning till 11 a.m., then I'd be fully available for them. Their co-operation was an important part of my being able to complete the work. Later, I added two chapters and my first book, *History of Methodism in Haiti*, was published in Port-au-Prince in 1991. Methodists have played a key role throughout Haiti's independent history. They were the only organized Church there during the period 1804–60 – the time between the declaration of independence and the signing of a Concordat with the Vatican. My work allowed me to discover and give value to a range of Haitian thinkers in the cultural, social, political and religious fields. I hope that my Haitian friends who read my work will feel some pride in the accomplishments of their predecessors. The thesis and the book were written at the behest of others. All my subsequent books (including this one), as well as my articles and chapters for other people's books, have been done at the invitation of publishers or editors. I'm grateful to them all. I've never really believed that I had enough time to undertake such projects and, had it been left up to me, my serious writing would have been very meagre indeed.

It was during these years that our two fathers died. My father visited us just once during our time at the West London Mission. One day, I took him around the various social work projects and he was visibly impressed. We returned to my office and he sank gratefully into a comfortable chair. 'Les, *bach*,' he said, 'your mother would have been so proud of you.' It was the only good thing that I ever heard him say about my mother. He died a few months later and I completed my filial duties by attending his funeral. I've rarely thought of him since.

Margaret's father died just 18 months later, in the early part of 1989. He continued faithfully to support the cause of discharged prisoners and their families, right to the end. And he was indefatigable as far as his work in the Sunday School was concerned. He wasn't a perfect man, wasn't always comfortable in his own skin, but his motives were always for the best. He loved his church and nothing pleased him more than a good sermon. He would always want to discuss mine, whether good or not. I found him so encouraging and told him many a time how important he'd been in my life. He was the real father figure who mattered most to me and it was so sad to see him suffering through his last weeks. He's left many a happy and inspiring memory.

I don't know what my father-in-law would have made of the great event which happened within a month or two of his death. Billy Graham was launching his last London campaign and the capital's churches were getting everything ready for it. To my great surprise, I was asked to be a member of the organizing committee. I had a lot of time for Billy Graham; so many of my friends and colleagues had been converted to faith during his first campaign in 1954. His theology was simplistic but his well-oiled machine could still be cranked up to powerful effect. Those who sup-ported Billy Graham wouldn't naturally think of me as a bedfellow. In their eyes, I'm a hand-wringing, sloppy-thinking liberal. And perhaps

I am. But I accepted the invitation to join the committee, especially when I understood that I'd be charged with oversight of the 'social need' dimension of the campaign.

Previous campaigns had been criticized for being too pietistic, too individual. Something felt wrong about Christians spending a lot of money on an activity that set its eyes on such holy outcomes while shutting their eyes to the needs of the city's poor. The organizers had taken this to heart. But I was horrified when I learned what was being envisaged to meet those needs. Baskets would be placed at every entrance to the stadium where the campaign meetings were being held. And those attending would be encouraged to bring cans of soup or other simple foodstuffs and leave them in these baskets for eventual distribution to 'the poor'. I expressed my profound displeasure at such tokenism and I made a counter-proposal. I challenged the committee members to remember the Bible and to commit themselves to dedicating a tithe, one-tenth, of the operating costs of the campaign, to the needs of the poor.

This set the cat among the pigeons. In effect, I was asking for something in the order of £500,000. There was much shaking of heads and an uncomfortable feeling in the air, one of deep embarrassment. Eventually, after much debate, it was decided to deduct the advertising costs from our calculations and to devote one-tenth of the operating budget to our cause. This would bring our working total down to about £100,000 and, after further passionate discussion, I accepted this as an honourable compromise. We were able to support some cutting-edge Christian social work from this money and most people seemed pleased enough with the results.

Donald Soper was livid with me for having anything to do with Billy Graham. He accused him, unfairly I thought, of 'fundamentalism'. There was something visceral about Donald's attitude on this point. It bordered on jealousy. I accused Donald of being pretty fundamentalist himself in the way he constantly bludgeoned the reputation and work of Billy Graham. Why, even the then current director of social work at his own beloved West London Mission had been converted at a Billy Graham rally.

In the course of the campaign, the evangelist had arranged to make a satellite communication to the Philippines. The technology went wrong and I had to entertain him in my office while it was put right. The two of us drank rather a lot of tea while we talked about anything that came into our heads. At one point in the conversation, I asked him whether he contemplated retirement from his globe-trotting ministry. He shrank from this with horror. 'But,' I persevered, 'you'd be able to relax and spend time with your grandchildren. Doesn't the prospect of sitting on your porch in your rocking-chair, looking at the world go by, fill you with pleasure?' 'On the contrary,' he replied, 'if I were to do that, I'd have to think about death and I'm certainly not ready to do that yet.'

I'd begun attending our annual Conference and, during these years, I was asked to chair a Commission tasked with forging a single London District to replace the segmented arrangement then in force. London Methodists were separated from each other by our structures and this prevented us from establishing ourselves as a presence in the nation's capital. At that time, Margaret Thatcher was dismantling the Greater London Council, making London the only capital city in Europe without its own metropolitan government. There was no better time, in my opinion, to act counter-culturally, to offer a kind of 'prophetic act' which made a loud statement to the effect that we, at any rate, believed in London whatever the government of the day chose to do. The Commission worked hard, consulted widely, kept to its timetable. Some circuits were ready for such a development, as it would give coherence to the Methodist presence in our capital city. Others were unsure but ready to listen to the arguments. Against all these, there were circuits which refused to engage in the discussion at all, who received us with poor grace, and who were only too ready to show us the door. Our proposal was defeated in the 1989 Conference, a great disappointment; but it eventually resurfaced and our present, unified, London District came into existence in 2004 – 15 long years later and, sadly, only after the Greater London Authority had been set up by the government of Tony Blair. Yet again, the Church proved better able to follow what was happening in the secular world than to stand up against the powers of the day.

I'd fully expected to keep my position as superintendent of the West London Mission for at least ten years. That was the normal pattern. But it was soon clear to me that my face didn't fit. In my third year there, I'd been asked to consider becoming chairman of the London North East District. I did not want to do it and my *noli episcopari* (I don't want to be a bishop) did eventually prevail, though it was a close shave. This distraction gave those who were unhappy with my performance the ideal opportunity to make things difficult for me. They did so in the typical English way, of course. They congratulated me heartily on what they called my 'promotion' and began thinking about my successor. When I turned down this 'promotion', they found themselves stuck for a while. But soon they were making my life difficult. I was humiliated again and again in public. My judgement was called into account. I was accused of having an arrogant readiness to ignore established policy in favour of my own 'solutions' to the deep financial crisis facing the Mission. And, it was said, I was lazy. The worst moment of all came when I was subjected to an attack in, of all things, a Pastoral Committee and for the astounding offence of preparing young people for confirmation without going through all the proper procedures. The discussion got so heated and the criticism so direct that I asked permission to leave for fear I'd say something stupid. I was shaken to the core at the viciousness of it and wept all the way home. Nothing like this has ever happened to me before or since.

It was obvious that I'd have to go. The vast majority of the church members were shocked to discover these goings-on. Our black members, young professionals, those who'd come from Kingsway Hall, to say nothing of our ecumenical partners, were stunned. I still have the dozens of letters from all of them. One circuit steward stood by me, a Sierra Leonean named Bankole Timothy who remained a staunch friend until his death some years later. Donald Soper told me that it would be wrong for him as a retired minister to intervene. That didn't stop two other semi-detached ministers, John Stacey and John Lampard, from making an open declaration of support. My working colleagues opted for a studied neutrality, keeping themselves available, they said, to play a pastoral role with both sides of the dispute when it was all over. It was wretched. I was wretched. I started looking around for jobs outside Methodism: a headmastership, a position with Christian Aid, a transfer to the Church of England – I flirted with all these. In the end, it was Margaret who kept me sane and held me fast to my calling. I shook the Hinde Street dust off my feet. In my farewell letter to the church members, I quoted a couple of lines from Tennyson's 'In Memoriam' which seemed to sum up the bitter-sweet experience of the previous few years. My time there seemed to have consisted of

> Short swallow-flights of song, that dip
> Their wings in tears, and skim away.

I was still licking my wounds when an invitation came from the Finchley and Hendon circuit to serve as minister of the Golders Green church. The chairman of the invitation committee, a renowned Professor of Medicine, Dr John Lennard-Jones, wrote me the loveliest letter. In it, he told me that everyone knew I'd be coming to them with a lot of extra-curricular activities. By that time, I was a regular broadcaster and a Board member of Christian Aid as well as having my fingers in several other pies. But they wanted me to come anyway. 'We would want you to continue to develop those interests,' he wrote, 'in the knowledge that when you are fulfilled we [at Golders Green] will be the first to enjoy the benefits.' A year or two later, John made it possible for me to join the Athenaeum Club. He wanted me to enjoy its rich programme of after-dinner speakers and to make new friends among its members. What a contrast to my previous experience! During our time in this north London circuit, we picked ourselves up, dusted ourselves down, and flourished all over again. Our faith in human nature began to be restored.

Within a year, and despite my efforts to get back into ministry 'on the ground floor', I was asked to take over the superintendency of the circuit. There were seven wonderful congregations, each very different from the others, and I spent the next five years criss-crossing this patch of north London, much of it the former constituency of Margaret Thatcher. The doyenne of the churches was on Ballards Lane in Finchley. Once, people used to draw up to its front door on Sunday mornings in carriages and wearing top hats. It still carried a kind of faded grandeur from those days. But it had also developed a social outreach ministry with a clothing store and a cheap and cheerful feeding centre. East Finchley, just across the North Circular Road, had an entirely different feel about it. A major refurbishment was just being completed as I arrived and this allowed a very flexible use of its space. Its leaders were the finest bunch of (somewhat eccentric) people, young and not-so-young, whose dedication and fondness for each other were very striking. They had a burning desire to serve their generation, both through local efforts and through their support for causes that were wider-flung.

The tiny congregation at Mill Hill had taken a battering. A dozen or so members had kept the flag flying for many years, even though their roof had been sold over their heads. I developed an early Sunday morning communion service in the front room of a house belonging to a retired deaconess. Sister Jessie Kerridge was a Lady Bracknell kind of person who, in her younger days, had done pioneering work in Jamaica and the West Indies. She was now nearly blind and over 90. But the force of her character (and her will) remained undiminished. Edgware, another church that had enjoyed a golden past, was just coming to terms with the multi-ethnic population which now surrounded it. Some old retainers from the age of glory were courageously bringing black people into positions of leadership. There was undoubtedly a sheen of gentility but it was laced with the strong flavours of social change. It was our Hendon church that struggled most. A new-ish set of buildings hadn't really worked but some faithful people dealt with demographic change and inadequate resources as best they could. What a contrast with the Queensbury church, the only one of our causes that lay beyond the borough boundaries of Barnet. Good lay leadership and a well-balanced programme gave a sense of purpose and excitement to all that happened there.

My own day-to-day pastoral responsibilities lay in Golders Green. For some years, this had been run jointly with the United Reformed Church.

Among its members were scholars and diplomats, school children and postmen, and an amazing group of young people. There was a sense of fun and energy, life and meaning, at the heart of worship. This was a joyous congregation and I loved it.

All this work was undertaken in an area that lay at the heart of the north London Jewish community. On the street where we lived in Temple Fortune, for example, we had secular Jews living on one side of us and a Greek family on the other. In the New Testament, the phrase 'Jews and Greeks' is another way of describing the whole inhabited earth. And that's just how it felt. The range and variety of Jewish groups was amazing. As well as the obvious divide between the religious and the secular, we encountered Ashkenazim and Sephardim, members of United Synagogue, Reform, Liberal and Masorti congregations.

I used to visit our Jewish neighbours when they were in trouble or in hospital. We'd stand and talk in the street. There was always someone to explain to me the intricacies of the various Jewish festivals. A family whose son wanted to become a rabbi sent him across the road to talk to me about the meaning of 'vocation'. I was soon chairman of the Hendon and Golders Green branch of the Council for Christians and Jews, which initiated a range of activities aimed at a better understanding and the building of a common front against intolerance. I found myself speaking in synagogues across the terrain and even appeared from time to time as the after-dinner speaker at events planned by the Friends of the State of Israel. Not that I found this last matter easy. I was highly critical of the policies of various Israeli governments and horrified at the never-ending injustices they imposed on Palestinians. Perhaps it was idealistic of me, but I felt that the Jewish diaspora could play a far more active role in applying pressure on those holding power in Jerusalem and turn them towards more moderate and creative ends.

When we were about to leave Golders Green, two of our neighbours invited us to have drinks with them after our Sunday morning service. To our great surprise, they'd invited the whole street and we had a merry time. Our host proposed the toast: '*L'chaim*,' he said, 'good health, to our

Methodist rabbi and his good lady.' It was very moving and reminded me of the farewell party organized for us in Haiti some years previously. Fritz Hunter, a leading member of the Methodist community there, had proposed a toast to *Pasteur Griffiths, ki bon nèg* – to Reverend Griffiths, who's a good chap. Except that the word I've translated as 'chap' really means 'black man'. It was a black gathering drinking a toast to a white man whom they are happy to salute as one of their own. And I suppose I ought to link these greetings with the initiative taken by the Ghanaian members at the West London Mission to enstool me as a chief, acknowledging me as 'Nana Kwesi the First of Hinde Street'. At one level, all this is just quaint. But at another, it's very profound. Here are groups of people paying what is surely the supreme tribute of saluting a stranger as one of their own, bringing an outsider within the ambit of their own cultural, racial or even religious circles. Whatever other honours I've received in life, none excels these simple tributes which I've come to see as beautiful and symbolic ways of declaring the graspable reality of a shared humanity.

A shared humanity didn't seem to figure high on the list of desirable ideals at the Methodist Conference during these years. The question of sexuality was rearing its persistent head and there was great pressure to resolve this matter once and for all. The Church was in danger of splitting open, with two groups going their separate ways. I couldn't avoid my own part in the debates of those years. After all, while at Hinde Street I'd presented Neil Whitehouse as a candidate for ministry. He'd made no secret of his orientation nor of the fact that he had no intention of opting for celibacy if he were accepted for ministry. Somehow he got through the selection process and was trained at Wesley House, Cambridge, and then stationed as a probationer minister in north London. All this had sharpened attitudes on both sides of the argument. Later on, a self-confessed lesbian, Sarah Coggins, offered for ministry. She was turned down, but only at the very last minute in a move that seemed unjust to many of us. She'd accumulated the very same recommendations as a number of other candidates but, following a little-used clause in our constitution, someone from the conservative side of the argument raised an objection, forced a vote, and succeeded in ousting her from the list of accepted candidates. I felt that this was unfair and brought a procedural motion before Conference later that week which, if passed, would rescind the earlier decision and allow Sarah Coggins in after all. It required a 75 per cent majority and failed only by a whisker.

My role in these two cases had made my position on the question at issue as plain as could be. It was at the Derby Conference of 1993 that we debated a specially commissioned report on human sexuality and defined a position (a fudge, some called it). The debate was highly charged and chaired with phenomenal patience by my old Wesley House tutor, Brian Beck. I'd consulted a number of people whose position was similar to my own and it was agreed that I should not enter the debate until the revered Donald English had made his move. Donald was one of our finest preachers and the leading figure on the conservative side of the argument. He had consulted his friends, too, and they'd decided that Donald shouldn't go to the tribune until he saw me go forward. We sat near one another, each waiting for the other to make his move. It was stalemate. In the end, neither of us spoke. When we discovered these tactical shenanigans later, we both had a good laugh about it. For all that, the decisions of the day gave everyone something that they could live with and that's how, more or less, it's continued ever since.

There was greater-than-usual interest that year in the choice of the next president of the Conference. Interest in the sexuality debate had ensured that there would be two strong 'camps' present and it was likely, therefore, that someone from one or other of them would receive the nomination. It was both humbling and frightening (in such charged circumstances) to hear that I was to be designated for this, the loftiest position in our Methodist Church. What gave me the greatest pleasure was that I'd received this honour as someone whose whole ministry had been served in the circuits, at parish level. I must admit also, however, that I took some delight from the fact that this sign of approval came from the Conference so soon after the debilitating experience that I'd undergone at the West London Mission. Indeed, my circuit steward from those days, Bankole

Timothy, was sitting next to me as the result was announced. He punched the air and said in a loud voice, 'The stone that the builders rejected has become the president-designate of the Conference.' His choice of scripture was wrong, his application of it even more awry. But his sentiments were very touching. His support had contributed materially and morally to my rehabilitation. None of us knew in that moment of elation that he wouldn't have the pleasure of seeing me sitting in John Wesley's chair when Conference met the following year in Leeds. The last thing that I did before leaving for that Conference was to visit Bankole in hospital. He was in a coma and died two or three days later, on the very day that I was being inaugurated as president. The funeral took place during the Conference. My whole family was with me in Leeds but we knew that we'd simply have to be represented at Bankole's funeral. We delegated Ruth for this task and she was proud to carry the Griffiths banner in this way. So we were able to give God thanks for the life of this African intellectual whose unfailing friendship had seen us through some dark and troubling times.

These years had given me rich and varied experience in three very different appointments. For almost the whole of this period, I was a superintendent minister. In all three places, I'd enjoyed strong ecumenical colleagueship. We built a new church in Loughton, drove forward a large social work programme in West London and forged unbreakable links with the Jewish community in Golders Green. But the main thrust of my 'day job' was to care for Methodist congregations and to exhort them to a deeper understanding of the faith that they'd embraced. It has always been the 'bread-and-butter' part of my work to respond to the charge which was made to me at my ordination – a charge which I repeat when, as a former president of the Conference, I preside at ordination services. They have never yet failed to move me almost to tears and there have been times when I've had to pause to get myself together again. The invocation is as clear as can be:

> Declare the Good News.
> Celebrate the sacraments.

Serve the needy.
Minister to the sick.
Welcome the stranger.
Seek the lost.

Be shepherds to the flock of Christ.
As you exercise mercy, do not forget justice;
as you minister discipline, do not forget mercy;
that when Christ the Chief Shepherd comes in glory
he may count you among his faithful servants.

When all else is stripped away, that's who I am. One of Mr Wesley's preachers, ordained to a ministry of word and sacrament and profoundly grateful for a life that's been rich and deeply satisfying.

And yet, alongside these duties and privileges, another set of responsibilities has developed with opportunities galore to reach a far wider audience than that offered by Methodism alone.

And that's where the story goes next.

5

A Wider Audience

I struck the board, and cried, No more.
                I will abroad.
What? shall I ever sigh and pine?
My lines and life are free; free as the road;
Loose as the wind, as large as store.

GEORGE HERBERT, 'THE COLLAR'

'Things must change,' the words thundered out across the tarmac. 'There must be a fairer distribution of goods, a fairer organization of society, more popular participation in its affairs, a more generous concept of service on the part of those who direct society. Those who have power, wealth and culture must understand their responsibility towards all their brothers and sisters. *Tout bagay douè changé*, everything must change.'

These were words delivered in the Créole language by Pope John Paul II on 9 March 1983. He'd touched down at Port-au-Prince where he intended to stay for as short a time as possible. A Mass was held at the airport with President Jean-Claude Duvalier and his government in attendance. Soon the pontiff was on his way again – he'd spent the merest moment on Haitian soil. But his visit sparked a revolution.

Haitians of all classes had been rocked by the arrangements made for the marriage of Jean-Claude Duvalier and Michèle Bennett. The couple had met while pupils at the school where, just after their time there, I became the deputy head. She was a mulatto and a divorcee. On both grounds this caused offence. The Duvalier revolution had sought to favour the black populations of Haiti against the traditional power-holders who were, on the whole, mulattos. The president simply ignored this detail. And he got the Archbishop of Port-au-Prince, Monsignor Wolff Ligondé, to declare Michèle Bennett's previous marriage null and void. She'd been an Anglican and her first marriage had been conducted without the presence of a Roman Catholic priest, so the archbishop found some small-print in the decrees of the seventeenth-century Council of Trent to prove that she'd never been married at all. Once this small matter had been settled, she went to Paris to choose her jewellery and her hairdresser. A refrigerated container brought flowers from Miami and the ceremony and ensuing festivities were jaw-droppingly lavish. For all the money spent on this event, however, it had felt cheap and tawdry and it certainly left a bad feeling right across the land.

When swine fever was detected in a few Haitian pigs near the border with the Dominican Republic, the World Health Organization decreed that the only way of dealing with this outbreak was a slaughter of the innocents. Every last local pig was done away with and, in the name of progress, big, fat, white pigs were brought in from Iowa to replace them. Soon, Haitian satirists were pointing out that this was a ploy on the part of big, fat, white Americans to undermine their economy. The imported pigs couldn't withstand the local conditions, they produced poor litters, they were expensive to keep and nobody wanted them. The Créole pig was at the very heart of the Haitian rural economy. For poor people, it was all they had. And now this had been ripped away from them.

So by the time of the Pope's visit, everyone was aching for a change. And those words of his proved a trigger that marked the beginning of the end for the decadent Duvalier dynasty. The Roman Catholic bishops, heartened by their pontiff's words, led the charge with a barrage of pamphlets and conference resolutions. On 6 February 1986, Duvalier and his family were flown out of Haiti under cover of darkness. It was the end of a 30-year nightmare.

These momentous events proved to have very unexpected repercussions for me personally. I was deep into my doctoral studies at the time.

I made a trip to Haiti shortly after the Pope's visit and found everything in ferment. I was able to use these impressions in one or two newspaper articles and I was asked to lead a seminar on my work at the Institute of Caribbean Studies. The interim military government which held power after the departure of Duvalier invited my friend Rosny Desroches to be Minister of Education and I had no doubt of his capacity to deliver. I just wish he'd been asked at a time of greater stability. Everything was moving fast, people were jockeying for power, terrible things were happening on the streets, and the *ancien régime* was finding surrogates through whom they could maintain their grasp on the levers of power. Under pressure from the international community, elections were called for November 1987. I was invited to join a group of election observers operating under the aegis of the World Council of Churches.

It was clear from the outset that things were fraught. We were holed up in a hotel across the public square from the presidential palace, along with a large team of journalists from all over the world. A petrol station next to the hotel was set on fire during the night and it went up with a huge explosion. Machine guns strafed the hotel and our electricity was cut off. I lay on the floor and got dressed in a horizontal position and then slid through into the corridor on my back. When dawn finally arrived, all hell had broken loose on the streets outside. Emergency vehicles were racing over the terrain, sirens blaring, and in hot pursuit were teams of journalists anxious to get eye-witness shots of whatever was going on. It was frenetic. There was mayhem. Gunmen in unmarked cars were shooting at the lines of people who'd been queuing to vote since before first light. Dozens were killed in cold blood. Those who'd dropped to the ground to take cover got up again and reformed their lines, ready to step over the bodies of the slain in their determination to lodge their vote. I saw a child's head cut in two by a thug's machete. And meanwhile, truckloads of soldiers stood by without making any response to what was happening in front of their very eyes. It was obvious that the election would have to be abandoned. The dead body of a young journalist was brought back to the hotel. He'd got too close to one nasty incident and paid for it with his life. By midday, we were all exhausted. Everything was calm by then and we sat silently in the shade of some trees outside the hotel, picking half-heartedly at our lunch.

I was wearing my clerical shirt and was amazed when hardened journalists, one after another, sought me out. They didn't want me to say anything. Some were crying, others just dumb. A touch, an embrace, an exchanged glance – such were the simple gestures that seemed to convey comfort or reassurance. I found it all very moving. It was at just such a moment, with a young *Miami Herald* journalist making in my direction, that I noticed a car stop in front of us and a gunman aim his weapon towards me. The journalist had also seen this; he gave me a flying tackle and bundled me to the ground. A bullet sped overhead as I lay there breathless but oh so thankful. It had been a very near thing.

Margaret, back in London, had been made aware that the election had been abandoned and that violence had claimed many victims but she had no idea what had happened to me. Nor could I easily reassure her. It was only when she saw me being interviewed by a BBC reporter on the late evening news bulletin that she could relax, knowing that I was safe and sound.

The media soon became aware that I might be one of the very few people in England with a detailed and up-to-the-minute knowledge of Haiti and soon I found myself very much in demand. There were whole days when I'd sit in a car being ferried from one interview to another. I became familiar with the labyrinthine layout of Bush House, the BBC and ITV newsrooms, and the busy breathlessness of local radio stations. I sat many times alone in self-operated television or radio studios, following instructions that were fed to me remotely and answering questions being asked by a faceless voice out there somewhere in the ether. I was interviewed by Jeremy Paxman on *Newsnight* and Jon Snow on *Channel 4 News.* But the bread-and-butter work of those years was on radio. The pace of the news-gathering industry is phenomenal, the deadlines they work to are always tight, their jealousy to be ahead of their rivals intense. It was in this context that I learned the need to be adaptable, available and comprehensible as I presented complicated stories within the short compass of a news bulletin or a three-minute recorded 'package'. Sometimes it all got scary.

One Sunday morning, on my way into church, I was given the phone. 'It's the BBC,' I was told. The voice at the other end explained that the World Service programme *Newshour* intended to make Haiti their main story later that day. Would I anchor a discussion which would include correspondents in Paris, New York and Port-au-Prince? I said I'd gladly address earthly mysteries when I'd finished dealing with the heavenly ones. So I put down the phone, donned my cassock and led that morning's services. We finished just after midday and I jumped into a taxi that took me to Bush House at the Aldwych. I'd never done anything quite like this before and I was more than a little on edge, only to discover that, since my early morning telephone call, there had been a *coup d'état* in Burma and the whole programme had been re-jigged. Instead of the ambitious, four-way conversation that would look at the Haiti story from a variety of angles, I was now allocated a three-minute, pre-recorded slot. I did the business there and then and got home for my Sunday lunch after all.

Things could happen the other way round, of course. I was called in on one occasion, again to the BBC World Service, to contribute a three-minute interview to a fast-moving news programme whose main item was going to be the arrival of Russia's President Gorbachev in Cuba. Apart from the team of reporters who were going to be involved in this 'breaking news' story, I was the only other live contributor. The rest of the programme would be made up of pre-recorded packages. That was the plan. The trouble was that the Russian president's arrival in Havana was held up by headwinds and, in the end, his plane didn't manage to touch down within our programme's allotted hour. So a whole raft of reportage had to be abandoned. The only person available to help the producers and presenters fill up rather a lot of empty airtime was me. So Haiti figured large that particular day and the material I'd prepared got stretched and added to until it filled all the available space.

All of this was going on before I heard from anyone in the world of religious broadcasting. I shall always be glad it happened that way round. When I'd been a Religious Education teacher, either in Haiti or sometimes in the United Kingdom, it was always important to me that I should teach something other than Religion too. And as a school governor, I always volunteered to monitor the Modern Languages or English department as well as keep an eye on Religion. I've never wanted to be 'religious'. My faith has to find its place in the secular world in which I live – only there does it play its part and add its value. In this instance, I was delighted to have served my apprenticeship as a broadcaster in the fast lane of news-gathering. It taught me how to let the facts tell their own tale. There was no need for special pleading or the introduction of a sanctimonious note. Religion, too, can have its truths presented with vigour and transparency. I could never move to religious broadcasting and forget the lessons I'd learned from trading my wares in the secular arena.

For all that, I was delighted to say yes when Beverley McAinsh, a senior producer in the Religion Department of the BBC, wrote and invited me to submit a couple of scripts to see whether I might be suitable to pre-sent 'Thought for the Day' on the agenda-setting *Today* programme on Radio 4.

I was less delighted with her treatment of what I'd submitted. Without writing a single note, she listened intently before taking my scripts and delivery apart, phrase by phrase, breath by breath. Something squirmed inside me. I had a degree in English, for goodness sake, I knew how to write and didn't need this kind of nit-picking over my stuff. But I kept my mouth shut, largely because I knew that Beverley was right. If she took my sentences apart, she also saw to it that she put them back together again. She was determined that I'd offer one thought for the day not two, that *non sequiturs* should be eliminated and 'literary' words sent packing. She urged me to climb down from my Latinized, polysyllabic way of speaking and thinking. She showed me how to write with a more Anglo-Saxon style and to settle for modes of expression that might, at least at first, offend my mental processes. She was brilliant. And she didn't limit her comments to the content of what I'd written. She went on to show me how to modulate my voice, measure my breathing patterns and lift what I'd written from the page so that it sounded conversational. I've never forgotten the 'master classes' that I went through at that time, and Beverley McAinsh's efforts were surely a large part of the reason that I was able to survive in the 'Thought for the Day' slot for 17 years.

In 1987, the *Today* programme was still being made at Broadcasting House in Portland Place. I took my seat very nervously alongside Brian Redhead, at that time the main presenter of the programme. He greeted me warmly, saw to it that there was a glass of water to hand, and generally helped me to feel at home. However much work I'd done in the newsrooms over the previous three or four years, I was now about to offer scripted material for the very first time. And I was perfectly aware of how the 'Thought for the Day' item was a football which everyone liked to take a kick at from time to time. The remit is simple – to offer a theological or spiritual reflection on something topical and in the news. Atheists and secularists hate it, partly because, in their view, it gives preferential access to people speaking out of religious conviction and partly because they'd love to get their hands on it themselves. One of the very few times a concession was made on this point, a morning when none other than Tyrannosaurus Rex himself (Richard Dawkins) was invited to fill the slot, all we got was a denunciation of religion. It just has to be the supreme irony that the stereotypical accusation laid against those who contribute to 'Thought' – namely that they use it to brainwash listeners with their own confessional viewpoint – was fulfilled that day by an arch-atheist. Contributors are as clear as can be that, as well as the passion that flows from their way of seeing the world, they also bring journalistic dispassion to bear upon their chosen subject. The piece has to fit in with the pace and agenda being set in the studio. The secret is to get as near as possible to something that's actually going to feature on the programme. If nothing grabbed my attention in the previous day's newspapers, I'd get my producer to let me have the putative running order for the following morning's programme and then fasten on to one or another of the items that figured there. I'd be adjusting my linking words in the car taking me to the studio and even in the studio itself. It seemed so important to me that listeners should feel that this slot hadn't been parachuted into the programme from a parallel universe but that it belonged there – that it fitted, moved and breathed within the programme itself.

My first piece picked up on the nurses' strike which was dividing opinion at that time and which was certainly a major item for reporters that day. But it was as much as I could do to deliver my script. I found myself worrying about the build-up of saliva in my mouth and had difficulty knowing when to swallow. I felt that my breathing was unnaturally loud and that I'd completely messed up. It didn't help that while I was on air, a guest of the programme was being shown into the seat next to me, the presenters were checking their papers in readiness for subsequent items and the person reading the weather forecast was having difficulty getting his notes together. It was with some relief that I brought this painful exercise to an end. Brian Redhead had introduced me and now he took the programme on to its next story, but not before he'd announced to his listeners that 'that was Leslie Griffiths with his very first "Thought for the Day"; the first, but I'm sure by no means the last.' That was hugely affirming. As was his personal word to me, uttered a minute or two later when the studio was 'dead'. 'Do you realize, Leslie, that you've just spoken to more people than John Wesley managed to in the whole of his ministry?' Of course I hadn't. But what a thing to think about on my way home.

I went on to give 198 such pieces over the next sixteen years, surviving more than one cull. I was put out to grass in 1996 because, with a General Election looming, I was thought to be too 'political'. In the end, it was politics that did for me. When I chose to take the Labour Party whip on entering the House of Lords in 2004, I was told that it was no longer possible for me to continue offering to 'Thought for the Day'. Rules are rules, I suppose, but my political leanings had been very public for a long time. I was a trustee and even a vice-president of the Christian Socialist Movement and had contributed to party political broadcasts – one, alongside Sir Alex Ferguson, in the not-too-distant past. Interestingly, the presenters of the *Today* programme, John Humphrys and Jim Naughtie in particular, couldn't see what all the fuss was about. They seemed to have confidence in what I was offering, and I certainly felt that I had much more to contribute. For all that, however, I can't really complain. To have had the opportunity to be part of a great team in the *Today* studio for such a long period was nothing other than a privilege.

Interestingly, the BBC in Wales didn't seem bound by the same rules. When I was dropped temporarily by the *Today* programme in 1996, they took me up at once. Roy Jenkins was in charge of religious broadcasting in the Principality at that time and he's never balked at courses of action that he thought were right. BBC Wales has a slot similar to 'Thought' but called 'Weekend Word' and, as its name suggests, it's done just once a week. I've almost reached 100 of these little pieces now and even my entry to the House of Lords hasn't led to my disqualification. One thing leads to another, I suppose, but Lisa Hawkins and Karen Walker have seen to it that I make regular contributions to non-scripted programmes, too, especially their flagship discussion programme, *All Things Considered.*

The amount of scripted material that I've written over the last 20 years is mountainous. I've been leading *The Daily Service* (or its Friday version, *Act of Worship*) since the late 1980s, first from the basement of All Souls Church, Langham Place, and then from Emmanuel Church in Didsbury, Manchester and latterly from a London studio. If anyone thought that this daily act of worship would fade away when it was shunted into its long-wave slot, they were very much mistaken. It's been wonderful to sense an audience of people for whom this is often a lifeline. The correspondence that I've received has been consistently steady over the years. And it's been a good challenge to offer something openly religious alongside my more nuanced offerings to the *Today* programme. I've passed the 100 mark on this score, too.

Other regular contributions have been made to Radio 4's *10 to 10* (until its demise), and also its early morning *Prayer for the Day*. Interestingly, this is the item which the people I meet in parliament these days tend to listen to, a pre-recorded piece which snuggles into the pre-*Today* airtime alongside news about farming, the iconic shipping forecast and other sundry items. Clearly our political leaders are early risers.

Beyond these regular items lie innumerable one-off efforts – live acts of worship (on radio and television), phone-ins (one with Edwina Currie, then at the height of her notoriety) and discussion programmes. BBC Radio Wales asked me to present a series of six programmes in which I'd interview some prominent Welsh men and women. I particularly remember interviewing John Humphrys in his own studio, a nice reversal of roles. Another featured Barry John, the iconic rugby international outside-half in what was arguably the best Welsh team ever. Like his great friend George Best, he was in the first generation of sporting stars and, again like Best, he's paid a high price for his fame. I discovered in these interviews that I didn't really have the killer punch with those I was interviewing, the courage to ask the really hard question that everyone knows needs to be asked if the programme is to work.

In the case of John Humphrys, I wanted very badly to push the point that our media have become the real questioning voice in our democracy rather than the opposition party in parliament or other more traditional parts of civil society – the church, trade unions and the like. Indeed, I wanted to ask him just what was in his mind when he interrupted, harried and was rude to the people he interviewed. He had a reputation as a rottweiler and I wanted to know just who he thought he was as he tore people, especially politicians, to pieces. After all, he was not accountable to an electorate. He took all this like the supreme professional he is. It felt like a boxing match. He played with me, swayed to right and left, feinted, urged me on, gave me space but I'm sure that I didn't get one real scoring punch on him, certainly nothing approaching a knock-out blow.

When it came to Barry John, I wanted to probe his relationship with the great Carwyn James, his schoolmaster and mentor and the coach of the victorious 1971 Lions team that toured New Zealand. James had a few years previously been found dead in mysterious circumstances, electrocuted in his bath in an Amsterdam hotel. It was known that he was gay – a somewhat rare thing in the machismo world of rugby. There were so many questions that I could have asked. My producer was shouting into my earphones that I should go for the jugular. Just what was their relationship? How had Barry John taken the news of James's death? How close had they been? But I didn't have the nerve. I just fed him soft questions and hoped that he'd let something out of his own accord. I was much too 'pastoral' for this kind of work.

Some programmes have been made about me. A series of four half-hour efforts, with my musical choices, pursued the major developments of my life and was broadcast in the mid-1990s. It was like being on four consecutive *Desert Island Discs* programmes. The first of these touched on my childhood and was recorded 'on location' in Burry Port. The folks there had never seen anything like it. I recall ambling along Glanmor Terrace, the street where I was born, with my sound man walking backwards in front of me carrying one of those fluffy mikes that resemble a hand puppet. My producer was at my side while I read my script out loud as we moved forward. We were a very cumbersome trio. To cover my embarrass-ment, I tried isolating myself in my own little world, looking neither to right nor to left, scarcely daring to think what the people who'd seen me grow up would make of it all. Then, suddenly, a first-floor sash window was thrown open and the head of an elderly lady of my acquaintance was stuck out of it. '*Duw, duw*, good Lord,' she said and shouted to someone inside the house. 'Mavis, Mavis, come over by here, girl. Come and see what's walking past our house. I don't know what they think they're up to but I think that's our Les they've got trapped between them.' That shout was enough to spoil the recording and require another take, but I've often thought that it deserved to be included in the programme in its own right. You can't invent little jewels like that or write them into a script.

At about this time, a 30-minute biographical sketch of my life and work was done for Harlech Television. A researcher and a producer were sent to London on two separate occasions and their preparations were meticulous. I so enjoyed working with professionals who knew exactly what they were doing. I went down to Cardiff and managed to put a 28-minute interview in the can at one take. On the whole, I don't like working on television nearly as much as radio. There's far too much to worry about. On one occasion, when I was working on a religious programme for ITV, I found myself with a whole team of people out in the wilds of rural Norfolk. I had to walk casually through a field talking about the glories of the natural order and then, with the merest nod, point viewers in the direction of a postcard-beautiful country church before bringing my little narrative to a close at the door of the village pub, at whose bar and in whose comfort the ensuing narrative was to take place. The trouble was that we couldn't get the kind of silence we needed for the outdoor speech. In the deepest parts of the English countryside, there seemed to be a constant and noisy activity on the part of either heavy-duty tractors or high-flying aeroplanes. It was a bitterly cold spring morning and I was not clad for the great outdoors, but I had to go back and repeat my efforts time and time again until I was a shivering idiot. I didn't dare to watch the finished item; it would have brought back too many painful memories.

One fascinating development occurred in 2002, later than other events marked in this chapter but which seems to belong here for all that. I was approached by the director of Premier Christian Radio, at that time a London-wide, faith-based station, while attending their Christmas party. They had a well-established programme called *Taking the Tablet*, which had been presented by a Roman Catholic priest who'd lately left the scene. The station needed someone to hold the fort while a successor was found. This was proving difficult – the Roman Catholic bishops hadn't come up with anyone and all other approaches had also failed. I agreed to help out. In those early days, it involved contributing 15 minutes of live comment on a Friday evening drive-time programme. All I'd have to do was choose a couple of articles and then engage in a kind of verbal jousting with the remarkable Cindy Kent as I unpacked the stories and made them accessible to a wider audience than that normally reached by *The Tablet*. Cindy has moved from the world of pop music into her career as a broadcaster with such effortless ease. She's a professional to her fingertips yet she's managed somehow to complete the necessary training to become an Anglican priest as well. That made it all so much more fun. It feels a bit edgy as a Methodist minister to be in conversation with a priest of the Church of England as we take a critical look at some of the key stories in a widely respected Roman Catholic newspaper.

It was meant to be for the short term yet, seven years later, I'm still doing it. It's now become a pre-recorded, half-hour stand-alone programme that's broadcast on Saturday mornings. For some peculiar reason, *The Tablet* withdrew its sponsorship of the programme and ceased advertising it in the newspaper. It felt like a very silly decision on their part – it cost them very little and gave them such a rich audience. It was something to do, they said, with their marketing strategy. That sounded bunkum to me but the great thing was that we seemed to keep many of our Roman Catholic listeners in tow. The main part of our audience is black and evangelical and, from all the responses that I've had, they seem to enjoy the programme very much. It's become an important part of Premier Radio's output, a key element in the case they put to the licensing authorities to prove that the station has a 'balanced' output and can properly describe itself as a 'Christian' radio station in the broadest sense of the word.

In the late 1990s, when requests to go on air reached their zenith, I decided to invest in an ISDN (digital) line and a small mixer-board. It seemed expensive at the time but it's more than justified itself. It's given me a little studio in my own home, a broadcasting point from which I can do so much of my radio work without leaving my workplace. I keep reminding myself of Brian Redhead's word about the number of people who were reached by John Wesley during his long ministry and I suspect that, were Wesley alive today, it wouldn't be so much the open air as the airwaves that would take his voice and his challenge abroad.

All this broadcasting arose out of my relationship with Haiti. And throughout these years something was stirring in that poor, benighted land, something startlingly new was beginning to emerge. And it all centred on a Roman Catholic priest, a young and prodigious liberation theologian named Jean-Bertrand Aristide. I first became aware of him in 1986 when a team of reporters from Channel 4 television asked me to look at some footage that they'd brought back from Haiti which showed Aristide at work in the slum parish of Port-au-Prince. I was soon hard at work translating and dubbing what Aristide was saying and this gave me a close understanding of his use of language and its effect on the dispossessed urban masses whom he was addressing. It was electric. He could galvanize crowds with a rhetorical style that seemed to direct words and images at their very souls. I've never known anything like it.

Not many months later, just after the aborted election of 1987, Aristide visited London and I met him at the offices of the Catholic Institute for International Relations. To my great surprise, he asked if he could see me privately. As soon as we sat together, he dropped into his native Créole (he'd previously been speaking English) and spoke with great passion. His country needed the support of the international community, he said, otherwise it would slide back into the hands of disenchanted former Duvalierists. Would I help? Would I approach Archbishop Desmond Tutu in Cape Town to see whether he would be prepared to visit Haiti and draw attention to its plight? My eyebrows were rising higher and higher. I'd never met Desmond Tutu in my life but there was something in the urgency with which Aristide was speaking that led me to agree to do what he was asking of me. After about 45 minutes together, his face broadened into a big smile and he embraced me warmly as we parted. I began to write letters to South Africa.

Before we could get very far with that project, however, events moved on in Haiti. Aristide had survived numerous attempts on his life, some of them the very stuff of legend. He was edging more and more closely to declaring himself a candidate at the next presidential election. In those fevered times, we entertained some of Aristide's friends on their visits to London. One, a fellow priest named Jean-Marie Vincent, will always stick in my memory. He'd been driving a car in which Aristide was a passenger when a troop of thugs descended on them. Only Jean-Marie's quick wits and steely nerve saw him through the circle of gunmen and away into safety. All the car's tyres and all its windows had been shot to pieces. Jean-Marie himself was cut about the face and the scar from that escapade was only too visible as he sat with us in our London home. He directed a coffee-growing co-operative in the north of Haiti and was in England to establish a network of trading partners. He was gentle and kind, intelligent and passionate in his commitment to justice. The Sunday after he left us, we heard that he'd been gunned down in cold blood outside the Port-au-Prince church where he'd been saying Mass.

In December 1990, I went out once more as an election observer. I took charge of a small team in Cap Haitien and we stayed with Monsignor François Gayot, the Roman Catholic Archbishop there. Gayot had suddenly turned against Aristide's candidature and stubbornly refused to vote. The nuns serving us at table ostentatiously held aloft fingers that had been marked with indelible ink; they'd voted and they were flaunting this fact under the archbishop's nose. Aristide won the election handsomely and, almost for the first time in Haiti's independent history, the previously disenfranchised peasantry felt that they had a champion. It was, in a phrase coined a generation later, an 'Obama moment', an election that brought into the political equation people who'd never figured there before.

A few weeks later, at the beginning of 1991, I received a phone call from Aristide. I must come to his inauguration, he said, he was expecting me. I was only just back from the election and didn't know how I could possibly justify another trip to the Caribbean so soon. I was pondering these things as Aristide continued. 'I also want you to get the Vatican to lean on the Haitian bishops,' he declared. 'We're just days from the inauguration, the results of the election have been out for weeks, and they still haven't announced their support for me.' I spluttered with incomprehension. Me? A Methodist minister? Telling the Vatican what to do? That's impossible! But before I'd conveyed any of my exasperation, he'd hung up with a final 'Let me know when you've made some progress.'

Once again, as with the Tutu project, he'd left me with an order – one that seemed impossible to comply with. But soon I formed a plan. I'd recently attended the consecration of Bishop Vincent Nichols at Westminster Cathedral. Since then, of course, Nichols has become Archbishop of Westminster. The letters patent which conferred the authority of the Pope on that act of consecration were read out over the name of Archbishop Luigi Barbarito, the Papal Nuncio at the Court of St James. I couldn't believe my ears – it was impossible that a second person of that name existed. It must surely be the same Luigi Barbarito, the

Nuncio to Haiti who'd been present at my ordination in Port-au-Prince all those years ago. I wrote to him, he confirmed that he was indeed the same person, and a friendship developed between us. We'd had lunch a few times and long conversations about Haiti, a country for which he still had great affection.

After Aristide's phone call, I sought an interview with the Nuncio. I explained that, however much His Holiness objected to a priest's entering the world of politics, it was far too late to intervene in the case of Aristide. He was already the president-elect. The people had spoken. The bishops simply had to make a public statement of their support. The Nuncio heard me out. He listened carefully. 'Put the gist of what you've told me on one side of A4 paper,' he said, 'and let me have it at once.' I did just that, outlining half a dozen points that needed to be made, then sealed the letter and left it with him. A day or so later, he dropped me a line saying that he'd written to the Secretary of State and laid the matter before him. He assured me that my concerns would receive due attention. After that, I heard nothing more before travelling to Haiti for Aristide's inauguration in early February. On my arrival, however, I was delighted to be told that the bishops had indeed now made a formal statement of support for Aristide. As I read their statement, my jaw dropped in amazement. There were all the points that I'd made in my letter and, what's more, they appeared in the very same order. I'll never prove that it was all of my doing, of course, but it was a welcome development and it's been a good after-dinner tale for a long time now.

Aristide's government lasted a mere seven months before he was thrust aside by a military junta. For over three years, he languished in exile. His detractors, especially United States Senator Jesse Helms, indulged in a campaign of character assassination while United Nations officials huffed and puffed, came and went, seemingly unable to do anything to regularize the situation in Haiti. Sanctions were imposed but were regularly broken. Huge petrol tankers were passing the United Nations blockade with impunity to offload their wares in the one and only oil terminal that exists in Haiti while tiny boats containing impoverished Haitians fleeing from their native land were regularly picked out, tracked down and returned to their port of origin.

During this unhappy period in Haiti's history, I set up and ran a Haiti Support Group that gathered together some of the finest journalists and aid workers in the United Kingdom. We campaigned for the restoration of legitimate rule in Haiti. We were able to bring Aristide to London and I accompanied him on much of his itinerary here. It was difficult to get the British government interested in his presence. At one time he suggested that, once he was back in power, I might consider becoming the Haitian consul in London – a lovely thought but one never destined to come to pass.

In November 1994, I was summoned to the Foreign Office. I'd paid regular visits there since setting up the Haiti Support Group to discuss various developments and to introduce visitors whom we'd brought over from Haiti, but this was different. The head of the Caribbean section was present and he introduced me to William Marsden, Assistant Under Secretary of State (Americas). He'd been reading my latest article in the Roman Catholic weekly *The Tablet* and he expressed respect for my analysis of Haitian affairs. 'I've asked you here,' he said, 'to give you advance news of the decision of the United States government to invade Haiti. We're supporting the Americans and I want to ask you what we're likely to expect and what mistakes we should avoid making.' A Methodist minister doesn't often find himself in a consultancy role for a military operation. I suggested, a little tongue-in-cheek, that 20 American soldiers would be enough. The Haitian people were longing for order to be restored. Two days later, Aristide was returned to his native heath by a military force of 21,000. He'd resigned from the priesthood, was now a married man with children, and was flown in (clearly a puppet of the United States) by helicopter. 'The second coming,' they called it. These were such sad times for Haiti, and the whole Aristide phenomenon – in the way it was so wilfully mishandled – represents a huge missed opportunity.

All this and much more I wrote up in a biography of Jean-Bertrand Aristide, which appeared in 1996. It was published by Lion Press as *The*

Aristide Factor, but they seemed to get cold feet at the last minute and started changing the terms of my contract. They 'pulled' the illustrations, limited themselves to a hard-backed edition, and seemed to want to get it out of their stockroom as quickly as possible. I felt as if my offering must have been an embarrassment to them. Nor were the reviews very cheerful – for the most part, they consisted of people using the space they'd been given to air their own opinions rather than assess the merits (or demerits) of my work. Yet I was immensely pleased with it. I felt that it gave a rounded picture of Aristide himself and set him within the context of Haitian history. I included my personal involvement with Aristide and explained in the Preface that this was more an *oeuvre engagée*, the personal account of a committed person, than simply a work of contemporary history. Yet I was taken to the cleaners by one reviewer for writing it that way rather than keeping it dispassionately objective.

Some years later, I was amazed to receive a letter from Kenneth Harris, one-time director and associate editor of the *Observer* newspaper and author of what is arguably still the best biography of Clement Attlee. He'd often judged Observer Mace university debates in the days when Neil Kinnock and I used to team up for such events. And I'd interviewed him at Wesley's Chapel, too. So we knew each other slightly. He'd discovered and, more importantly, read a copy of my book and felt moved to write. His words were manna to my soul and I hope it won't be mere self-indulgence to quote from his letter here. This is what he said:

> I knew next to nothing about Haiti but, within a few days, I was engrossed. It is extremely well written – the very first page, for example, which introduces Aristide, is a model – and though it is packed with fact throughout, it keeps the reader hooked all the time. There are many, many gobbets of remarkable information. I thought, for example, that the pages dealing with Marjorie Michel's relationship with Aristide were fascinating. I was struck by your exchange with Monsignor Barbarito; I imagine 'the contents of your letter . . . made known to the Holy See' would be the only letter written by a Methodist minister ever to be given that highly complimentary attention. Chapter 3, 'Just Who Are You, Father Aristide?' is a splendid chapter. Much of the book, for

all its authority and factual realism, reads like a novel. I hope it got the critical reception it deserved.

It didn't really. On the whole, it fell by the wayside but I wouldn't have missed writing it for all the wool in Wales.

The developments marked in this and the previous chapter were occurring in parallel. So much was happening as a consequence of my ministry and it wasn't always easy keeping together that and the demands of my 'day job'. So it was in addition to an already charged agenda that I found myself designated by the 1993 Derby Conference as its next president. I took up this position in Leeds a year later.

Many people have asked me to explain exactly where the role of president fits into the way Methodism works and I've yet to discover an easy answer to such an obvious question. It all began with John Wesley – an autocrat to his fingertips. He *was* the Conference for virtually the whole of his lifetime. Ministers met and conferred but their decisions were generally heeded only if they coincided with Wesley's own. Towards the end of his life, in a humble admission of his own mortality, he made legal provision for the continuation of the Methodist cause beyond his death. A body known as 'the legal hundred' was set up by a Deed of Declaration lodged in Chancery in 1784. One hundred ministers were chosen for this exercise and, of course, those who fell outside the charmed group resented their omission. Others, notably the ambitious Welshman Doctor Thomas Coke, started jockeying for position well before Wesley's death. It was unwholesome, to say the least.

The challenge was posed in its most radical form when Wesley finally shook off his mortal coil in March 1791. Biographies started rolling off the press almost at once, both the hagiographical variety and also something altogether more scurrilous, the former to secure the Wesley 'myth', the latter to rub his nose in the dirt. Lay Methodists fought for a share of power with the preachers. Splits occurred and separate Methodist identities were soon being forged. Meanwhile, back in the fold, the body that would soon be known as 'Wesleyan Methodists' (to distinguish them from the more corybantic 'Primitive Methodists') took steps to curb the ambitions of people like Thomas Coke. The cry went up: 'Never another king in Israel,' a theological version of *Le roi est mort, qu'il reste au tombeau* – The king is dead; let's keep it that way.

And so an annual presidency was born – the Conference was the real thing, the body in which the legal identity of Methodism rested. But everything was arranged so that no power was vested in any individual. It seems appropriate that, as Methodism moved into its 'mahogany phase' – its bourgeois, stuffy period – its supreme office should most resemble that of a municipal mayor, someone who came and went with some alacrity. I was to find that, in an era where the media play such an important role, the office has become virtually meaningless. Who wants to learn the name of the latest president when Methodism itself pays such little heed to his or her voice? I was flabbergasted to learn, for example, that the outgoing president, at the Conference where he or she lays down the mantle of office, is forbidden to speak. This gagging convention has come into existence so that the ex-president doesn't steal the thunder of the successor. So just at the moment when someone acquires a knowledge of the whole of his or her Church, they are denied the obvious opportunity to share that experience. Daft! – that's what I say.

During my year in office, for the one and only time in my life, I was presented to Her Majesty the Queen. I was introduced as 'The President of the Methodist Conference', a title which clearly bewildered her. She responded in the way she does so often and so brilliantly: with an obvious question. 'What exactly does the President of the Conference do, Dr Griffiths?' It's simplicity itself but answering such questions isn't as straightforward as you'd expect. I didn't think Her Majesty would want a mini-lecture with details of Dr Coke, the legal hundred or the constitutional nature of the Methodist Conference thrown at her. So, instead, I heard myself explain how half the job is spent going around the country rallying the faithful, cheering them up, offering them encouragement and listening to their stories. The other half, I continued, consists in representing the faithful to the big, wide world beyond Methodism. She listened intently. 'That's strange,' she said. 'It sounds just like my job. Perhaps we should share notes some time.'

The vice-president during my year in office was Christine Walters, the head of the Diaconal Order, and we undertook a punishing schedule of visits across the length and breadth of the country. Margaret joined me whenever she could negotiate time off from her hospital duties. We visited all 32 Methodist 'districts' (dioceses) and I asked those organizing our time if they could take me to visit prisons in their area and also to any church-run projects that served the needs of homeless people. The homelessness charity Shelter had agreed to provide me with statistical information for each of the areas I visited and I was fascinated to see the range of services being offered by day and night shelters, advice centres, clothing depots, hostels, drop-in centres, as well as personal friendship and hospitality. The Christian community in general, and Methodism in particular, has sometimes seemed as if it believes that it's past its sell-by date. On the basis of the astonishing work done, disinterestedly, to relieve the plight of the poor, I can only state the evidence of my own eyes, that Christians today are as dedicated to proclaiming what they call 'Good News' as they ever were. All the tales of numerical gloom and statistical doom should be set alongside the huge scale of the involvement of ordinary believers in doing exactly what Jesus asked his followers to do.

As for the prisons, my visits left me much more pessimistic. In a very short period during the early 1990s, for much of which my old school friend Michael Howard was Home Secretary, the prison population had soared above 51,000 (shamefully, it's very much higher now). The cry had gone up: 'Prison works' and the Gadarene rush to fill all existing penitentiaries had generated a discussion about using large ships anchored off our shores as holding places until new prisons could be built. It will always be a subject for debate, of course, as to how to balance the duty to protect the public from dangerous criminals with the need variously to persuade, shock or equip offenders to abandon crime and to become contributing members of society again. Prison should never foreclose on the possibilities of rehabilitation. That *cri de coeur* can surely go up without stimulating in return a visceral accusation that those emitting it have gone soft on crime and soft on the causes of crime.

I visited two prisons, Blakenhurst in the West Midlands and the other near Middlesbrough in the North East, which had been built to an identical architectural specification. One was in the private sector and the other was under public control. They were identical except for the size of their population. The privately run prison was being run strictly according to its contract – staffing levels were guaranteed, rehabilitative and educational services were readily accessible, and the number of inmates never exceeded the agreed ceiling of just over 400. The state equivalent was at the mercy of the needs of the moment. When I visited, it held over 600 prisoners. That meant prisoners sharing cells, and staff being directed towards surveillance – and very often away from rehabilitative and educational services. Inmates were spending up to 23 hours a day in their cells and the whole place, newly built, felt heavy and repressive.

Throughout this extraordinary year, I kept on uncovering the work of various kinds of chaplains – in schools, the armed forces, prisons, industry, hospitals and the like. Again and again, I heard tales of how they felt semi-detached from the churches they belonged to. Yet they were doing front-line work – extending the hand of friendship, exercising pastoral care, giving a steer to policy directives, keeping whole shows together – work of which the organized Church should have been immensely proud. But the Church seems constantly beset with the need to keep itself alive and all too often obsessed with the boringly familiar but shockingly disruptive questions relating to human sexuality – so much so that it loses sight of real and genuine outreach work that takes its message into some of the neediest and even darkest corners of our national life.

Another revelation that came to me during my year as president relates to the role of district chairman. (How I wish I could, once and for all, obliterate this title from our records!) I met these chairmen three times during the year and it dawned on me that, within one room, I could ask a question about any one of the 7,000 Methodist chapels within Great Britain or any one of our 3,000 ministers and I had 32 people in front of me who could have given me an informative reply. Here were our bishops! It's not the Conference but these people who, between them, are pastors to the flock, overseers of the whole show. The Conference knows very little about anything. Every year it emasculates itself further in the name of egalitarianism and inclusivity – politically correct but formulaic ways of giving a voice to anyone who wants to speak. Young people and those attending for the first time are often prioritized to speak in debates which demand great wisdom and a sense of history. The district chairs should be encouraging those qualities (egalitarianism and inclusivity) in the areas where they work but they, corporately, should be entrusted with the leadership of the Church. One of their number, elected by them, should be the presiding bishop for a period of years. It's a simple model and it actually relates to facts on the ground. But it hasn't a chance of winning support because Methodists will suspect 'bishops' of personalizing power and being potential abusers of that power. Since the days of John Wesley and Thomas Coke, this paranoia about power has entered our DNA. We're genetically predisposed towards flat management styles and government by committee. How narrow-minded and self-serving can you get?

Since 1991, I'd been a member of the Board of Christian Aid and chairman of its Africa and Middle East Committee. Wearing both my Methodist and Christian Aid hats, I visited Southern Africa in the summer of 1994. I spent a short time in Johannesburg where I discussed the scaling-down of support for the South Africa Council of Churches – part of a general response to South Africa in the years following the end of apartheid. I had a long conversation with a remarkable Methodist minister, Mvume Dandala, who was at that time superintendent of the Johannesburg Central Mission but contemplating the position of general secretary of the South Africa Council of Churches in succession to Frank Chikane, who'd accepted a position in government. Dandala himself went on to hold various positions in African National Congress governments and became a member of parliament himself in due time.

My short visit to Zimbabwe allowed me to stay with old friends Richard and Elizabeth Dales. Richard was at that time our High Commissioner there and I was able to see the still-flourishing tobacco floors and other evidence of a country that was still, just about, the 'bread basket' of Southern Africa. Richard saw Robert Mugabe on a regular basis and, soon after my return home, organized a state visit to the United Kingdom for Zimbabwe's president. Margaret and I attended the Guild Hall dinner organized by the Corporation of the City of London – a dinner held to enhance trading links with this important sub-Saharan partner. Who could have foreseen later events?

Malawi and Mozambique were the other countries which I visited at this time, both ravaged by drought and desperate poverty. The civil war which had been tearing Mozambique apart for the previous twenty years had only just ended. I travelled hundreds of miles within its borders, visiting one refugee camp after another, and was struck by the fact that I saw almost no animals in its fields. All had been slaughtered for food during the war years and programmes to replace them were only just getting under way. I sat with rural farmers looking out at land that they were trying to irrigate, heard their tales of tough times and tried to imagine what hope there was for the country's future. It was a similar tale in Malawi, where the Banda years were just finishing and new government was waiting to emerge. But the land was dry and the population suffering from the rampant advance of AIDS.

My 'official' overseas visit as president should have been to Burma, but I failed to get a visa and at the very last minute we had to call it off. I'd asked for permission to call on Aung San Suu Kyi, even then being held under house arrest. That, together with my request to the military authorities to visit Methodist work on the ground as well as in Conference in Mandalay, led to the refusal. Perhaps I'd tried too hard and presented myself as a potential nuisance.

I tried even harder to gain access to the Conservative Party Conference in September 1994, but again to no avail. Despite my membership of the Labour Party, as president of the Methodist Conference I'd wanted to visit the annual jamborees of all three major parties, but the Tories balked.

Every week of this very demanding year, I managed to write a 1,000-word article for the *Methodist Recorder*. What's more, I wrote an imaginary letter per week to various members of my family and this appeared as a little book called *Letters Home*, which appeared just in time for the 1995 Conference. This was a sales wheeze from Brian Thornton, the very entrepreneurial head of the Methodist Publishing House. These two items allowed me to feel that I was keeping up a conversation with the Methodist people. So, too, did my occasional visits to my own congregations at Mill Hill and Golders Green.

As a late substitute for the aborted visit to Burma, I was able to travel with Margaret (and our daughter Ruth, as well as old friend Patricia Smith) to Haiti in the period between Christmas and the New Year. President Aristide had just been flown back after his years in exile and I was able to pay him an official visit during which we exchanged gifts and made small speeches. I had been critical of the way Aristide put his governments together, packing them with his most avid supporters. If ever there was a time in the history of Haiti for a government of national unity, it was surely then. I particularly arraigned him for leaving out of his administration my good friend Rosny Desroches. He assured me that he'd give the matter his close attention. Nothing, however, came of the suggestion.

So many other events were crammed into this momentous year. I appeared on Melvyn Bragg's Radio 4 programme *Start the Week* when one of the other guests was Salman Rushdie, whose works I'd been avidly reading over the years. I gave a Prestige Lecture at the annual gathering of the British Association for the Advancement of Science on the well-worn subject of 'Religion and Science'. And also the Tawney Lecture for the Christian Socialist Movement on 'The Survival of Hope'. I met more than once with George Carey, the Archbishop of Canterbury, and Basil Hume, Cardinal Archbishop of Westminster. In their company, setting agendas for inter-church action, I was once again conscious of how stupid our annual presidency really is. Most of the events we discussed would take place when I was no longer in office.

The whole of this year saw one well-planned itinerary followed by another. This was entirely due to the organizational skills and unflappability of Kath Booth, wife of Mark who was acting superintendent of the Hendon and Golders Green circuit during my absence. I've long discovered that every 'successful' person in the public arena is likely to be supported by at least half a dozen others who are glad to perform repetitive, necessary and routine operations with little if any public acclaim. The one at the front gets all the praise showered on them but they, of all people, know who should be getting it.

In May 1995, Margaret and I travelled to Edinburgh. We'd booked the cheapest and most restrictive tickets available and sat uncomfortably for hours in a heavily overcrowded train. Stepping onto the platform at Waverley Station, we entered another world. We were met by a pennant-bearing Rolls-Royce and greeted by a driver and a military aide-de-camp. We sat in the back seat and, since a number of heads were turning in our direction, couldn't help giving an occasional wave. We were whisked into Holyrood Palace, guests of Lady Marion Fraser who was representing the Queen for the duration of the General Assembly of the Church of Scotland. Marion was also chair of the Christian Aid Board and we'd worked closely together for three or four years. We were given a fantastic room looking out onto Arthur's Seat and were awoken the following morning by a piper's playing of doleful tunes on his mercifully distant instrument. There was dinner, breakfast, amazing company and good conversation. We looked at the changing of the guard from inside the Palace, the only time I'm ever likely to have that experience. Margaret was given the Duchess of Argyll as her 'minder'. The following day, we swept up the Royal Mile, again in a huge car, to attend the opening of the General Assembly. We sat in the Royal Box. Then back to the Palace, out of our glad rags, and off to the railway station for the return trip. We stepped out of our vehicle, our aide-de-camp handed us our baggage and, fully conscious of what it must have felt like for Cinderella, we got into the mouse-drawn iron pumpkin that took us back to London.

It was a great privilege to be president of the Conference and especially as a serving circuit minister. But it was a great relief to get back to my normal work and my own bed again. How Margaret had found the energy to share as much of the year as she did and still hold down a demanding and full-time job, I shall never know. But it ensured that we'd be able to share memories of that year and that was a great thing. We'd celebrated 25 years of marriage and Margaret had reached her fiftieth birthday in that time. Our boys had begun university courses and then thrown them over, preferring to get out into the world of work. They both ended up running wine shops! After a few years of that, they both went back to university and completed their studies. Ruth, meanwhile, was completing her own degree at Cardiff, in French and Spanish, and I had the great pleasure of seeing her walk across the stage of St David's Hall wearing my own hood, gown and mortar board. She graduated from the same faculty as I had 32 years earlier.

About a year after I laid down the presidency, I received a phone call in our Golders Green home from Garth Rogers, my district chair. It was very late on the evening of 24 May, the great high day for Methodists since that's when we remember the conversion of John Wesley. In a sombre voice, Garth informed me that a vacancy had unexpectedly occurred at Wesley's Chapel – 'the mother church of world Methodism', as it's fondly styled – and that the committee meeting to consider who might be sent there had placed me as their number one choice. The gap would have to be filled within a few weeks. Would I go? I must inform him by 6 a.m. the following morning, before he set out for his family holiday in Cornwall. I told him that he could go to sleep with a peaceful mind. It's part of our discipline. Of course I'd go.

6

Wesley's Chapel

A serious house on serious earth it is,
In whose blent air all our compulsions meet,
Are recognised and robed as destinies,
And that much never can be obsolete.

PHILIP LARKIN, 'CHURCH GOING'

Simon Jenkins is the son of a famous Congregationalist minister, who's become a latter-day guru commentator – a man who always these days seems to speak from Mount Olympus. A few years ago, he published *England's Thousand Best Churches*, in which he included roughly 20 non-Anglican churches. One of these was Wesley's Chapel, which, while glad enough to be included in such august company, had to be satisfied with its one-star rating. Judged against the criteria set by Jenkins, no one can complain about this but it wouldn't be difficult to make out a case for an entirely different categorization. After all, this is the 'mother church of world Methodism'. It was built by John Wesley and opened in 1778. Wesley's architect was George Dance the Younger, who had also designed the Mansion House within the City of London. Wesley had asked for an interior that would be 'neat but not fine'. He got a wonderful Georgian church which, though now carrying a great deal of the impedimenta of the Victorian age, retains her sense of the numinous. Jasper pillars, oak pews, stained glass have not withered her nor the years condemned; many a visitor is reduced to silence and awe in a place whose walls seem soaked in prayer.

The Chapel was built on a parcel of land that lies just outside the historic City of London, a place where the garbage and waste from the St Paul's Cathedral building site had been dumped. The Good Book (Hebrews 13.12) tells us what a miracle of love was wrought on a rubbish heap outside the city, a perfect place for putting out the message of redemption and reconciliation. The front of the site snuggles into the very southernmost tip of the London borough of Islington, while the back gates open onto the mysteries of Hackney. Here is to be found the interface between social deprivation and almost unimaginable wealth. Here is a trysting place between past and present. Local people cross our threshold and rub shoulders with visitors from the far corners of the earth. And, with 5,542 of the earliest Methodists buried on this blessed plot, the veil between heaven and earth is at its very thinnest in this place.

Wesley's Chapel is both a parish church and a cathedral; it serves its neighbourhood while relating to metropolitan, national and, indeed, international agendas. Its forecourt is dominated by a statue of John Wesley, which shows the founder of Methodism looking away from the church building and out into the busy world that lies beyond the gates. The plinth bears his well-known statement: 'The whole world is my parish'. These days, those words have come home to haunt him. The present-day congregation is drawn from three dozen national backgrounds and we've counted over 20 first languages other than English. The extraordinary expansion of Methodism in the century following Wesley's death has created a worldwide communion numbering tens of millions. In these days of rapid demographic change and global migration, significant numbers of the sons and daughters of this scattered family have 'come home' and entered our fellowship.

Simon Jenkins felt overpowered by what he called 'the hagiography' of Wesley. From his sceptical and aesthetic point of view, that's perhaps understandable. But another secular observer may have summed it up more tellingly. Roy Hattersley is another widely appreciated writer and social commentator. He's a former deputy leader of the Labour Party, a non-believer, who in 2002 published *A Brand from the Burning*, a biography of John Wesley. In it he argued that whatever opinion one forms of Wesley himself, no one can deny the huge influence which Methodism brought to bear on the social and political history of Britain in the century following his death. And no single place focuses or symbolizes those developments better than Wesley's Chapel, which for millions of Methodists across the world is holy ground, a place of pilgrimage.

It is not without a sense of irony that I came to Wesley's Chapel in the summer of 1996. After all, I'd once raised my voice to demand that it be demolished, disposed of, and the money realized given to the poor. That was in the mid-1970s when the Chapel was closed for a number of years after a coping stone fell dangerously near one of my predecessors and almost brought a glittering career to a peremptory end. It appeared that the foundations had crumbled and the building was moving. It would need serious and costly attention. All this irked me considerably. I'd just returned from Haiti, the poorest country in the Western hemisphere, and the thought of spending a million pounds on an ancient and useless pile seemed almost blasphemous to me. So I raised my voice in protest. I'm only glad that we'd returned to Haiti by the time the Queen and the Duke of Edinburgh re-opened the Chapel on 1 November 1978, the bicentenary of its original opening. Her Majesty would not have been amused at my antics if she'd perchance spotted me standing there waving a placard and shouting my iconoclastic slogans at the top of my voice.

Now, all these years later, here I was, appointed by the Methodist Conference to serve the Chapel as its superintendent minister – surely a clear sign that God is possessed of a keen sense of humour. I became the fifty-ninth holder of the post in a direct line running from John Wesley himself – this is as near as we Methodists get to the notion of an apostolic succession. From my two remarkable predecessors, I'd inherited an astonishing legacy. Ron and Olive Gibbins had laboured here for ten hard years. They'd turned the membership around, taking it from 25 to 96 and establishing a strong commitment to Eucharistic worship. This was such an appropriate development in the very first Methodist church that had been specifically built for the celebration of Holy Communion as well as the (more normal) preaching of the Word. Indeed, as I've often reminded my High-Church friends, it is quite wrong to refer to the events which regenerated Anglo-Catholicism in the nineteenth century as the 'Oxford Movement'. These events should, properly speaking, be referred to as the 'Second Oxford Movement' for it was in that same university city, 100 years before John Keble or John Henry Newman or Edward Bouverie Pusey, that John Wesley and his friends began a similar High-Church movement of renewal. The spirituality of those first Methodists came to be just as much focused on the Eucharist and auricular confession (in groups rather than one-to-one to a priest) as was its successor movement a century later. In its doctrine of grace (Arminian rather than Calvinist) and its affection for the Cambridge Platonists, Thomas à Kempis and the Greek Fathers, Methodism also showed a readiness to keep its distance from some of the more severe and sectarian forms of Protestantism. Alas, Methodism lost a great deal of these defining characteristics in the course of the nineteenth century and it rejoiced the hearts of many of us when Wesley's Chapel, a showcase for the Methodist Church, strove with such determination to reconnect with them; these, after all, were the forces which brought Methodism into being.

Paul and Hilary Hulme followed the Gibbins and immediately struck up a good working relationship with Neville Ashton, minister of the nearby Leysian Mission. The Mission was a kind of 'settlement', a piece of outreach work from The Leys School in Cambridge. It had done sterling work among the teeming slums of Moorfields for over a century but its work had been overtaken by the provisions of the welfare state. It had served its purpose and the various officers of the two churches set about shaping a plan that would unite both causes in one set of premises. This came about on Easter Day 1989 and bore a great deal of fruit in the years that followed. It helped me greatly, from the start, that our two sons had been pupils at The Leys and that the headmaster, John Barrett, was an old college friend. All this allowed me to hit the ground at least trotting as I set about working to strengthen relationships with the school and with its alumni.

One of my predecessor's great innovations was the custom of holding

Thursday lunchtime 'Conversations' with people prominent in public life. I was able to develop this model and gather speakers around some key themes. One such series looked at issues arising within the financial sector of our national life. I was able, on successive weeks, to interview the chairman of the Stock Exchange, the governor of the Bank of England, the dean of King's College London, the chairman of Lloyds, the Lord Mayor and the financial correspondent of one of our television channels. Large crowds gathered for these events but none of us quite expected Eddie George's opening remarks. 'Before I answer your first question,' he said, 'I want to explain what my wife is doing here. She very rarely accompanies me to meetings like this but she insisted on coming today. That's because, and she told me to say this, we met in a Sunday School class and coming here today would inevitably remind us of that. So, on her behalf and mine, thank you for asking me to come.' Thus spoke the governor of the Bank of England, with whom I went on to enjoy a brief friendship before his untimely death in 2009.

Another of our series was held in partnership with the British Association for the Advancement of Science. Peter Briggs, the chief executive officer of the association was (and is) a good friend and together we were able to build a very strong list of speakers which ranged from the Astronomer General to a clutch of professors working in the field of molecular and genetic biology and also the government's Minister for Science. I found myself reading a couple of serious books per week as I prepared myself for these interviews. Some of the contributors were fierce atheists but, in all cases, the exchanges were positive and highly stimulating. It was particularly interesting to hear Steven Rose (of the Open University) explain how divisive a figure Richard Dawkins was within his own field of genetic biology. Dawkins is considered by some of his peers to hold views that seem potentially dangerous, in social terms. His famous notion of the 'selfish gene' can so easily lead to a kind of determinism which gives every impression that we can be genetically predisposed to become racists, misogynists or whatever. It smacks of Calvinism, a scientific equivalent to the doctrine of predestination. Having come to recoil from Dawkins' irrational lunges at anything to do with religious belief, I found it truly fascinating that some people within his own discipline were just as upset at some of his scientific writing.

Few people in Britain have forgotten Arthur Scargill, the firebrand leader of the National Union of Mineworkers during the 1980s, who led his troops into a long strike to save the mining industry from being closed down. He met the determined resistance of Margaret Thatcher's government and, in the end, both the strike and the pits were doomed. When Scargill came to us, he insisted that we talk as much about his Methodist mother as his communist father. It was a fascinating discussion. At the end, he asked us to substitute the hymn we'd chosen for one of his mother's favourites, 'O Love That Wilt Not Let Me Go, I Rest My Weary Soul in Thee'. He sang all four verses without once looking at his hymn book and with tears running down his face.

Ron Davies was Secretary of State for Wales when his life fell apart after some strange happenings on Clapham Common. Details of the events that happened at that time filled our daily newspapers and Davies, who'd been obliged to resign from the government, kept a very low profile for a while. We were scheduled to host his first public appearance since the scandal erupted. It was very brave of him to come and he was ready, in a guarded way, to discuss the whole affair. He was clearly glad to have such a safe place to face people again and gave every appearance of being self-aware and even contrite.

Other series included the likes of Jeffrey Archer, Melvyn Bragg, Hanif Kureishi, Neil Kinnock, representatives from the embassies of every country in the Middle East, Ann Widdecombe and John Humphrys – these and so many others gave our lunchtime audiences some very enlivening and thought-provoking sessions.

I was often asked if I'd allow these interviews to be broadcast or, at the very least, if we could make available a recording of them subsequent to the event. I always refused. My guests seemed to appreciate being able to have a sensible discussion about the issues of the day without feeling the need to 'go on the record' or to guard themselves against the press or dig deep for a sound bite. I tried to make these occasions warm and relaxed; I wanted them to be conversations, just like it says on the tin. After ten years, the model got tired and we suspended it. But it's an idea just waiting to have its second wind and one of these days we'll start it up again.

Shortly after my arrival at the Chapel, I brought out my fourth book, *Worship and Our Diverse World*. It was published by Stainer and Bell in a series called *Touching the Pulse* and was the brainchild of Bernard Braley, the managing director of the company. Two other volumes had preceded mine. One of these offered an array of devotional material for different avenues of work, while the other presented prayers for various aspects of the everyday lives that most of us live. In my volume, I either wrote material myself or gathered together the material of others from a wide variety of sources, to focus the thinking of individuals or even a worshipping congregation on places in the world or on activities which often get ignored. So I composed prayers or meditations for (among other places) Angola, East Timor, Uruguay and China. And others highlighted the plight of hostages and writers in prison, and reflected on the Mostar Bridge and some of the horrors of history. I even wrote a meditation on charcoal, the only fuel available in so many developing countries, a household commodity made by cutting down precious trees. 'Strange to think,' my piece concluded, 'that a cheerful boiling pot and the smell of the next meal might well announce so many dreadful woes with loss of Eden and the inexorable onward march of the desert.'

I also wrote modern versions of ancient prayers and canticles – items like the *Te Deum* and the *Nunc Dimittis*. And this extended version of 'The Lord's Prayer', which I've used several times on radio, has proved very popular:

> **Our Father in heaven,**
> remind us constantly that you are parent
> to all your children, whoever and
> wherever they are or come from
> **hallowed be your name.**

Your kingdom come,
establishing peace and justice,
hope and life for all peoples,
your will be done on earth as it is in heaven.

Give us today our daily bread,
disturb us into an awareness of the needs of others.

Forgive our sins,
our pride and also our prejudice,
as we forgive those who sin against us.

Lead us not into temptation,
especially keep our hearts and minds
open to see the good in others;
deliver us from evil.

For the kingdom – just and true,
the power – gentle and fair,
and the glory – shot through with the colours of love,

are yours, for ever and ever. Amen.

This little book represents my only attempt to offer any 'creative writing' to the public. I enjoyed doing it but I know that I'm just not good enough to write poetry or other imaginative material on a more regular basis.

The membership of the Chapel, which stood at 204 in 1996, rose steadily towards the 400 mark in the decade that followed. We began to get involved in inner-city regeneration schemes, the government-sponsored EC1 New Deal, the Central Foundation Schools, as well as a ministry to neighbouring businesses and offices. We were soon working in close collaboration with our local Lutheran, Roman Catholic and Quaker congregations as well as with St Giles, Cripplegate, our parish church. My pastoral work seemed to be weighted towards helping people with problems arising from their immigration status. I found myself a member of the Court of City University and was soon invited to become a Freeman of the City of London. I got drawn more and more closely into the life and work of St Paul's Cathedral.

On an entirely different front came something with which I'd had no previous experience at all. I became responsible for a very significant heritage site – centred on John Wesley's House and the Museum of Methodism, but including the Chapel and grounds, too. We attract pilgrims from all over the world and the service is offered by an imposing band of volunteers drawn from all over London. The operational oversight of this service is fulfilled by a full-time curator. It was my task to manage this professional worker and a new person had been appointed to this post when I arrived. She was an Iraqi woman, a Sunni Muslim, and she was quite brilliant. Noorah Al-Gailani's father had once been professor of Fine Art at Baghdad University. That's where she'd been educated as well and, in her teenage years, she had been required by the regime of Saddam Hussein to do military service. Hardly surprising, then, that she soon set about licking us all into shape. During her six years with us, she got our museum registered and all our procedures regularized. She ensured that we worked in close collaboration with other nearby museums and institutions in the heritage sector. When she left us in 2002, it was to become curator of Islamic art at the prestigious Burrell Collection in Glasgow. She had introduced me to a number of Arab intellectuals and I date my real knowledge of Islam from the time of my acquaintance with Noorah. Her family had ancient connections with a shrine outside Baghdad which is held in high esteem by Sufi Muslims. She made us a wiser (as well as a better-regulated) bunch and her influence lives on long after her departure.

The other person who became an integral part of our operation virtually from the day of my arrival was Jennifer Potter. She'd spent 25 years in southern Africa, five in Zambia and 20 in Botswana – mainly as a teacher but latterly as an officer of the Botswana Council of Churches. She became widely involved in educational and development networks across the whole continent of Africa. She'd once nurtured a sense of vocation to the ministry but because, in the days of apartheid, she'd have been required to study in a whites-only college, she withheld herself from that path. After all, her daily work was with black people and she could not have borne the pain of being trained in a context that diminished or marginalized them. After an honourable career in southern Africa, Jennifer applied for and was appointed to the position of international affairs officer of the British Methodist Church. She was looking for suitable accommodation and wrote to me asking whether she could avail herself of one of the bedsits that we have at City Road. She came to live here just a few months after we did. And she's still here.

Jennifer soon equipped herself for her new responsibilities with yet another Master's degree and immersed herself in her work for the Connexional Team, Methodism's civil service. But it was clear that her sense of vocation had never left her and soon we were exploring ways of testing that through study and discussion. One thing led to another and it was with great joy that we accepted her as a probationer minister in 2002 and saw her ordained to a full ministry two years later. Her contribution to the development of every facet of the church's life is considerable. She works tirelessly. Her intellectual stimulus gets the best out of others, especially me, and it's been simply wonderful to be working in harness with a person of such exceptional ability.

Ever since my days as a university lecturer, I've relished any opportunity to take students under my wing. Wesley's Chapel gave me an opportunity to work alongside a steady succession of very talented and mainly young people as they offered themselves for ministry. From the moment I arrived at City Road, I had the thrill of seeing Hannah Faal, a young professional woman of Gambian origin, leap all the hurdles of our byzantine selection procedures as she completed her candidature for the ministry. She went to Cambridge and later into a London circuit where I was delighted to conduct her marriage to another minister, a German Old Testament scholar of some distinction, Knut Heim. She bristles with energy and enthusiasm and has just begun her first stint as a superintendent minister in Dudley.

Nigel Cowgill was a lay worker at the Chapel and had obvious, if unpredictable, charisma. Everyone enjoyed his lively presence. But a touch of dyslexia which hadn't been discovered at an early age had stopped him from achieving academic success. Once that was sorted out, and with appropriate technological support, he took everything in his stride. He studied at our Bristol theological college and he, too, has just taken up his first superintendency. He and Jennifer Potter began their studies together and became as thick as thieves – a friendship that's gone on developing with the years.

I first met Claire Taylor as an undergraduate and became her work consultant as she completed two stints as a lay worker, in Woking and Smethwick. I preached when she was accredited as a local preacher. She eventually candidated and went to Cambridge, where she completed a Master's and a Doctor's degree with ease. She went on to marry John Potter (no relation to Jennifer) at Wesley's Chapel. After serving two circuits, in Yorkshire and London, she decided to take some time out from circuit ministry to become the curator at Epworth, the childhood home of John and Charles Wesley.

Claire was a contemporary at Cambridge with Hannah Faal and also with Jonathan Dean. Jonathan distinguished himself with a very fine doctoral thesis on the Reformation. He spent a summer with us at the Chapel and the relationship has only strengthened since his placement came to an end. He's subsequently settled into church life in Chicago where he and his partner, Trey, must be two of the brightest young people for miles. He's written his first book and keeps up his scholarship through teaching. Although ensconced in the United States, he remains very much part of our extended family.

Things were a little different with Nina Johnson. I'd known her as a teenager in Loughton, where I'd been immediately impressed by her gifts, especially her ability to say very profound things in the simplest possible way. She went to theological college and was badly served by a system that seemed to process and stereotype people rather than forming them. She was appointed to a circuit in Gateshead, where she married the undertaker and brought three fantastic children into the world. But her ministry went onto the rocks and she took some time out. We remained in touch and I was delighted to hear that Nina had equipped herself with some impressive qualifications from the world of counselling and that she was thinking of returning to ministerial life. She and Steve and the children are now delighting their congregations in Hertfordshire and I look on with considerable pleasure from a distance.

People sometimes come to us in strange ways. When a brilliant young Korean mathematician, Chin Baek, asked us if we'd help him to improve the English language skills of his younger brother, Kido, we said we'd do what we could. Kido arrived in England in the summer of 2008 and was soon doing full-time duties alongside our rota of heritage stewards in the museum. That forced him to listen to a wide variety of accents and speech peculiarities – those who come from Surrey have a smooth way of speaking that differs from the more glottal, cockney style peculiar to the earthy East End of London. Kido was soon flourishing and we got him a place to study for a Master's degree in Pastoral Theology in Cambridge. Now all the talk is of his entering the ministry. He'll make such an accomplished and joyous addition to our ranks.

I take the trouble to offer these sketches for a simple reason. It's true that I've played a part in some of the key developments in the lives of each one of these people but it may be less obvious what they've contributed to mine. Every one of them is possessed of great talent. As a representative group of people they could hardly be more inclusive, since they cross the categories of gender, race, orientation, marital status and age. As I've got older, the stimulus of the company and friendship of such bright people has been so important to me. I feel proud to be a minister in a church that continues to attract men and women of this quality. One of the most charming works of Francis of Assisi is called 'Little Flowers'. I always thought that these *fioretti* were his companions, the people he attracted to himself and who gilded his daily life. I may well be wrong on that score, but that's how I like to think of these (mainly) young men and women who've added so much to my life – my own little flowers, loving and stimulating companions, ensuring that I continue to be young in spirit, too.

One day, out of the blue, I received a telephone call from Colin Kinnear. There was something he wanted to talk through with me and he wondered if he could see me for a few minutes. My only previous knowledge of him was from one or two social functions organized for former pupils of The Leys School. He's a successful businessman who's now beginning to relax and think about how to apply his wealth. The proposal he made took my breath away. He wanted to establish a scholarship, a full scholarship, for pupils chosen from the Wesley's Chapel congregation that would enable them to attend The Leys. This would amount to several thousand pounds a year and I found myself both intrigued and suspicious at the same time. How would one such pupil from the inner city fare among the self-assured children from much wealthier backgrounds? He soon knocked that one on the head. 'It's not one pupil I'm interested in,' he explained, 'it's one per year, up to seven at any one time. We'd have to kick-start the project and get a few in straight away. Then we'd have to keep the levels up on an annual basis. I agree with you that the school might suffer from a little complacency, situated as it is right at the heart of Cambridge. It's my judgement that the antidote to that is a good dose of streetwise, inner-city kids.' We were now talking about rather more than several thousand pounds per annum. And there was something about the eagerness with which he wanted to spend all this money that I found attractive. I was later to find that his wife, Brenda, was fully behind him in this project, as indeed (perhaps even more extraordinary) were his children and their families.

I was still a little hesitant. My only previous dealings with wealthy people had been uniformly negative. I'd several times tried to interest rich men in supporting worthy causes – they usually hid behind their account-ants. Or else they wanted to give their money with strings attached. Sometimes they wanted some publicity in return for their altruism, at other times they sought to have some kind of control over the good cause I was asking them to support. I've met several mutations of what I can only call 'paternalism'. So I eyed Colin Kinnear warily. The last thing I'd consent to would be a scheme that would subject the children of Wesley's Chapel to someone who wanted fodder for his own glory or to turn them into forelock-touching vassals who somehow felt obliged constantly to acknowledge the munificence of their benefactor. I'd been poor once myself and I still cringe with embarrassment or writhe with anger at my memory of the way some people offered me their help as I struggled to find my way forward in life.

But I needn't have worried. Colin and Brenda Kinnear gave over the entire operational management of the scheme to the school and to ourselves. They've certainly got to know the children who've benefited from this scheme and also their families. The downright pleasure they get when one of the children writes them a letter or bestows a hug is a joy to behold. It's unasked for and always so touchingly received. In fact, quite simply, it's a moment of grace. I and one or two others keep an eye on the way the scholarship works out. It pays for equipment, school uniform and trips. I once told Colin and Brenda that I'd withheld permission for one of the children to sign up for an expensive skiing trip. It seemed to be more about fun than education and I wondered whether we shouldn't be drawing a line between the two. They gave me a kindly but severe telling-off. What's the point of sending the children to such a school and then not allowing them to join their friends when something a little out of the ordinary is on offer? The children must enjoy the whole experience, they insisted. No scrimping. No dumbing down. The children must draw the maximum benefit from everything that the school offers.

There have now been well over a dozen beneficiaries. Some have gone off into university studies and the world of work. They are a very multi-racial crowd of young people and this scholarship has invariably given them a huge break in life. In addition to funding the scholarship, the Kinnears also send a regular and generous gift to the Chapel that enables us to help all our young people in higher education. I've never met such generosity nor such cheerfulness in parting with wealth. It's so pure, so unalloyed and the pleasure it bestows is so childlike. It's love in action – disinterested and unconditional. Colin and Brenda are not conventional churchgoers but I feel certain that I've seen in them something that's as profoundly spiritual as anything I've ever met.

Moments of grace seem to occur again and again at the Chapel. Imagine people's surprise one day in February 2004 as two chauffeur-driven cars pulled up in our courtyard minutes apart. Out of the first stepped the Most Reverend and Right Honourable Rowan Williams, Archbishop of Canterbury. He knocked on the manse door and was duly admitted. Close behind came the unmistakable figure of John Humphrys, senior presenter of the *Today* programme, a man who's been variously described as 'the nation's conscience', 'the rudest man in Britain' or, just simply, a rottweiler. He, too, entered the manse. Those who witnessed these arrivals were bristling with curiosity.

The idea had been born a week or two earlier as I was being driven to the *Today* studio early one morning to deliver my 'Thought for the Day'. I was captivated by a newspaper report of an incident which had occurred in the studio just the previous day. John Humphrys had thrown a fit – he'd stomped around the studio swearing and threatening what my mother used to call 'blue murder'. It had been volcanic and he took a long time to calm down. When I entered the studio, I asked him if he'd recovered and he nodded affably enough. He asked me if I could hang around for a few minutes so that we could speak when the studio was 'dead'. I gladly assented and he told me the whole story.

He was furious with what he called 'the archbishop's praetorian guard', or his 'Lambeth minders' or other things ruder and cruder by far. It was a whole year since Rowan Williams had been enthroned as archbishop and John Humphrys felt that he had been systematically denied access to him. So when Anglican primates from all over the world came to London to discuss the thorny question of homosexuality, the *Today* team tried again. This time, Lambeth grudgingly relented but only on condition that the interview would be pre-recorded and given 'down the line' from a radio car. This was truly preposterous but Humphrys had no choice in the matter. He did manage to get agreement for a supplementary question about the Iraq War. With these understandings in the bag, both parties prepared themselves for the interview.

Everything went well enough until Humphrys asked his question about the Iraq War. How moral was it, he wondered? Thirteen seconds of silence followed and was broken eventually by Humphrys. Silence is the commodity radio finds most difficult. 'You seem to be having some difficulty with my question, archbishop,' he said. Rowan Williams retorted that any question about morality required careful consideration. It certainly couldn't be summed up in a sound bite. Humphrys has always maintained that this part of his interview, including the dramatic silence, was good radio. After a few further exchanges, he brought the interview to an end and then returned to the main studio.

It was to be put out after the eight o'clock news and John Humphrys himself trailed it just before the Greenwich pips, promising listeners that the archbishop would be answering his questions on the Anglican Primates' meeting and also on the Iraq War. Unknown to him, Lambeth Palace had taken objection to the line of questioning on Iraq, no doubt thinking that the long silence would make their charge sound uncertain and even bumbling. They insisted that the second half of the interview be scrapped. And so it was. But nobody had told John Humphrys. He felt that this incident showed unwarranted levels of paranoia within a BBC newsroom still reeling from the criticisms of the Hutton Inquiry into the Iraq War. He accused its decision-makers and controllers of behaving 'like boy scouts'. He felt that his professionalism had been impugned by their prevarication.

John was still clearly angry when he told me this tale. I suggested that the best course of action would be for him and Rowan to meet. I felt that they were made for each other. 'They won't let me near the poor bugger,' he said. I assured him that it could be done and, in the end, he gave me permission to try to pull it off. He went away convinced that it would not happen.

But it did. Over lunch in our kitchen! Within seconds of meeting, the two of them relaxed with each other. Both men had recently lost a parent and were soon in deep conversation. Margaret fed what she called her 'three Welsh boys' and then she and I quietly left the two of them to themselves. They were still enjoying each other's company when their chauffeurs insisted that it was time to go. Since that day, I've listened to on-air conversations between them and been struck by the obvious respect and even affection that they seem to display towards one another. As I'd said to John Humphrys, they were made for each other.

Not all our moments of grace are resourced from outside our congregation. The marriage of two young Africans produced its own source of wonder. The groom had arrived in the United Kingdom after fleeing from war-torn Sierra Leone. He'd taken up work with the United Nations and was sent on a peace-keeping mission where he met his fiancée. She hailed from Rwanda and had only just escaped the genocide there, somehow getting over the border into what was still Zaire. Her family, including her baby boy, were all killed. She, too, found a job with the United Nations and it was in Kosovo that the two of them met, both refugees from human atrocity helping to save others from the same. As they stood in front of me on their wedding day, I marvelled how, between them, they had direct experience of all those places that we'd been so regularly praying for. Some time later, they ventured to pay a visit to Rwanda. It was a brave thing to do. While wandering through the streets of Kigali, someone recognized her and, in a moment of indescribable joy, told her that the child she thought she'd lost all those years ago was still alive. They brought him to her, a lovely ten-year-old lad, a little miracle. He came home with them and, a few weeks later, to great rejoicing, we baptized him and gave God thanks for this wonderful act of deliverance.

One of our young men survived a gang attack in which his best friend was killed. The courage he showed in the aftermath of the attack has been inspirational. Two refugees from political turmoil in Peru and Colombia had become friends while in a reception centre after fleeing the repressive regimes in their respective countries. One was a Roman Catholic, the other a Methodist, and they thought that they'd never see each other again once they'd left the centre. And here they were, obviously astonished and delighted to be meeting each other, in the foyer of Wesley's Chapel one Sunday morning. Such stories could be multiplied but I must forbear. I look out every Sunday and see before me the whole world in microcosm.

I see educated and barely educated people, rich and poor, many lawyers and dozens of young professional people, a Fellow of the British Academy (one of the world's leading experts in medieval Arabic) and the parents of a child who's been excluded from school. There are always battles to be fought, burdens to be carried, joys to be shared. To be the minister of such a congregation has truly been one of the great blessings of my life.

Dozens of dedicated volunteers make sure that a huge burden of responsibility is taken from my shoulders. This gives me room to breathe and attend to the multiple demands that come my way. It also allows me to 'specialize' in the pastoral care of those whose immigration status is in question – people without work visas, those who've overstayed or been given deportation orders or gone underground, those who've been tagged and those who hide behind several identities. And it gives me time to press officials of the United Kingdom Borders Agency on their own irregularities, inefficiencies and plain wrong-headedness.

From the work that I do in this field and the misery that I experience day after day, I can come to only one conclusion. Our country's immigration policy doesn't work. Those responsible for administering it cannot cope either with the backlog or with the ongoing demand. One injustice is committed after another. The new points-based system, the country-of-origin granting of visas and the privatization of the visa-issuing service are producing their own tangled bureaucracy and will soon be shown to have created an unsavoury mess. And very little concern seems to exist for the human dimension of all this. The endless hours that I spend assessing one problem after another are akin to shovelling shit in the Augean stables. The more you dispose of, the more there seems to be. It's astonishing how significant a proportion of my pastoral work is now focused on this area of life.

In Methodist polity, the key role for lay people is held by the quaintly named circuit steward. We have three of these and each of them has given outstanding support to me personally and also sacrificial service to the church. There are days when I think that they'd have provided great characters for Jerome K. Jerome, on others they look like characters from

Last of the Summer Wine. But of their excellence, there can be no doubt. They've each drawn me into a world of experience that I'd never otherwise have accessed.

Paul Appafram is Ghanaian, an electrician by trade, and responsible for the oversight of property at Wesley's Chapel. The years he spent in the engine room of large ocean-going liners is obvious from the look on his face as, in dungarees or overalls, he stands proudly in charge of our basement boiler house. With his wife Marian's permission, he's at the Chapel most days. In 2001 he accompanied me and Margaret to Ghana, where I'd been invited as the main speaker at the fortieth anniversary Convention of the Sacred Order of the Silent Brotherhood at Akropong. It proved to be not at all the work of a 'secret society' as its name seems to suggest. Thousands of white-robed members of the Order came together for this annual convention and I was very touched that Margaret and I were the only non-Ghanaians present. This commitment gave me the opportunity to travel a little and we spent time on the coastal belt between Accra and Cape Coast.

In Cape Coast, we were able to visit the colonial fort through which thousands of African men and women had been trafficked on their way to slavery in the New World. There was something sinister about the fact that hundreds of manacled or fettered people could be held awaiting transportation in grim dungeons which were situated directly below a fine chapel with stained-glass windows and all the trimmings. This was where the 'masters' said their prayers while, under their very feet, groaning men and women abandoned hope and prepared for their hell on earth. I conjured up vivid pictures of those places in Haiti where the *bossales*, the chattels, were bought and sold with no regard to their humanity. They'd begun their journey somewhere like this. What wickedness! How could it have been perpetrated under the banner of Christian nations?

Also in Cape Coast, we were able to visit the two Methodist schools, Mfantsipim School for boys and the Wesley Girls' High School, two of the finest such institutions in Ghana. Both of these impressive institutions were founded by British missionaries. But it was while standing in the

pulpit of the Wesley Methodist Church, the first church to be established
in Ghana outside the direct protection of the Castle, that I found myself
most deeply moved. Buried beneath me, directly under the pulpit, lie the
bodies of the first Methodist missionaries to the Gold Coast – Joseph
Dunwell, the Reverend and Mrs Wrigley, and the Reverend and Mrs Peter
Harrop – who died of malaria in their early twenties, an incredibly short
time after their arrival in their new homes. My thoughts reeled. Over there
in the Castle, I'd stood in a fine place of worship that stood directly above
the dark dungeons which dashed the hopes of so many young Africans
who were sold into slavery and died in faraway places. And here was I,
in another fine place of worship, standing directly above the remains of
those young English men and women who'd so readily given themselves
to Africa for the sake of the Gospel and who themselves had died in
faraway places across a different ocean. The contrast could hardly have
been greater.

Some years before this trip, I'd been made an honorary Ghanaian
chief and it was wonderful to pay a visit to Anna Budu Arthur, sister of
a paramount chief and the architect of my enstoolment. I'm proud to
be known as Nana Kwesi the First of City Road and my chieftain's stool
remains one of my proudest possessions. It was Anna, while still living in
London, who'd introduced Margaret and me to Maya Angelou and enabled a friendship to flourish between us. We saw each other whenever she
was in London and we still send each other samples of our latest writing.
I was greatly honoured to play a part in her seventieth birthday celebrations at the Dorchester Hotel. Throughout that 2001 visit to Ghana, Paul
Appafram acted as our interpreter and go-between. His companionship
was invaluable.

Five years later, it was the turn of another of our circuit stewards,
Naibuka Qarau, to accompany us on a visit to his homeland, Fiji. Margaret
and I spent three weeks among the scintillatingly beautiful islands that
together constitute that faraway nation. I was the principal guest at
the annual Conference of the Methodist Church and preached at the
inauguration of their new president. We were given the use of a house

that belonged to a one-time vice-president of Fiji on the royal island of Bau. This is where the redoubtable Fijian chief Cakobau held court in the middle decades of the nineteenth century and where he finally yielded to the preaching of Methodist missionaries, abandoning his warlike and cannibalistic ways in favour of the Christian path. The baptismal font in the church on Bau was once the stone on which the heads of those needed for the cooking pot were smashed to pieces. We may dream of a world where swords will be beaten into ploughshares. This was a notable variant on that theme.

We attended rugby matches, paid an official visit to the President of Fiji, travelled among the islands of Taveuni, Rewa and Viwa. I wore the *sula*, a skirt-like garment meant to show sturdy, dark-skinned legs to advantage (as opposed to my white, stick-like ones). We were royally entertained by the Boladuadua family – he'd been High Commissioner to London and they'd worshipped at Wesley's Chapel. I preached, lectured, took part in one welcome ceremony after another and drank *kava* (a milk-like drink made from the bark of a tree and used for ceremonial purposes). I visited the theological college and came to an agreement with the principal that this was where I'd send my theological library when I retire from active ministry. We listened to one male voice choir after another – each of which could have held its own with any from the valleys of Wales.

But it was the social aspects of Fiji that I liked best of all. I met a number of those ministers who were later to fall foul of the military government. They were such good company and imaginative and creative thinkers. I became aware of the unresolved and explosive question of land tenure as raised by Fiji's Indian population. I was given an insight into the workings of the Council of Chiefs – an indigenous body of very conservative leaders whose role will need careful understanding in any eventual settlement of the problems of Fiji. Events have recently turned Fiji into a repressive state and one day soon the whole social and political framework of that lovely land will have to be re-imagined.

We came away greatly refreshed and profoundly inspired. Naibuka Qarau and his wife, Makarete, had been our guides and it was so special to see our circuit steward in his own milieu. Naibuka had been a serving soldier and, since settling in London, he and Makarete have taken on a kind of parental and pastoral role for numbers of young Fijians coming to the United Kingdom to enlist in the British armed forces. Some of those who pass through their hands end up serving in Iraq or Afghanistan. One was killed when a roadside bomb exploded and the whole of the Fijian community were stricken by grief. In our liturgical life, we shared the obvious pride of our Fijian members at the young men who pass through our hands on their way to active service. And we weep when one of them is afflicted. In a congregation like ours, we're never far away from so many of the places that we pray for.

We visited the home patch of Paul Appafram by taking a plane from Heathrow airport to Accra. Our travels with Naibuka Qarau were even longer, for we reached Suva via Tokyo. In Peter Baugh's case, it was much easier. We hopped on a number 43 bus at the Chapel gates and travelled no more than a couple of miles. Peter is a lifelong resident of Islington. After a series of jobs as one kind of office boy or another, he was called up for National Service. I don't think that Peter would have won us the war, but his time in the army gave him a taste for learning and, after his demobilization, he got himself a Bachelor's degree and went into teaching. He'd just retired from a headmaster's job when I first met him. He comes in to the Chapel every day and takes responsibility for a thousand and one administrative tasks as well as keeping a kindly eye on the museum. In retirement, he registered for an Oxford degree in Theology and, soon after we met, we agreed that I'd be his local tutor. For six years, we saw our way through one module after another. We engaged with the intricacies of inter-faith studies, Christian ethics, biblical exegesis, Old and New Testament theology, Christianity and the modern world. Indeed our theological journeyings seemed sometimes more demanding than those expeditions to Ghana or Fiji. But the company was just as good. Peter is blessed with a wickedly dry sense of humour and a keen, questioning mind. I and his elder brother Johnny sat so proudly in Oxford's Sheldonian theatre to witness Peter in his cap and gown take a degree, *magna cum laude*, from the vice-chancellor of the university. Not bad for a 70-year-old.

In November 2000, as I was getting into my stride with my work at Wesley's Chapel, I got the devastating news that my brother Jim was near to death. Margaret and I had seen him in hospital a few days earlier, just before he went home to die. We knew, and he knew, that it was all up. Our elder son, Tim, insisted on driving me down to Kent where Jim and his family lived. Jim was in a coma when we arrived; on hearing my voice, however, he rose in his bed and gave the two of us a hug and his blessing. He was just 57 when he died. His death left me quite desolate. He was the companion of my earliest days. We'd pulled each other out of one scrape after another. He was my buddy. A few days later, in my monthly *Methodist Recorder* article, I poured my heart out. 'My kid brother died last week,' I wrote. I continued:

> A horrible cancer in his lungs ate away at him until it left him barely recogniz-able. He'd always been so big and strong. At the end, he was a poor shadow, a hollow shell, a breathing skeleton.
>
> Seeing him just a few hours before his end might have been a very painful experience. And yet it wasn't. From within that wasted frame there came such a surge of recognition, for me and for my son, as we stood by his bed, that we both felt we had encountered the raw life force that inhabits us all more deeply than consciousness or cognition. This surging of the human will, this reaching out in love, seemed so elemental, indestructible, something near the essence of whatever it is that we call 'eternal life'. Jim's faith remained firm to the very end and he'd constantly tell me how unafraid he was of death, how ready he was to go and how he'd be waiting for us all to rejoin him. What's more, he told me to say so at his funeral service. At two o'clock in the morning of All Souls' Day, he breathed his last.

> For the sword outwears its sheath,
> And the soul wears out the breast;
> And the heart must pause to breathe,
> And love itself have rest.

I loved him so very much. May he rest in peace.

I conducted his funeral service a few days after his death. He left a wife and son. I still miss him terribly.

During these years, all three of our children were married. Tim and Dru, Jon and Susanna, were wed at Wesley's Chapel. Ruth had fallen in love with Bunna Sat, a young man whom she met while working in Cambodia, and they were married in that beautiful, still-traumatized land on Christmas Day 2005. A few months later, Margaret retired from her work at St Bartholomew's Hospital. A big leaving party was thrown for her and I felt as proud as Punch as I listened to the rich plaudits given her by her workmates – everyone from consultants to ancillary staff. She has since settled into a busy life filled with all her interests and so many things she's waited years to have an opportunity to do – singing, genealogy, being useful to disabled people, as well as a range of services to the church.

Meanwhile, I don't feel at all ready for retirement. Every day still seems so full of challenge. Not, of course, that there aren't aspects of the work that I could well do without. There's so much bureaucracy to contend with. We're only a small organization but we seem increasingly to find ourselves battered by the necessity to formulate Health and Safety policies, emergency evacuation procedures and compliance with the exacting demands of English Heritage. We have to be familiar with the expanding demands of employment and charity law, grievance procedures, the re-accreditation of our museum, risk assessment and management and, of course, the safeguarding of children.

Our pastoral team meets every week and allows me to focus on the core activities of any church – its liturgical life and the pastoral oversight of those who come our way. It was one of the early challenges that I set myself to build a team that would reflect back to our membership something of its own diversity. It's been so important that Jennifer Potter and I could bring our years of experience in the Caribbean and southern Africa to our work with such a cosmopolitan congregation. We're joined by Brian Goss, a retired minister who puts his long pastoral experience at the disposal of the team. He is an indefatigable visitor, a wise old bird and a holy man to boot! He and Zena have been a real blessing to us. Peter Baugh meets with us too, bringing his dry humour and wry observation to our discussions. Joy Leitch, who was born and brought up in Guyana, has been a team member for over ten years. She spent her professional life in the world of education. She's a local preacher and her contribution to our worship is widely appreciated. And Abe (Abena) Konadu-Yiadom is proud of being an Ashanti and sports the title 'Leysian Missioner'. She came to us from the Citizens Advice Bureau and helps members of the congregation to find their way through our labyrinthine benefits system and the byzantine ways of statutory and other services. The latest member of our team is Peter Briggs, now retired from his duties at Roehampton University, work which earned him a richly deserved OBE. He's our education consultant. This is our team and it has meant so much to me to be a part of it.

It's a team that enjoys working together. Yet, as I found in Loughton, it's pure grace when we can say that we like one another too. Here again, I sense myself surrounded by my *fioretti*. They've helped me in a thousand ways to juggle my multiple activities by sharing so many of the routine tasks of ministry.

On 15 September 2003 a very significant event took place which bound Wesley's Chapel in a covenanted relationship to the parish church of St Giles, Cripplegate. This is the church where John Milton was buried, where Oliver Cromwell was married, and where Samuel Annesley, the grandfather of John and Charles Wesley, was incumbent until he, together with so many others of that epoch, was ejected in 1662 for refusing to sign the Act of Uniformity. Both Wesley brothers were curates in the 1730s at St Luke's, Old Street – a church which now forms part of the St Giles parish. And it was within the parish that these brothers had their 'Aldersgate experience' – that heartwarming encounter with God which has become enshrined in the popular imagination as the effective beginning of the Methodist revival.

It was a fine day as we all gathered in the forecourt of Wesley's Chapel. We made a very colourful procession as we marched behind two matching banners which had been made especially for the occasion. The Bishop of London and the chairman of the London North East District of the Methodist Church brought up the rear. We'd trawled a number of eighteenth-century archives and come up with a collection of denunciations of John Wesley made by various clergymen of the Church of England, in particular those which barred him from preaching in so many of London's churches. The plan was that these relics of ancient animosity would be handed to the bishop at the door of St Giles and he would proceed to tear them up in a public renunciation of long-dead hostility. That was the plan, but we became aware that the bishop wanted something altogether more dramatic. Before we set off on our procession, he phoned down to St Giles and demanded that a special vessel with an arcane liturgical name should be produced to await our arrival. He intended not only to tear up the offending documents but to burn them to a cinder.

Bishop Richard Chartres cuts an imposing figure and has a voice to match. He clearly took great pleasure in setting fire to those hostile remnants of a divisive past and, I must say, the physical disposal of them in that way made a much stronger point about Church unity than the tentative findings of a thousand well-meaning committee meetings. It looked and felt like a prophetic act, an acted parable, and everybody present loved it. And so it was that we put the past behind us and gave ourselves permission to enter the church where we signed a covenant which committed our two churches to develop a shared eucharistic ministry and to work together on outreach and study programmes. This was followed by a service of Holy Communion when the celebrant was Ermal Kirby, our Methodist chairman. The first to take communion from his hands was the Bishop of London.

This relationship has gone from strength to strength and the dream I've nurtured since the day of my ordination has been, at least in part, realized. And it's all led me to wonder. If we can go this far, what's to stop us going even further?

7

A Bigger Stage

To see a world in a grain of sand,
And a heaven in a wild flower,
Hold infinity in the palm of your hand,
And eternity in an hour.

WILLIAM BLAKE, 'AUGURIES OF INNOCENCE'

On Monday, 4 April 1997, our newspapers were abuzz with the news that Martin Bell had announced his intention to stand as the anti-sleaze candidate in the Tatton constituency at the forthcoming general election. He would have the backing of both the Labour Party and the Liberal Democrats and neither party would field a candidate against him. Bell was an immediately recognizable knight in a shining white suit, a veteran BBC war correspondent and a former pupil of The Leys School. He'd be standing against the Conservative sitting member of parliament, Neil Hamilton, who'd disgraced himself by accepting money from Harrods' owner Mohamed Al-Fayed in return for political favours.

The news delighted commentators and intrigued the public. I was among those anticipating a fascinating campaign. But for me there was an added *frisson*. Just a couple of days before this news hit the headlines, I had myself been asked if I would be the anti-sleaze candidate for the Tatton seat. I received a phone call from Labour Party headquarters asking me to consider such a possibility. It took me completely by surprise. I protested that the Liberal Democrats wouldn't want a card-carrying member of the Labour Party for this exercise. They'd surely want someone more independent. But this convenient line of argument was knocked on the head that same evening when a voice from the Liberal Democrat campaign office confirmed the offer. I spluttered something incoherent and asked to be allowed to sleep on the matter. First thing next morning, I was called again from the Labour dugout and asked for my response. 'I don't think so,' I said. The voice at the other end showed considerable impatience. 'Why ever not?' it demanded. 'Because I'd win,' I retorted. I wouldn't have minded standing against Neil Hamilton as a gesture, to make a point about probity in public life, but the political scene was moving away from the Conservative Party so fast at that time that I was sure I'd have a pretty good chance of overturning even a 20,000 majority. I'd only moved into my new responsibilities at Wesley's Chapel six months earlier and it was far too soon to contemplate a change of direction. In any case, I was a Methodist minister, not a member of parliament. I'm sure that I did the right thing. Even so, it's remained one of those 'what if' moments which we all live through from time to time.

Through the mid-1980s, I'd played a key role in the refocusing of the Christian Socialist Movement (CSM). I argued strongly that it should affiliate with the Labour Party rather than remain a glorified talking shop. Affiliation would bring the right to attend the annual conference and have a voice in the shaping of policy. So many members of parliament, including key members of the shadow cabinet, were members of CSM that it didn't make sense to keep a *cordon sanitaire* between ourselves and the parliamentary party. This was the point of view which eventually prevailed and I was then leaned on to become chairman of the CSM Executive Committee, a position I declined because of the increasing pressures that were coming my way from a number of other directions at that time. In the end, the chairmanship went to Chris Bryant, a former Anglican priest who went on to become the member for Merthyr and Minister for Europe in Gordon Brown's government.

It was on behalf of the CSM that I offered prayers of intercession at the memorial service in Westminster Abbey for the much-lamented John Smith, leader of the Labour Party, who'd died suddenly of a heart attack in May 1994. It was a remarkable service in which Elizabeth Smith and her three daughters offered such a poignant presence. The Abbey choir sang beautifully, a poem by Gerard Manley Hopkins was read with great feeling, and the sanctuary was filled with light. But nothing quite matched the music offered by the Grimethorpe Colliery Band which filled the whole place with mellifluous sound and evoked profound emotion from the souls of anyone present who carried a candle for the labour movement in general and, in particular, the part which coalminers had played in its history.

When people ask me how I got into the House of Lords, I generally say that I haven't a clue. But I suppose that quite a number of the activities that I was heavily involved in well before 2004 must have given some people the idea that my name was worth considering for such a role. Before anything of the sort came to pass, however, something of an altogether different nature stopped me in my tracks. In May 2000, I received a letter from the Bishop of London inviting me to become an Honorary Canon of St Paul's Cathedral. It was followed by a further invitation to become one of the founding members of the Cathedral Council. I accepted both with great pleasure.

And so, just a few weeks later, I underwent a twee little ceremony which culminated with the bishop's commanding the Dean of St Paul's to take me to my stall in the quire. John Moses, the dean, held out a clenched hand, his index finger alone protruding from his fist, and I did similarly. Our fingers touched and, in this guise, like two roué ballerinas, we minced our way to the seat assigned for me. It was great fun.

I was to find myself in very distinguished company on the Council. It met three times a year under the chairmanship of Dame (since Baroness) Elizabeth Butler-Sloss, the distinguished former president of the Family Division of the High Court. Other members included Eddie (later Lord) George, governor of the Bank of England, Frank Field MP and Simon Thurley, the chief executive officer of English Heritage. All these years later, I'm still a member of the Council though many of its original members have been replaced. It's given me an amazing opportunity to discover how a cathedral works. Under John Moses' leadership, a younger and more focused group of residentiary canons was brought in and this changed the atmosphere of the place overnight. St Paul's used to be a kind of siding where clerics of a certain age were shunted to see out their ministries, a kind of consolation prize for never having got a bishop's hat. Now, it was run by dynamic and gifted people who would probably go on to some significant position after leaving the cathedral. Already two of these are bishops and another a dean and yet another a sub-dean. What's more, we began to see women in key positions of leadership. The dean had to overcome serious resistance from senior colleagues to achieve this obvious development. It's inconceivable now that the cathedral's senior team would ever again become an all-male preserve.

Over the years, I've preached several times from the lofty St Paul's pulpit and taken a regular part in its public worship. The Wesley's Chapel congregation attend the midnight Christmas Eucharist at the cathedral and special seats are always held for them right at the front. I and all my ordained colleagues are welcomed into the team distributing communion. It's a truly awesome experience to be part of such a service with a packed cathedral enjoying the drama of the occasion.

I've been present for many a national observation and played my full part in them. The service held for the Queen's Golden Jubilee (with the whole Royal Family present), the quickly arranged but brilliantly implemented service put on just four days after the 11 September 2001 terrorist attacks in the United States, and the triennial service for the Order of the British Empire give some idea of the range of events catered for in worship on the cathedral floor. I'm welcome at anything I care to attend and, duly robed, I wend my way in procession to my stall where I have a bird's-eye view of everything that goes on.

During John Moses' time as dean, both the interior and the exterior of the cathedral were totally refurbished and cleaned. A truly mind-boggling fund-raising campaign raised the £41 million it took to achieve this. I looked on with green eyes from the sidelines. I'd love to find just £1 million to reorder our museum, but Methodists are either poorer or

meaner or else just less well connected than Anglicans. I just don't seem
to have found the secret as far as fund-raising is concerned. Whenever
I talk to a potential donor, I see the glaze come over his eyes as I move the
conversation from general bonhomie towards the question of money.

The other great initiative taken at that time was the setting-up of the
St Paul's Cathedral Institute. I'm a patron and enjoyed working with
Canon Ed Newell (now sub-dean of Christ Church Cathedral in Oxford)
as he set up programmes which focused on key issues of our times. World
debt, the collapse of our financial institutions and the role of the family
have all been addressed in a variety of ways ranging from grand events on
the cathedral floor to retreats and breakfast seminars, prayer meetings and
smaller teaching sessions. Major speakers like Kofi Annan, Gordon Brown,
Kevin Rudd, Rowan Williams and my own guru, Hans Küng, have all
drawn in full houses. There's something special about seeing the snaking
queues of professional City workers wending their way into the cathedral
for one of these events. If the Church can tune in to the questions people
are really bothered by, it can still play an important part in forming the
conscience of our present generation. St Paul's Cathedral offers an object
lesson in this regard.

Through the covenant arrangements that hold Wesley's Chapel in a
close relationship with its parish church and through the role I'd been
invited to play at the cathedral, I felt as if we were storming the bastions
of the Church of England. But it was when I was invited to become an
Honorary Fellow of Sion College that I knew I'd arrived. I've heard Sion
College described as the clergy's Livery Company. Its splendid theological
library has long since been dispersed and its buildings disposed of. It sur-
vives as a fellowship. Its rich endowment allows seminars, dinners, visits,
family days and study projects to take place. My membership has allowed
me to get to know dozens of Anglican clergymen and women across the
diocese of London and to preach in some wonderful parish churches.
As far as I know, I'm the only non-Anglican member of the College and
I count it a great honour to have been asked in.

I've since been given honorary fellowships of Sarum College (Salisbury),

Southlands College (Roehampton University), the University of Wales (Lampeter) and Cardiff University. Rotary International has made me a Paul Harris Fellow. And it's 20 years since I was made a Knight of the Order of St John of Jerusalem. These awards have all been gratefully received and I sport a range of splendid certificates across the wall of the corridor leading to my study. But none has led to such an ongoing involvement in its affairs as Sion College.

More and more doors seemed to be opening to me and I found myself taking on an ever-widening set of responsibilities. My political activities were increasing, I was broadcasting regularly both on radio and television, my church duties had increased at local and national levels and my ecumenical work was expanding exponentially. I succeeded the Roman Catholic bishop, Crispian Hollis, as chairman of the Churches Advisory Council for Local Broadcasting (later to be renamed The Churches Media Trust). It was all go. Then, out of the blue, I was invited by the Archbishop of Wales, Rowan Williams, to write his Lent book for 2003. I found myself agreeing to do this even though I knew that I'd just have to get up a little earlier every day to get it written. And thus *Voices from the Desert* came into being. By the time it was published, of course, Rowan Williams had become the 104th Archbishop of Canterbury. He was amazingly generous in his Foreword and I had the rare honour of seeing my book serialized in the *Church Times*. None of my previous literary efforts had gained such notoriety.

This was a book that I enjoyed writing. I don't think I've ever entirely shaken myself free from my childhood experience of religion with its strictures and its poses. I've often contrasted a truly terrible incident in Richard Llewellyn's *How Green Was My Valley* with the evening prayer of the Reverend Eli Jenkins in Dylan Thomas's *Under Milk Wood.* In the former, when a young girl named Meillyn Lewis becomes pregnant, she's brought before the chapel deacons and berated for her sinfulness. The sneering judgementalism and the heartless cruelty of the religious officials make grim reading. It's no wonder that Meillyn Lewis just wants to run away from her interrogation, ready to make a pact 'even with the Devil himself in a stink of sulphur, only to be out of that Chapel and running up the mountain away from those nodding heads of Ha's and Hmm's and the eyes of Mr Parry [the greasy inquisitor] and his voice.' The clergyman in Thomas's play stands in total contrast to all this. When he hears Polly Garter, the village prostitute, singing her melancholic song about the lovers she's known, he's driven to lift his voice for all to hear, 'Praise the Lord!' he exclaims. 'We are a musical nation.' And in his evening prayer, his warm humanity shines out like a beacon: 'we are not wholly bad or good, who live our lives under Milk Wood,' he intones before completing his thought, 'and Thou, I know, wilt be the first to see our best side, not our worst.'

I'd grown up in a 'thou shalt not' environment where the religion was miserable and finger-wagging. I remember my mother's refusal to go to church because she'd be preached at, looked down on, because she was a divorcee who liked her little pleasures – a cigarette, her beloved bingo, an occasional bet on a horse. I grew up with a deeply engrained dislike for that kind of religion and must have retained an ultra-sensitivity to its continuing prevalence. Indeed, I suspect that this is my only known allergy.

Voices from the Desert allowed me to look at the writings of people with whom organized religion had always been uncomfortable. I looked at the work of people like Andy Warhol, George Harrison, Eldridge Cleaver, Maya Angelou, Niall Griffiths, Salman Rushdie and Hanif Kureishi and tried to tease out – not really a difficult task – a preoccupation with (or at least a discussion of) the spiritual. Again and again, in music and art, poetry and prose, I found people wrestling with what it means to be really human in today's world. I remember the way religious voices were so dismissive and censorious, for example, when the musical *Hair* took to the stage. Church leaders were incensed because this production showed naked people on stage. Their fulminations seemed to me to prevent them from hearing the questions that all of us, within and beyond the fold of formal religion, are surely wrestling with:

Where do I go?	Where do I go?
Follow the river.	Follow my heartbeat.
Where do I go?	Where do I go?
Follow the gulls.	Follow my hand.
Where is the something,	Where will they lead me?
Where is the someone	And will I ever discover why
That tells me why	I live and die,
I live and die?	I live and die?

What could be more haunting than that?

In the years following the Second World War, Christians were faced with the fact that, in the popular mind, their faith was increasingly being associated with industrial and militaristic capitalism, an inevitable ingredient, it was supposed, of so-called Western values. It was being seen as a cause of war rather than a cure for it. In my chapter on 'The Beat Generation', I examined the escapism and hedonism which energized a group of young people to gorge themselves on the fruit of previously forbidden trees – the joy of random sex, the mind-expanding possibilities of drugs, the sheer *élan* of a life free from bourgeois responsibility. Jack Kerouac gave up his college and sporting career, Allen Ginsberg became a wandering and poetical prophet and William S. Burroughs abandoned his family fortune and courted notoriety in a very public and sensational exploration of new sexual freedoms. All this provided a 'thrill factor' and made iconic figures of these three men and their associates. The fact that they ended their lives so wretchedly – one in alcoholism, another insane and the third spaced out by drugs – is usually overlooked. They portrayed the idea of a search for something other than conventional wisdom to live by. They were ready to seek out at any cost what the French philosopher Michel Foucault would later call 'the limit-experience'. They believed that they would only ever discover exactly who they were and what their lives could amount to by living beyond the suffocating constraints of bourgeois convention.

All this led me to look at the part played by the 'beach Buddhists' in the story of the Beats. Later in the book, I went on to examine George

Harrison's flirtation with Hinduism and the flight of alienated African Americans into the Nation of Islam, as well as the strange love–hate affair of Andy Warhol with the byzantine Catholicism in which he'd been brought up. People were fleeing conventional Christianity in all directions. And, in all of this, I found that people who were looked on with suspicion by organized religion, 'beat-up' people, were again and again put centre stage – bums and dropouts, the homeless and the unloved – as if in protest at the way society in general, and religion in particular, had marginalized them. From somewhere deep beneath all this surface activity, however, there seemed to be a common cry from a disenchanted generation which could be summed up in the scream of Allen Ginsberg's poem 'Howl', where conventional Christianity is identified with the Moloch figure who dominates the closing section of the poem. 'In a set of nine maledictions,' I wrote,

> Moloch, the child-devouring god of ancient times, is blamed for all kinds of social ills. He it is who brings sorrow to young men conscripted into the army and old men weeping in the parks. Moloch is named as 'the Congress of sorrows', whose mind is 'pure machinery', whose blood is 'running money', whose fingers are 'ten armies', whose breast is a 'cannibal dynamo'. This is the god of impassive skyscrapers, satanic factories, banks, urban pollution, weapons of mass destruction, robot apartments, the god from whom there is no escape except, perhaps, that afforded by drugs. Visions, miracles and ecstasies have 'gone down the American river'. The only way to break free from Moloch's grip is somehow to break out and cross this river.

This massive rejection of what these writers perceived to be 'Christian' society was hugely influential in turning a whole generation away from organized religion. The Manic Street Preachers, a group of college-educated young men from a Welsh mining valley, had drunk deep from the wells of Kerouac and Ginsberg. Their 1994 album *The Holy Bible*, like the name they'd chosen for their group, seemed like a deliberate ploy to put themselves and their message where religious belief had always prevailed. Their songs are angry screams, often very brave efforts to rail against a world where racism and sexual exploitation seem rampant. They address uncomfortable subjects, too – themes such as anorexia, bulimia and self-mutilation. One critic described their music as a meeting place for anger and despair. The churches then, as now, were preoccupied with homosexuality, sabbatarianism, gambling, contraception, abortion and the evils of cohabitation outside marriage. The politicians were calling the nation 'back to basics'. The population at large were seeking their escape from all this through expensive holidays, home improvements and the latest gadgetry. The Manic Street Preachers were struggling to drag something out of the despair and alienation of their generation and to wave it in front of a public which preferred to look the other way. Their manifesto appeared prominently on the cover of their album; it was a provocative quotation from Octave Mirbeau's *The Torture Garden*:

> You're obliged to pretend respect for people and institutions you think absurd. You live attached in a cowardly fashion to moral and social conventions you despise, condemn, and know lack all foundation. It is that permanent contradiction between your ideas and desires and all the dead formalities and vain pretenses of your civilization which makes you sad, troubled and unbalanced. In that intolerable conflict you lose all joy of life and all feeling of personality, because at every moment they suppress and restrain and check the free play of your powers. That's the poisoned and mortal wound of the civilized world.

As a Methodist, I cherish the belief that God's amazing grace flows for all, without distinction. *Voices from the Desert* represents an ongoing effort on my part to keep listening to the uncomfortable voices of secular society whose spiritual needs are as great as anyone's and whose struggle to express them is often so haunting and compelling. Why, in any case, should I suppose that the operation of God's grace takes place only within the confines of organized religion? No one could ever persuade me that the kingdom of God is coterminous with the church.

Throughout my years at Wesley's Chapel, I've travelled extensively not only across the United Kingdom and Northern Ireland but also to distant destinations on several continents. The United States comes top of my list. I've made 17 visits to 16 states in a dozen years. Sometimes these are mere weekend preaching trips; I leave on Thursday or even Friday, preach or teach on Saturday and Sunday morning and then catch the overnight plane that brings me home in time for my Monday morning staff meeting. I've been invited to give keynote speeches on Methodist history, or multi-culturalism, or on more general theological themes to annual Methodist Conferences across the United States. When I visited Georgia in 2001, it was just a few days after the terrorist attacks of 11 September and my meetings turned out to be great rallying points for the traumatized community of Savannah. People queued to get into church and the events were highly charged. I've never experienced, night after night, such profoundly emotional moments. It was as if I'd been given the role of drawing nasty, pain-creating pus from a wound so that it could have a chance to heal.

Short twinning arrangements were made between Wesley's Chapel and the Foundery United Methodist Church in Washington, DC, as well as the church at the Chicago Temple in downtown Chicago, and I changed places for a few weeks with American colleagues there. This kind of arrangement allowed me to visit political leaders, university campuses, cultural centres and seminaries, as well as all kinds of imaginative work in the not-for-profit sector. We were even able to watch some football and baseball – never basketball, which has always been beyond me. Margaret generally accompanied me on these visits and we made some very good friends. Our travels ranged from Alaska to Florida, from Michigan and Rhode Island to Texas and the Mexican border, and I found myself again and again spending quality time with influential people and able to catch the mood of a punch-drunk America in the grim days of the late Clinton and entire George W. Bush presidencies, the one overshadowed by foolishness and the other shot through with the ineptitude of the holder of the most powerful office in the world.

Without any doubt, my most memorable visit to the United States came in March 2005, when I was invited to be part of a Congressional visit to Selma in Alabama to commemorate the fortieth anniversary of the crossing of the Edmund Pettus Bridge by those demonstrating for civil rights. My visit began with a posh dinner on Capitol Hill when I met the senators and congressmen who would be making up the visiting group. The following morning, we left Washington from a military airport and were given top-grade security for the whole of our journey. I still haven't worked out how I got to be invited to join the group in the first place, but I was determined not to miss out on any aspect of the experience.

The event which drew us to sleepy Selma had occurred on 25 March 1965, a Sunday morning when a large but apprehensive crowd gathered under the leadership of civil rights activist (later congressman) John Lewis. Martin Luther King had had to fly back to Atlanta to fulfil his preaching duties. He expected to rejoin the campaign later that day as they began their march to Montgomery, the state capital. The march got underway but, once they reached the brow of the bridge, it was immediately obvious they were not going to make much progress that day. A massive force of mounted police with dogs, together with contingents of state troopers armed with tear gas and clubs, awaited them. For a moment there was a pause, then John Lewis rallied his forces, and they moved forward. All mayhem was let loose. Dozens were injured. The skull of John Lewis was cracked open by a brutal blow and soon the march came to a shuddering halt.

This was to be the last major campaign of the civil rights movement. Its main objective was to win voting rights for African Americans. Because everyone in the state of Alabama was required to take a literacy test before registering, a ridiculously low number of black citizens were entitled to vote. The outrageous behaviour of the Alabama authorities that day was captured on television. President Lyndon B. Johnson himself was one of the viewers. He was immediately galvanized into action and his memorable speech which ended, most movingly, with the words 'we shall overcome' (the watchword of the campaigners), gave the clearest signal to the whole nation that the days of discrimination were over and that decisive action would now be taken to see that it never occurred again. Johnson put all the weight of his presidency behind this move and there can be little doubt that this cost him and the Democratic Party dearly for many years to come. Effectively, it lost the South to the Republicans.

I walked over the Edmund Pettus Bridge that Sunday morning, the very

Cambridge – 1967

Haiti – beyond the mountains are more mountains

Class of happy kids –
Nouveau Collège Bird

Deputy head giving prizes –
the school was destroyed in the
earthquake of January 2010

Hyde Park – Speaker's Corner, 1989   President of Conference, 1994–95

Broadcaster – 1980s onwards

With Margaret at Golders Green, 1994

With Jennifer Potter at the Chapel

Lord Griffiths of Burry Port and Lady Griffiths

Canon of St Paul's Cathedral

The day John Humphrys and Rowan Williams met

Haiti – February 2010 alongside the ruin of a school we built in the 1970s

David Carr's narrative portrait showing the story of my life

Haitian woodcut representation of my ministry

day that marked the fortieth anniversary of that poignant occasion, with a feeling of great privilege. I was at the shoulder of John Lewis himself and in the company of Harry Belafonte, the daughter of Lyndon B. Johnson, and several veterans of the original campaign.

In a curious way, I'd always felt that I had a link with the leaders of the civil rights movement. One of my closest American friends, Wesley Williams, is the son of Willard, both of them Methodist ministers. Willard is now dead but I lapped up the stories he used to tell of the time when he and Martin Luther King were students together at Boston University. The Kings would babysit Wesley when he was a child and the two families remained in touch after they'd moved back south. A photograph of Willard alongside King on the road from Selma to Montgomery has always had pride of place on my mantelpiece. I know that this is only friendship by association and that it's stupid of me to make any capital out of such a tenuous link, but I can't help it. Just to think that my wonderful friends were themselves that close to one of the great leaders of the twentieth century sends shivers down my spine.

On our way to Selma, we visited the city of Birmingham. I sat on the front seat of the air-conditioned coach alongside Fred Shuttlesworth. Fred was one of the campaign veterans. He was a founder member of the Southern Christian Leadership Conference and it was he who'd first invited Martin Luther King to come to Birmingham to give some focus to the campaign there. He'd suffered an attempt on his life, been beaten with baseball bats, and imprisoned again and again. His monumental confrontations with Birmingham mayor Eugene 'Bull' Connor and, not far behind him, the Ku Klux Klan, were at the heart of the struggle. Fred shared his memories freely with me on that bus ride into Birmingham. His voice broke into a chuckle as he pointed to the police outriders who flanked our bus, their sirens wailing as they drove other traffic out of our way. 'To think,' he said, obviously enjoying the thought, 'that I once had to run the gauntlet of their truncheons and witness the hatred in their eyes as they beat me and clapped me in handcuffs. Now look at them. My heralds and my protectors.'

During this same period, I visited a number of countries that bore the scars of long and heavy conflict. In April 1993, I represented Christian Aid at the plebiscite which brought Africa's newest nation into being. For many years, Christian Aid had supplied the humanitarian needs of the Eritrean People's Liberation Front. It had done this by shipping its aid secretly across Eritrea's border with Sudan. Technically, it was against international law to supply one side in a conflict of this kind across the border of a neutral state. Christian Aid took serious risks in doing this. It also opened itself to the criticism of uncomprehending supporters who might argue that supplying humanitarian needs is just a euphemism for supporting one side in an armed struggle. Once the 30-year war with Ethiopia was over, a way needed to be found to give the embattled people of Eritrea a legitimate place among the family of nations. They were to be consulted in a national poll, an exercise which would be overseen by a large team of international observers. As part of this, I was asked to lead a small group of election monitors who'd operate in Keren, the country's second-largest city. My team included the Somali ambassador to Eritrea and a law professor from Copenhagen. The welcome that I (as the representative of Christian Aid) received was overwhelming. On the list of official government guests, my name figured between those of Mikhail Gorbachev and Neil Kinnock! Christian Aid was given pride of place for all the solidarity and courage that it had shown over the years.

The day was a triumph of hope over the years of despair and it seems so sad that the optimism of that time has been dashed again and again as Eritrea's leaders have refused to grasp the opportunity that was theirs. Continuing border disputes and repressive government have contributed to heavy loss of life and great impoverishment for a people who had struggled so hard over so many years to gain their freedom. A real tragedy.

The lovely West African country of Sierra Leone was another troubled place which I visited in these years. The atrocities perpetrated during its civil war were truly horrendous – children were being held upside down by their ankles and ripped apart, neighbours were setting fire to the homes of people they'd lived alongside for years, an army of child soldiers was roaming the land fiercely focused on killing anyone who blocked their way. I was part of a team of three whose two other members were magnificent African leaders – Dr Emmanuel Lartey and Professor Kwesi Dickson, both Ghanaians. They were universally respected and it was a privilege for me to stand in their company. The Sierra Leone Council of Churches was well placed to play a positive role in the search for peace but, unfortunately, its officers had turned the Council into a tribal fiefdom, using its powers of patronage to favour members of their own families or tribe. This had to be addressed and my colleagues were relentless in their investigation. While there, we had radio contact with the rebel leader and direct talks with a number of leading political and military officials. When later Prime Minister Tony Blair sent contingents from the British armed forces to play a restraining and retraining role alongside the Sierra Leonean army, his initiative was received with joy and led directly to the resolution of conflict there.

In 1998 and 1999, under the auspices of the World Council of Churches, I paid two visits to Sudan. On each occasion I chaired a round table that brought together major non-government organizations (NGOs) from across the world and officials of the Sudanese as well as the South Sudanese Council of Churches. A nasty war had been simmering in Sudan since the withdrawal of the British in the 1950s. This was a country the size of Europe and almost impossible to administer efficiently. The 'Arab' north and the 'African' south were in a state of conflict (Darfur wasn't on our radar screens in those days) and various efforts had been made to resolve this. When drought and famine, as well as tens of thousands of internally displaced people living in camps, were added in, it was hardly surprising that the country had undergone a humanitarian disaster of the first order. Memories of this crisis were still very vivid at the time of my visits.

Sudan was being governed by an Islamist group which, under the leadership of Omar al-Bashir, had seized power in a bloodless coup in 1989. After the events of 11 September 2001, it was considered a rogue state by the United States whose government fired an intercontinental missile at Khartoum as well as Kabul to make its displeasure known and felt. Oil had been discovered in the south and a long pipeline was being constructed to bring it to Port Sudan in the north. Any proposal to divide the country into two (and this was being looked at seriously at that time) would have to include a resource-sharing formula that would enable both entities to enjoy the wealth generated by this discovery.

The particular business for me was to get those present at the round table to commit real money to their Sudanese partners as they continued with the ongoing reconstruction and development work that inevitably follows a crisis. But there was a problem, one that I had found in various forms in other countries too. Since this was at the very heart of what I'd gone to Sudan to do, it may be worth rehearsing the matter here.

The world community has shown itself again and again immensely generous when disaster strikes one of the poorest countries of our planet. A tsunami, earthquake, hurricane, flood or drought will touch the hearts of ordinary people around the world. Increasingly in latter times celebrities have wanted to play a part and our media have made their own efforts too. Soon, huge amounts of material aid are on their way to the afflicted country. And soon, this exposes the lack of capacity within that country to handle the well-meant support that floods in. Sudan had only recently found itself in this position. The Councils of Churches (north and south) had been among the small number of organizations which appeared to have structures capable of handling such aid and soon their officers were purchasing trucks, organizing a logistical base, hiring scores of people and establishing bank accounts to deal with the activity. They made a reasonably good fist of it, although there were inevitable glitches. Not everything went to plan. But on the whole, by common consent, things went well.

It was when the immediate crisis was past its peak and the interest of the outside world diminished that the problems began to emerge. Attention drifted elsewhere and a general downsizing of the operation was left in the hands of the local people. Employees had to be dismissed, properties sold, vehicles disposed of. It inevitably takes time to do this. What's more, where do the costs of such disengagement come from? The Sudanese Council of Churches found itself crediting its 'ordinary account' with monies that had been sent to support the aid effort. How else could the Sudanese have financed the winding-down of the disaster activity? This was an obvious question but didn't represent the way that some of the major funders saw things at all. They accused the Sudanese church leaders of corruption and refused to continue their support until their house had been put in order. They refused to see the logic of the case. Their overriding concern was to be able to show a 'transparent' set of accounts to their own supporters in their countries of origin.

I found all this very upsetting. International NGOs are as capable of neo-colonialism as any government or political system. Some of the self-righteous and arrogant attitudes on display were quite objectionable and I had to say so. Undoubtedly, mistakes had been made by the Sudanese but they were certainly not guilty of stealing, cheating, lying or anything else like that. They'd done the best they could and now needed help over a longer period of time if they were to get things back into shape. That was the thrust of my argument from the chair and I refused to entertain the sort of criticisms that some had come with. At one point, I adjourned the meeting until the funding agencies could agree a budget of support and warned that I would not reconvene the meeting until and unless there was a fair outcome to their deliberations. We got our budget in the end but I didn't make many friends among the international agencies. I found it frightening how some very intelligent people, once in a position of power over those who are weak and vulnerable – the very people whose needs they are supposed to serve – seem capable of parading and strutting that power around like disagreeable demigods.

In October 2009, as part of a group of Muslims and Christians, I visited Bosnia, another country with a mixed ethnic population and a violent recent past. Fifteen years previously, while preparing to take on my duties as president of the Methodist Conference, I'd witnessed with horror Bosnia's unfolding tragedy. I found myself having to address this as the leader of the Methodist Church. Genocide and ethnic cleansing were resorted to by those seeking mastery in their respective countries and the international community watched the pictures on television with a feeling of utter helplessness. The United Nations was found wanting. It seemed incredible that such crimes against humanity could be committed on European soil within living memory of the crimes of Hitler against Jews, homosexuals and gypsies during the Second World War.

Bosnia hangs by a thread, a mish-mash of a country on the edge of Europe, saddled with a peace agreement which, while it settled hostilities for a short time, was bound to become part of a bigger constitutional and political problem that would return to haunt those who had framed it. Officials of the European Union were in Bosnia at the same time as our group and they were giving their attention to precisely this question: 14 years after the peace agreement, how do we lay the basis for a true peace? Croats, Serbians and Bosniacs vie for position in this balkanized corner of the Balkans. And their communities correlate roughly with distinct faith communities – Roman Catholic, Serbian Orthodox and Muslim. Our aim was to test the minds of those in the religious communities to see if they could play a significant part in helping their political masters to reach just and binding agreements for the future. On the whole, we were not reassured on this point.

To stand in Sarajevo and imagine Slobodan Milosevic's big guns thundering down during the three-year siege suffered by the citizens of that wonderful place is almost unbearable. To imagine the destruction of the truly beauteous Mostar Bridge and those multicultural communities linked by it is to envisage wanton savagery. And to speak to mothers and brothers of some of the 8,000 Muslim men and boys who were slaughtered by the soldiers of Ratko Mladic in Srebrenica in 1995 is to realize just how deep and open the wounds of war still are. On all hands there is denial. Trust has been destroyed. A shadow economy based on the trafficking of women and children and the sale of human organs is just about the only profitable activity around. The people wait helplessly. The international community dithers interminably. Hostility could so easily break out all over again. I ended our visit wondering how, if a situation like that facing Bosnia (or Haiti) can't be successfully dealt with, there can be any hope at all of finding a way through the byzantine complexities of larger problems in Afghanistan, Iraq and Israel–Palestine.

It was these experiences that led me and my colleague Jennifer Potter to write *World Without End?* in 2007. That book represents a serious attempt to question the mechanisms available to us for resolving our contemporary crises. The United Nations and its agencies had been part of a brilliant attempt in the years following the Second World War to build a new world order where the risks of a repeat of such conflict would be minimized. The Bretton Woods Agreement, the Marshall Plan and the United Nations achieved a significant part of their aims and objectives. But all these mechanisms were posited upon the nation state as the cornerstone of the way the world was organized. Borders were inviolable and the sovereignty of the state unquestioned. Understandable, perhaps. Everyone remembered the way Hitler's Germany had invaded Czechoslovakia and Poland. And the newly independent countries of a post-colonial world would demand and cling to clearly defined borders. And yet, the world was about to become such a different place.

At the heart of our book lie two matching chapters. The first, written by me, sets out half a dozen case histories of conflicts that have erupted since the fall of the Berlin Wall and the end of the Cold War. In Bosnia, East Timor, Eritrea, Haiti, Iraq and Rwanda, countless lives have been lost while the international community huffs and puffs with indignation, unable (or unwilling) to intervene. Borders, even ridiculous ones drawn by distant colonial masters in an entirely different age, are not to be crossed. The nation state is all.

Meanwhile, the world has quite simply become a different place. Almost everything that affects and shapes our lives most directly holds no regard whatsoever for borders. In her chapter, Jennifer sketched six such forces – crime, the environment, finance, health, the media and migration – where our everyday lives are constantly affected by developments that are global rather than local, where borders seem to be irrelevant. We argued that, in these circumstances, it's vital that we reshape the mechanisms set up over half a century ago to make them fit for purpose in our global era.

Otherwise, we shall go on witnessing one conflict after another, with no methodological or logistical capacity to affect outcomes. We shall have to sit idly by and watch while the world consumes itself with rage or greed.

During these years, I developed a number of interests on the home front, too. As a trustee of Art and Christianity Enquiry, I found myself enjoying the company of experts who sought to relate the visual arts to 'sacred space'. The Trust put on a number of important exhibitions and lectures as well as making annual awards to those who had contributed significantly in this field. The Sir Halley Stewart Trust makes generous grants to innovative projects in the medical, social and religious fields. As the lead trustee for religious applications, I've had years of enjoyment getting to know some very creative people in broadcasting, the creative arts, education, inter-faith relations, evangelism, community work and so much more. The Trust tries to support interesting people and to balance pro-active initiatives on our part with responses to applications for support. This means that I can keep my eyes open for stimulating pieces of work and begin the discussion that might lead to a grant's being made.

I've mentioned my role as chairman of the Churches Advisory Council for Local Broadcasting. This put me in touch with broadcasters and programme-makers of all kinds, some of whom have gone on to do extraordinary things in the media. More recently, I've chaired the College of Preachers, steering it through its fiftieth anniversary celebrations. I think it's true to say that I accepted both these positions out of a sense of duty. After all, I've had a great deal of experience both in the world of broadcasting and preaching. But I can't truly say that I've enjoyed either of them. Not because they're uninteresting or unimportant, for indeed they've both allowed me to work with very creative people in areas that I'm totally committed to. And therein, of course, lies the rub. I'd prefer to be at a microphone or in front of a camera, I'd rather be doing the work of broadcasting than to talk about it. And I find discussing preaching dull compared with actually doing it. So I've been happy enough to give something back to both these activities in the way of organizational input. But it's no substitute for the real thing.

Right on the Chapel doorstep stands the Central Foundation School for Boys. Its most famous alumni is Jacob Bronowski, whose *The Ascent of Man* remains one of the seven wonders of world television 40 years after it was first shown. The boys' school in Islington is matched by a girls' school in Tower Hamlets. Our son Jon is a governor of the girls' school and it's a real delight to see the hijab-bedecked pupils, who make up more than half the school population, making their way to their classes or else performing (as unlikely as this might seem) in Shakespeare's *Macbeth*. I'm a governor of the boys' school and also vice-chairman of the foundation which stands behind the activity of both schools. This has been such an interesting vantage point from which to look at educational provision in two multicultural and impoverished London boroughs. My roles here have allowed me to make contributions to debates on education in the House of Lords and also to see just how Acts of Parliament (which I've played my own small part in promulgating) impact on the daily life of such schools. The work has been demanding and engrossing. I'm constantly amazed at how two splendid head teachers can give schools which operate in difficult social environments such a progressive feel and sense of purpose.

Perhaps the most unusual of the trusts and charities that I've found myself involved with over the years has been the Addiction Recovery Foundation (ARF). It began when I was working in West London. About a dozen self-help groups met on our church premises, mainly Alcoholics Anonymous and other agencies committed to the twelve-step method of recovery. One day, a delegation from one of these groups asked if they could see me. They wished, they said, to set up a body that would launch a journal where twelve-step treatments could be discussed and publicized. Apparently, no such publication existed and my interlocutors were convinced it would meet a real need. They invited me to be one of the founding trustees of the body that they were about to create. Those who called on me that day were themselves all in recovery from the misuse of one kind of substance or another. I said that I'd be delighted and honoured to be one of their number and that's how a 17-year involvement with the ARF began. Soon we had published the first number of our title *Addiction Today*. It took well over a decade to turn this into a viable publication and our whole operation was long run on a hand-to-mouth basis. When eventually ARF merged with another specialist group and the financial situation became regularized, I made my withdrawal. I remain an honorary president to this day.

A key figure in the whole of this development was Benjamin Mancroft. He was in recovery from an addiction to heroin and the story of his pathway to 'clean' living reveals enormous courage on his part. His father was a peer and, when he died, Benjamin inherited the title and took his seat in the House of Lords. I was present to hear his maiden speech in which he recounted the dangers of drug dependency. He was a leading provider of modern forms of gambling – lotteries of one kind or another – and it was income from such sources that underpinned the activities of ARF in its earliest phase. I entered the House of Lords just when everyone was getting into a lather about a proposal to ban fox-hunting. And there was Benjamin, leading the pack in support of that activity, jumping his fences and sounding his tally ho with great aplomb. We developed a great warmth for one another and I still marvel at the irony of a Methodist minister from humble beginnings who can boast the friendship of a hereditary peer who's pioneered significant developments in the field of gambling, whose leisure time activities included fox-hunting and who sits on the Tory benches in parliament. One day in the middle of winter, noticing that I seemed to be very tired, he put an arm around my shoulder and said, 'Leslie, you must get away. Why don't you spend a few days on my estate in Scotland? We have 17,000 acres, so you'll find plenty of peace and quiet. The house is always staffed up and you just have to say the word.' It was a characteristically generous offer but, in its very essence, it spoke of an existence I knew nothing about, of two people who might have been born on different planets.

And so I entered the House of Lords.

Hilary Armstrong, Tony Blair's chief whip and an old friend, asked if she could see me. The government had been going through some tough times and Hilary herself had had more than one sleepless night in her efforts to organize increasingly turbulent backbench members of parliament in support of government proposals. In particular, of course, she'd had to deliver support for the decision to invade Iraq. I remember her saying to me, just ahead of that vote, that she wasn't at all sure she could get a majority. If not, she assured me, the prime minister was resolved to go to the country. In the end, the House of Commons gave its grudging assent but the toll of this and other pressures on Hilary was immense and, when she contacted me that day, I was sure that she wanted to see me on something related to the pressure she was working under. But I was wrong. I sat her down and produced a cup of tea. Margaret was in Newcastle-under-Lyme visiting her mother. 'Tony wants you in the Lords,' she said – words that came like a thunderbolt from a clear blue sky. I felt my jaw continuing to make pleasant conversation while my head went into a complete spin. How would I explain all this to Margaret when she got home later that day? Would she believe me? I heard Hilary say that the prime minister was offering me the Labour whip though he'd quite understand if I wanted to sit on the cross-benches. That brought me out of my reverie. Who would want to go into a political arena and deny himself the chance of doing the politics? And hadn't I been part of the labour movement for much longer than I'd been a Christian? In any case, politics was far too important to leave to politicians. I jumped at the chance, accepted the whip and have never regretted it since.

Now I had to visit some very colourful characters, officers of the College of Heralds, often referred to affectionately as 'the playing cards' because of their titles and the uniforms they wear. Fellow-Welshman Peter Gwynn-Jones, Garter Principal King of Arms, and Clive Cheesman, Rouge Dragon Pursuivant, helped me to choose my title though there wasn't much to discuss. I wanted my new identity to be linked to Pembrey and Burry Port, where I'd been born and where I'd grown up, and this proved easy to arrange. Much easier than was sometimes the case, they told me. One postulant had asked, somewhat timorously, whether he could include a city outside the United Kingdom in his title. 'What do you have in mind?' Garter enquired. 'Damascus,' came the reply. Thumping his fist on the desk in front of him, Garter's reply was classic. 'Not unless you've sacked or relieved it,' he said peremptorily. And that was that. The poor peer-to-be had to content himself instead with a leafy London suburb.

I received shoals of letters, nearly all of them from people wanting to share my pleasure. There were a few which were more critical. How could a minister of religion compromise his calling by entering the political world? And why on earth had I sacrificed my freedom and endangered my conscience by taking the Labour whip? Wasn't my ego big enough already? But this was a rare note. Far more common were the numerous letters of affirmation I received. Among these was a handwritten note from my old school contemporary Michael Howard. 'Warmest congratulations on your peerage,' he wrote. 'It is richly deserved and will give great pleasure to your legion of friends and admirers – not only those who are old boys of Llanelli Grammar School. I am not sure how much I look forward to your contributions in the Upper House but I shall read them with inter-est! With every good wish, yours ever, Michael.' I just hope that it doesn't sound too self-serving to quote this in full. Michael and I have had one bust-up after another over the years, especially during the time he was Home Secretary. And I'm sure we'll never see the world the same way. All of which makes his note seem so generous and the bonds that hold us together so strong.

I was introduced to the Lords in July 2004 by Margaret Jay and John Habgood. Margaret is the daughter of Jim Callaghan and the sister of Michael Callaghan, who was a contemporary of mine in my under-graduate years in Cardiff. John had been Archbishop of York before his retirement. So a scion of the Labour Party and a much-respected Christian leader accompanied me as I made my oath (in Welsh as well as in English) and took my seat on the red benches. Whenever possible, I like to sit immediately behind and above the bishops – how much pleasure a Methodist minister takes from that little ploy! This proximity to the bishops has allowed me to enjoy some good company and make one or two nice friendships.

I have been constantly struck by the consensual approach that prevails in the Lords. The arithmetic makes this inevitable but it is nevertheless most agreeable. Roughly speaking, there are 200 Labour peers, an equivalent number of Conservatives, about 70 Liberal Democrats, 26 bishops and 250 cross-benchers. So the governing party, despite always being able to force its legislation through in the Commons, has to find other ways of getting its proposals accepted in the Lords. Conversations take place and deals are struck through what are called 'the usual channels'. This cosying-up to one another doesn't temper the passionate arguments that are sometimes put forward on one side or another of a controversial issue, but our debates do seem so very mature so much of the time. I must admit, however, that 'sedate' or even 'soporific' would be a better qualifying word at times.

I have been greatly impressed by just how representative the House is. Women are present in numbers and many of them have taken significant leadership roles. The last three leaders of the House, the Lord Speaker and several government ministers or their shadow equivalents are women. There are representatives of various ethnic minority groups and non-Christian faiths and several members are wheelchair users or disabled in other ways. Once you factor in the experts, leading voices from the judiciary, the armed forces, the worlds of diplomacy, politics, the trade unions, business and industry, science, medicine, the arts and academia, you have a really impressive line-up. I've found their company inspiring and have made several friends from their number.

I certainly haven't become the country's legislator-in-chief. I spend a fair chunk of time in parliament but, because of multiple other duties, I've found it impossible to give the kind of time necessary for following a piece of legislation through all its stages. Even when I speak at the second reading of a Bill that interests me, for example, I can rarely synchronize my diary with the sequence of days then set aside for its committee and report stages. It's considered discourteous to dip in and out of these debates (except, of course, when a particular amendment assumes an importance all of its own), so I content myself largely with listening to others, or else questioning ministers outside the Chamber.

On the other hand, the House of Lords offers many opportunities to take part in discrete debates where points of principle can be argued out without being shackled to, or deeply immersed in, a legislative proposal. On the whole, this is where I've made my contribution with speeches on subjects as diverse as international development, assisted suicide, civil society, the role of the Churches and faith communities in contemporary society, the future of religious broadcasting at the BBC, education and other social issues. I've paid particular attention to the repeated attempts by Lord Joffe and others to weaken current legislation on what they insist on calling 'dying with dignity'. I've enjoyed standing behind Baroness Finlay, professor of Palliative Care at Cardiff University, in her attempts to put the other side of the argument and to staunch the rising tides of secularism. I try hard to make my speeches in a manner that resonates in such an arena. There must be no claiming of special privilege on the grounds of my religious beliefs. Nor must my interventions sound sanctimonious or otherworldly. A touch of humour always works but mustn't be overdone. And reason must prevail at all times. It's quite a challenge. One, in all honesty, that I relish.

I take groups and individuals from all kinds of background into the Lords. A-level Law students at our local school, members of the Church Sisterhood (a group of feisty women of a certain age), my ecumenical colleagues, the ten-year-old pupils from our daughter-in-law's inner-city school, members of the Boys' Brigade, visitors from Burry Port – all have enjoyed personal tours. I think of this as a major responsibility. After all, parliament belongs to the people and the more who see it at work, the better.

Both houses of parliament have been racked recently with revelations related to the way members claim their expenses. The indiscriminate and uncritical way that these were published, putting every case on the same footing as every other, has been one of the major factors that has stirred up the general distaste and public anger that have ensued. Undoubted abuses were put forward on the same basis as acts of carelessness or negligence. It was assumed that every infraction involved deliberate deceit. Tiny amounts, especially if they could be associated with the purchase of insignificant items such as toilet rolls or a pound of sausage meat, were placed in the same category as mortgage repayments on second homes and the refurbishment of moats or the payment of expenses into personal business accounts. It's all felt like a hatchet job. And if it was, then who can doubt its success? It has destroyed public confidence in our political system and thrown members of both houses, across the political parties, into a deep slough of despond.

Again and again in this narrative, I've given vent to the visceral dislike I formed as a boy for the self-righteousness and Holy-Joe-ism which I found among the adherents of organized religion. I now find similar feelings evoked by the sanctimonious judgementalism of our press. Journalists are accountable to their editors, who seem driven by a need to boost the sales of their newspapers or improve the ratings of their programmes. Under this pressure, they so often reveal themselves only too ready to humiliate people in public life, to invade their privacy, to expose them to ridicule and to leave off their gang-bashing only when their victim is either reeling abjectly from their attacks or driven glumly from office. Fox-hunting (which we've outlawed) has nothing to compare with the man- (or woman-) hunting that has become such a regular feature of our public life. And what an ugly manifestation of wanton human cruelty it all is! Politicians are slated when they claim only to have acted 'within the rules'. And quite rightly, too. It's such a weak defence. But why aren't journalists condemned when they retreat to their own default position and justify their brazen tactics by a too-ready claim to have acted 'in the public interest'?

I've had one experience since entering the House of Lords that suggests an entirely different possible dimension to the question of improper activity on the part of our public representatives. I was approached by the whips at short notice and asked if I would be interested in a fact-finding trip to Darfur. I jumped at the opportunity. An all-party group (which included some prominent figures) would spend four days in Sudan. They needed a couple of people from the Labour Party, and I and Denis Tunnicliffe declared ourselves available. It was only when I was told that we'd be travelling by private jet that I began to ask myself questions. Whose private jet? What would be our itinerary? Who would we meet? What outcome would we be working for? The answers to these questions were disquieting to say the least.

We'd be travelling in the private jet of one of Britain's richest men. Most of the time would be spent in Khartoum. It seemed to me that our experience of Darfur would amount to little more than crisis-tourism. We'd have our photographs taken with various government figures and sit through several set-piece or carefully staged meetings.

The man in whose plane we'd be flying had been convicted of fraud and given a 15-month suspended sentence for taking illegal payments from a French oil company. The Serious Fraud Office once raided the offices of one of his companies in connection with an alleged attempt to swindle the National Health Service. He has been linked with various other high-profile scandals and has been the subject of a number of investigative articles in a variety of newspapers and journals. His lawyers are currently alleged to be making strenuous efforts to close down public debate about him. His name has figured in an adjournment debate in the House of Commons – parliamentary privilege allows an openness that's becoming more difficult in the public arena. Most of these concerns, it needs to be said, are still at the level of suspicion and allegation. And they should be balanced by a recognition of his altruism, for which he has been honoured by the Roman Catholic Church with a papal knighthood and by various other public institutions, too.

One journalist described the boast of this man that he 'has been able to collect British politicians the way other people collect stamps'. And here was I about to be stuck into his album. I felt uneasy, so much so that I decided to withdraw from this venture. Dennis Tunnicliffe came to the same conclusion. This meant, of course, that there would no longer be any Labour representation. Soon the phone was ringing. A prominent British politician made several attempts to get me to change my mind. In the end, in exasperation, he exploded. 'Oh Leslie,' he said, 'stop being such a . . . such a . . . such a . . . Methodist!'

As a postscript to this little incident, I was surprised to read in a sad volume of memoirs written by Father Michael Seed (*Sinners and Saints: The Irreverent Diaries of Britain's Most Controversial Priest*) how closely linked he has been in the affairs of this millionaire. He writes about a visit to Beirut to an ultra-expensive hotel with 'spectacular meals' and where guests were 'entertained by beautiful hostesses . . . with a selection of belly dancers weaving their magic'. Those who'd accepted invitations to attend this lavish function included 'an interesting mix of politicos and various City bigwigs'. And he names a number of British politicians who 'leapt impulsively' onto the floor to dance well into the night with these 'voluptuous ladies' and 'enticing dancers'.*

I've never regretted my decision not to go. But I've wondered again and again about just what is happening when people prominent in our public life accept such hospitality and allow themselves to get caught up in such activities.

It would be completely wrong of me to end this chapter with these glimpses of decadence. They stand in stark contrast to the disinterested and self-sacrificing hard work of the large majority of those who serve us in parliament. They work long hours. They serve the common good with great commitment. They give encouragement to so many and put their often considerable experience at the disposal of a wide variety of good causes. I am very proud indeed to have joined their ranks.

One of these knights of our democracy was Lionel Murray. It gradually became obvious to me just how hard he had worked, with others, to secure my peerage. I so wanted him to introduce me to the Lords but, alas, he died just weeks before I took my place there. I conducted his funeral at the Loughton Methodist Church where I'd been minister in the early 1980s. That was in May 2004, just days after the news of my impending peerage had been made public. Just before he died, Lionel had sat down to write a note of congratulation, a message he never completed. His family found

---

* These allegations (amid others) are made by Nick Cohen writing in the *Observer* newspaper on 16 November 2003, reiterated by Keith Dovkants in the *London Evening Standard* on 27 February 2008 and underlined by Melanie Phillips in the *Spectator* on 19 December 2008.

the postcard on which he'd begun this note when they were tidying up his affairs and they sent it to me. It was so deeply moving. 'Dear Leslie,' it read, 'Congratulations. At last they've seen sense. Now an old man can happily say his "Nunc dimittis" . . .' and that was that.

I just want to be worthy of the confidence that Lionel and others have placed in me. There's work still to do.

Epilogue

We shall not cease from exploration
And the end of all our exploring
Will be to arrive where we started
And know the place for the first time.

T. S. ELIOT, 'LITTLE GIDDING'

When I was first asked to write this account of my life, I balked at the very idea. Not only would I have to find the time to do it but, or so I felt, an autobiography is just an exercise in self-indulgence. In the end, the persistence of those who wanted me to write it, together with a distinctly pleasant feeling of being flattered by such an invitation, saw me cave in without too much of a struggle and I duly signed the piece of paper put under my nose. One of the things that I was most fearful of in attempting such a task was that my efforts would leave readers thinking I'd written my own obituary and that I was offering a retrospective look at a life now well over and effectively done with. I thought that people might imagine that I wanted to get all this down on paper before second childishness or mere oblivion came along to end my strange, eventful history. Obituaries (like funeral eulogies) often turn the rough and tumble of a man's life into a tale that's overdosed on sugar and spice and all things just a little bit too nice. So I hope this tale has reflected the ups and downs of my life with some accuracy and that I've avoided taking myself too seriously. Nor will this last word tie things together neatly or bring everything to a tidy end. It will simply open on to a future that's still waiting to be grasped.

An earthquake registering 7.0 on the Richter scale struck Haiti with devastating effect on 12 January 2010. It drew me into a flurry of activity from the outset. A capital city virtually destroyed, up to a quarter of a million dead, hundreds of thousands rendered homeless – these headline facts hid a multitude of less obvious sufferings and deprivations and brought a real (though unspoken) sense of uncertainty about the very future of Haiti. Within a few weeks of the disaster, I headed out to Haiti at the invitation of our Church leaders there. Until that moment, my efforts on behalf of my beloved Haiti had centred on a plan to bring parliamentarians from the United Kingdom, the Dominican Republic and Haiti into a working relationship to see whether we could contribute towards the building of an ethos of parliamentary government in that poor, benighted land. All that now assumed lesser priority behind the primordial needs of feeding the hungry, caring for the sick, giving shelter to the homeless and reconstructing a devastated city.

I talked with so many people who'd witnessed the full force of the earthquake. Some had been pulled out of the rubble; others had watched loved ones die just inches away from them. All of them had been part of the panic and chaos that followed the shaking of the foundations. Many were homeless. Cathedrals, government offices, commercial premises, schools and people's homes were all indiscriminately destroyed. I walked among buildings that had lurched like drunkards, all their weight resting unsteadily on one unbending limb, everything else sloping away into a grim shapelessness. Many a multi-storied building had quite simply collapsed like a pancake to a total height now less than mine, making it possible to look across the flat concrete roof of what had once been a tall building. Others had had their fronts ripped away, a pile of rubble standing like a pool of vomit in front of their open throats.

Half a million people were without adequate shelter. They were huddled in 400 tented 'villages' with little but a small tent or a sheet of blue tarpaulin to give them privacy or protection from the sun. Whether these sad compounds would withstand the rain when it came was anybody's guess. It didn't look like it to me.

I'd been invited to preach a sermon at the end of the annual Conference of the Methodist Church in Haiti. The new president, Gesner Paul, reminded everyone that I'd confirmed him and then, some years later, taught him New Testament Greek before he set off for his theological studies in Jamaica. That led his three predecessors to remind us that I'd done exactly the same for them. Any hesitation I may have had about being parachuted in from the outside world to preach a cheap sermon to a group of people who'd suffered so terribly was removed by these and other similar remarks. They made it so clear to me that I was there as a kind of father figure for them all and they seemed eager to hear a word from someone who was fully in sympathy with them but who had some detachment from their immediate worries. As was so often my experience in Haiti, I found all this very humbling. I was glad that I'd not lost my ability to speak Créole (it had been 30 years since I'd spoken it in everyday settings) and that allowed me to preach in all the three languages of my congregation.

During my stay in Haiti, I'd learned that the contract for the reconstruction of Port-au-Prince had been given to John McAslan, a leading London architect whose interest in Haiti had arisen out of conversations that he and I had had in the previous year. He'd visited several times since then and become involved with the work of former US president Bill Clinton, the United Nations envoy to Haiti. McAslan is currently responsible for massive urban projects including the development of the King's Cross area of London and much of the site of the forthcoming Olympic Games. But without question, the rebuilding of Port-au-Prince will be his ultimate challenge.

So Haiti keeps a corner of my heart, more now than ever. And it's Haiti, of course, that's been key to everything else I've tried to do in the field of international relations. I think of the dozen visits I've made to the continent of Africa – trips that took me to Eritrea, Ghana, Malawi, Mozambique, Nigeria, Sierra Leone, South Africa, Sudan and Zimbabwe. I've worked at relationships between British Methodism and its sister churches in West Africa. I've chaired important meetings to sort out funding agreements for the two Councils of Churches in Sudan. I led a team of election observers in Eritrea. I inspected Christian Aid projects in southern Africa and played a small part in the search for peace in Sierra Leone. I've preached and lectured, stood in solidarity with some embattled people, wept and laughed in so many places. Africa has great needs. And this is a key time for finding a way to respond to those needs. But Africa has great character, too. I cherish my memories of the African people I've met in all corners of the continent who work day and night to bring dignity and hope to their communities.

My 17 visits to the United States have had a different flavour. But I think of the talks I gave on 'Racism and the Church' in West Virginia and 'Social Inclusion and an Inclusive Church' to a huge national Conference in Houston, Texas, when these were the burning topics of the day for my listeners. Our visits to Washington have given us opportunities to meet people on Capitol Hill and in various departments of government. I was in Georgia at a highly charged moment after the terrorist attacks of 11 September 2001; in Alabama with a Congressional team for the fortieth anniversary of the beginning of the march from Selma to Montgomery; I undertook a fact-finding visit to the Haitian inmates of the Krome Detention Center in Florida; and Margaret and I found ourselves in a hyperventilating Chicago around the time of Barack Obama's inauguration. I've formed precious friendships with so many African Americans and gained from them a working knowledge of their culture and world-view. We visited Alaska, a real frontier state, during the governorship of Sarah Palin and Washington at the time of the Monica Lewinsky affair. If I had to guess which one of them will turn out to be America's *femme fatale*, I think my money would be on Palin.

From the day of my ordination, I felt a compulsive need to do whatever lay in my power to bring peoples together, to create better understanding between nations, and to work hard for justice and peace. I little realized in January 1973 just what opportunities would come my way. Even now, with recent visits to Fiji, Cambodia and Bosnia still fresh in my mind, I find myself with opportunities to develop interests in so many different directions.

The unity of the Church has also continued to be at the top of my agenda. I've worked consistently in an ecumenical way – in Port-au-Prince, Aux Cayes, Cap Haitien, Reading, Loughton, in London's West End, Golders Green and the City of London. Many people see ecumenical work as adding another layer of meetings to their already charged diaries. For me, it's always been the opposite – working with others seems to give us all a greater output than anything we'd have achieved if we'd worked separately. We established a local ecumenical project in Loughton and we enjoy a covenanted relationship with our parish (Anglican) church in the City of London. I'm a canon of St Paul's Cathedral and a founder member of its Council. I've preached in 19 cathedrals and in innumerable churches of every denomination. I cannot envisage working in any other way and it's always been one of my earliest endeavours when arriving in a new posting to get to know my ecumenical colleagues there.

That continues to be my stance. Now more than ever. So imagine my delight when, one day and out of the blue, I received a letter from the Right Reverend and Right Honourable Richard Chartres DD, the Lord Bishop of London, in which he made a most interesting proposal. The bishop shared his disquiet with me that there seems little progress in the search for unity between Methodists and the Church of England. In order to take the process out of the hands of our church bureaucracies and into the realm of practical outcomes, he's come up with a bold suggestion which, in his view, would move the ideas that we've been wrestling with for the last half-century from the realm of abstraction and into the real world.

The bishop is conscious that he's the successor to the man who denied the repeated requests of John Wesley to send priests to America in the aftermath of the revolutionary wars there. No doubt, Bishop Lowth felt that it would be inappropriate to send any help whatsoever to the very people who'd only recently defeated the British armies and declared their independence from the British Crown. In John Wesley's eyes, the political realities were less important than the pastoral ones. People needed the succour of priests and the only person who had the constitutional power to send any was the Bishop of London. When the prelate refused to do so, Wesley took unilateral action and ordained four priests himself for immediate service in America.

If Richard Chartres is the successor of Bishop Lowth, so too, he argues, am I the successor of John Wesley, both by dint of having sat in his chair as the president of the Conference and also because I preach Sunday by Sunday from his very own pulpit in the City Road Chapel. So, the bishop prods, why don't we think the unthinkable? He suggests that a ceremony might take place in St Paul's Cathedral where he would make a fulsome apology for all the ways in which the Church of England has mistreated Methodists over the years. I would accept his apology and offer some kind of 'absolution'. He would then proceed to lay hands on me and bring me into the threefold ministry of the Church of England, but only on the strict understanding that this would not, as might be the case in every other such act on his part, bring me under his authority. I would remain the minister of Wesley's Chapel and under the authority of the Methodist Conference. The reach of my ministry, however, would now extend well beyond Methodism and be acceptable anywhere within the Anglican Communion.

I've found this proposal ingenious and generous. At a stroke, it establishes a basis – without denying the validity of my present ordained status – to bring the ministries of our two Churches together. That, it seems to me, is a huge first step towards restoring the unity of our Churches after all the false starts and pious words of the past. And, argues the bishop, the disunion which began in London would be brought to an end in London. It would be fitting if those who move this process forward were the successors of those key players whose actions (or whose inaction) brought about the event that took our Churches so decisively towards their eventual separation.

Unfortunately, the Methodist Conference poured cold water on the proposal when it sat in judgement in Scarborough and Wolverhampton in 2008 and 2009. It reckoned that such an act would in fact amount to re-ordination and, thereby, a denial of the validity of my present ordained status. I feel that this judgement is profoundly wrong. Nothing is being proposed that hasn't already been agreed in principle. Nothing is being suggested that hasn't already taken place with one form of subterfuge or another in a number of cases. I am left wondering what to do next. And it's possible that I shall ask the Bishop of London to move forward in line with his proposal, even though that would be in defiance of my Conference's declared position. I'm fully conscious that such a decision would, in all likelihood, create the possibility of my being expelled from my ministry I suppose that there would have to be a trial of some kind – would I be charged with disobedience? Or heresy? It's become a matter to which I know I must give my most serious and prayerful thought.

At Wesley's Chapel, too, there's work still to be done. We commissioned a major study of our museum with a view to conducting a radical refurbishment. Everyone who's seen the concept design brochure raves about it, but the beginning of the fund-raising campaign coincided almost exactly with the start of the recession. We're playing this one long but our tired facilities need freshening up; so much has changed in the world of museums and we need to catch up with some of that. I want to get back to this as soon as the international financial climate seems more settled.

The other aspect of our work that's been begun in my time at the Chapel and which has produced undreamed-of results is our website. It draws visitors from far and near and those who worship with us go on following us well after they've returned to their country of origin. Well over ten thousand 'hits' are registered each week and we get some very touching testimonies from all over the world. Wesley's dictum that the world was his parish is the perfect strapline for our website. Now we post our weekly sermon in audio as well as written form. And we're investigating the use of cameras, too. I find the challenge of keeping abreast of modern technology breathtaking. Indeed, just being at Wesley's Chapel offers me a constant stimulus. I know that Margaret and I will find it quite a wrench to leave this wonderful, historic place as one day, of course, we must.

Meanwhile, there's so much to look forward to on the family front. Our eldest son, Timothy, produces golf magazines, one of which is under license from the Royal and Ancient (Golf Club) of St Andrews. He has a freelance publishing business and happily deals with every aspect of magazine and book production other than authorship. His interest in sport has seen him launch into a Master's course in Sport Law – which, once you look at it, seems to have a far greater range of applicability than you'd ever imagine. His younger brother, Jonathan, has survived the downsizing of the workforce at Westminster City Council and is responsible for a number of the services they provide to residents. His wife, Susanna, a dedicated schoolteacher in a difficult inner-London borough, gave birth to their first child, a bouncing baby boy named Thomas James Mellor Griffiths in March 2010. They live in Bow, just a stone's throw from us, and clearly there's a great deal to look forward to on their part. Ruth, our youngest, is far away in Cambodia where she works as an economist. Her husband, Bunna, is from a Buddhist background and their marriage, which took place on Christmas Day 2005, was one of those wondrous experiences that I could never have dreamed of. Half a dozen village ancients chanted endless mantras while a number of traditional rituals were performed by members of both families to indicate that they were now bound to each other through the nuptials of their offspring. It was very moving, though I don't think that either Margaret or I could have maintained the lotus position for one minute longer. Now we must add to the world's carbon footprint as we make serious efforts to spend time with each other either in Cambodia or in the United Kingdom.

Perhaps it's appropriate that my narrative should end where it began – in Burry Port. My links with my hometown had become tenuous. I had two cousins living there but nowhere to stay if we wanted to visit, so on the whole, we just didn't go there. We'd take flowers for my mother's grave if we were passing through or in the vicinity, but to all intents and purposes the association had ended. Then, suddenly, I became Lord Griffiths of Burry Port. And I began to feel that I should work a little harder at developing and maintaining contact with the place of my birth. How could I justify using it for my title otherwise? And it didn't take long before Burry Port was making approaches to me. The town council held a reception for me and accorded me the supreme honour of opening a snooker room in the

Memorial Hall. I became honorary president of the Burry Port Historical Society and gave them an inaugural lecture on the developments which had turned a sleepy fishing village into a thriving industrial town. I've got to know the vicar of Burry Port, Paul Davies, and his lovely family. Astonishingly, for the first time in my life, I've visited (and worshipped in) the parish church. Paul has even asked me to be patron of the St Mary's refurbishment appeal, with an invitation to preach at the opening of the newly ordered church towards the end of 2010. I've been made an honorary member of the Burry Port Reading and Social Club as well. I speak out of ignorance on this one, since I've never yet penetrated its mysterious interior but I'm told on good authority that, while plenty of social activity goes on, it's unlikely I'll get much of a chance to do any serious reading. One of these days I shall knock on the door and find out for myself.

The Bache was hemmed in by an ugly, sprawling industrial complex when I was growing up. Now all the industry has gone. Even the three-stacked, coal-fired power station has been taken down, brick by brick. The land opened up by these developments has been transformed. The old docks have become a marina, social and pleasure amenities are being installed, chic houses are being built and Burry Port's centre of gravity has moved south of the railway line to a rapidly changing waterfront. Our side of the tracks is no longer thought of as the rough end of town. It's not even referred to as 'the Bache' any longer. It's now 'the south side' and all the fashionable developments are taking place there. And the English Methodists are the only religious body with an organized presence in the area. The chapel that I attended as a boy is getting its second wind and shows every sign of bucking the trend as it builds a stronger membership base and offers its services to its neighbourhood.

Pauline Barnett, the dynamic superintendent minister of the Llanelli and Carmarthen circuit, had the bright idea of demolishing the school-room attached to the chapel (where I'd once taught Sunday School) and replacing it with a comfortable suite of rooms that could host a whole range of community activities. She got most of the money from the Welsh Assembly's development agency and, in May 2009, I was invited to cut the ribbon and declare the new facility open for business. It was decided to call it:

Canolfan
Leslie Griffiths
Centre

On the day we opened it, I addressed a packed church from the pulpit where I'd preached my first sermons almost half a century previously. From the window beside the pulpit I could see, just 50 yards down Glanmor Terrace, the house where I was born, the house we were ejected from in October 1947. Running away from the Chapel at 90 degrees to Glanmor Terrace is Silver Terrace and, a mere 16 houses down its length stands the house where my mother was brought up. And all this is just 100 yards from the Building Trades Supply where I'd lived with Jim and our mother until my departure for my undergraduate studies at Cardiff. It was here that I'd officiated at my mother's funeral service. This is a place that played such a striking part in my early days and has underlain the direction in which the whole of my subsequent life developed. 'The Leslie Griffiths Centre', though a modest enough facility, sounds so very grand. 'Les bach,' my mother would have said, 'there's posh!' No one who saw my rough beginnings, and certainly not I, could have imagined that this simple edifice, built originally for Cornish metalworkers, would one day sport my name in this way. I don't think that it will boost my ego too much. At least not as long as the *Llanelli Star* continues to carry advertisements like this one:

Fish and chip supper followed
by a quiz will be held at the
Leslie Griffiths Centre
behind the English Methodist
Church on Glanmor Terrace.
Tickets at £6.

This appeared in the section of the paper headed 'Community News'. A quiz and fish and chip supper – lots of laughter and fun, simple food and fellowship. And all in a building that bears my name! That's as satisfying a legacy as I could ever have dreamed of.

Acknowledgements

For a number of years now I've valued the friendship of Huw Edwards. We hail from the same neck of the woods. We went to the same school and, although he's a generation younger than I am, he was taught by some of the same teachers as I was. We don't lack for things to talk about – from Welsh culture and chapel architecture to the latest happenings in the world of politics. He's become one of Britain's most trusted voices, a latter-day Richard Dimbleby, with endless demands on his time. I knew that he was as well placed as anyone to write a foreword to this book but I had no right to suppose that he'd be able to find the time to do so. Yet he has, and I'm grateful. My efforts have certainly acquired a little glamour as a consequence.

I've had the space to write this book because so many others have been quietly and efficiently at work on tasks which, if they'd been less dedicated, would have required a great deal of my own time. In the financial affairs of Wesley's Chapel, Roger Chapman, John Gibbon, David Tee and Alan Watts (all volunteers) together with Robin Kent, our finance officer, have lifted heavy burdens of dutiful bureaucracy from my shoulders and given me the space to do more creative things. Throughout the time needed to produce this book, the museum we run has been without its full-time curator – a consequence of the economic downturn. This has meant that the onus of co-ordinating the input of the dozens of volunteers who cheerfully come in from all parts of London (and beyond) – to serve the needs of the thousands of visitors who come our way in the course of a year – has fallen to Thea Scott and Peter Baugh, two stalwarts of the first order, and so once again I've been the direct beneficiary of other people's hard work. Zara Adato, Margaret Hazard, Beatrice Sarsa, Becky Venn and Adrian Bevis have, between them, ensured that everything needful for the management of our day-to-day lives in a bustling church with its excitable and energetic congregation has been done and done well. Elvis Pratt brings brilliance and reliability to the musical life of the chapel and his quiet efficiency has meant, once again, that I've had no anxieties in that direction. The work done by Tracey Smith, my personal assistant, is prodigious. She licks complicated documents into shape, organizes events, keeps our website up to date and, the hardest of all tasks, keeps me in order. It really is no exaggeration to say that the kind of service rendered by these (and so many other) people has made it possible for me to write not only this book but the seemingly endless articles and scripts that seem to be required of me on a regular basis. I couldn't allow this book to appear without ensuring that due recognition and an adequate expression of gratitude to all of them stands clearly on the record.

Jo Baxter has put her considerable professional experience as a photographer at my disposal. She was egged on by her insuppressible sister-in-law Katherine and I'm grateful to both of them for their time and efforts.

I really must say a word of thanks to my son Tim for his considerable help during the editorial stages of this book. His skill, sense of style, affection and patience saved a non-computer-literate dad from panic and the book from oblivion.

There would have been no book but for the enthusiasm of Continuum's commissioning editor, Caroline Chartres. She's urged me on, kept up my spirits and persuaded me that this was a book worth writing. We'll see about that, of course, but no one should doubt her constant and cheerful stimulus in pushing the project forward.

There may well be errors of judgement or mis-remembered detail in my narrative and I can only offer my apologies if that turns out to be the case. A biography, and even more an autobiography, reveals those flaws of character and missed opportunities which, if only one had had greater wisdom and all-round vision at the time, might have made for better outcomes. And yet I don't think that I'd have wanted much in my life to have been very different. So I offer these pages, for what they're worth, to anyone interested and hope that they bring a little colour and even a modicum of pleasure to those who read them.

Index